ESSAYS ON SOUTH INDIA

ASIAN STUDIES AT HAWAII, NO. 15

Essays on South India

Edited by Burton Stein

ASIAN STUDIES PROGRAM
UNIVERSITY OF HAWAII
THE UNIVERSITY PRESS OF HAWAII

Manufactured in the United States of America

Library of Congress Cataloging in Publication Data
Main entry under title:

Essays on South India.

(Asian studies at Hawaii; no. 15)
Essays originally presented at a conference of the Society for South Indian Studies held at the University of Wisconsin Apr. 7–9, 1970.
Includes bibliographical references.
1. South India—Congresses. I. Stein, Burton, 1926– II. Society for South Indian Studies. III. Series.
DS3.A2A82 no. 15 [DS484] 954'.8 74–620104
ISBN 0–8248–0350–7

Contents

Editor's Preface

The essays of this volume were first presented to a conference of South Indian specialists convened at the University of Wisconsin on 7–9 April 1970. This was the second such conference of the Society for South Indian Studies, the first having met at the University of Texas on 5–7 December 1968, from which came a valuable set of essays entitled *Symposium on Dravidian Civilization*, edited by Andrée F. Sjoberg.*

Robert E. Frykenberg, Department of History, University of Wisconsin, the convenor of the second SSIS conference, intended that the papers and discussion should be a comprehensive "stock-taking" of scholarship on South India. Each of the scholars invited to present papers was specifically asked to make such an assessment in the field of his or her competence and was also asked to suggest potentially useful lines of future research in the light of that assessment. Participants in the conference comprised both Indian and American scholars; there were also graduate students—both Indian and American—from a number of universities. Discussion of each paper was lively and vigorous, and the ambience within which each session took place was conducive to the most complete discussion and debate of issues raised in the papers. For this auspicious context, a word of gratitude must be registered to the conference convenor, to his colleagues at the University of Wisconsin for their intellectual contributions as well as their hospitality, to the Department of Indian Studies of the University of Wisconsin for its support, and, finally, to the University of Wisconsin for having provided the necessary facilities.

* New York: Jenkins, 1971.

A larger measure of gratitude is reserved for the people and scholars of South India to whom the volume is dedicated. All but one of the authors of these essays are American scholars who have sojourned for a greater or lesser time in South India. Each essay bears the mark of valuable—indeed essential—dependence upon the South Indian scholars among whom all the writers have lived and worked. There is perhaps no really adequate way to express the gratitude which each American essayist feels toward his South Indian friends and colleagues. These essays, as works of the mind, bear the heavy burden of conveying heartfelt friendship and thanks to them.

The scope of the essays is broad; they reflect the range of interests and scholarship of Americans in South India. And, though each of the writers accepted the charge of Professor Frykenberg to survey some portion of the totality of knowledge of South Indian society, culture, and history, some essays provide new and sometimes startling formulations. This was an unexpected dividend of the conference.

While not intended, this identification of new emphases in the study of South India could have been anticipated. As much as any part of India, South Indian scholarship has been the result of both Indian and foreign scholars. One has but to think of the honored names Caldwell, Foote, Oppert, Rice, Heras, Slater, and Fleet. Several generations of Western scholars have brought to the study of South India views formulated in other, non-Indian contexts. These have enriched South Indian scholarship. The number and variety of foreign scholars have increased over the years and now include Japanese and Soviet scholars as well. It is inevitable that such diverse scholarly traditions and interests should raise different kinds of questions and bring forward somewhat different kinds of answers. But all such efforts—the present volume included—are minor eddies in the stream of knowledge about South India which is essentially the work of South Indian scholars who have been and will continue to be our teachers as well as our colleagues.

BURTON STEIN
Honolulu

Archaeology in South India: Accomplishments and Prospects

CLARENCE MALONEY
Montclair State College

Claims are often put forward for high and distinctive early civilization in South India, and in Tamiḻ Nāḍu in particular. These claims, however, are based on literary references that are often enigmatic, and there has been little effort to support them with solid archaeological evidence. Such evidence as there is will be presented in this essay, including pertinent data from Śrī Lankā (Ceylon). We shall survey the archaeology of all South India from earliest times, but we shall not attempt to go beyond about A.D. 300 nor shall we take up temple archaeology.

Part I briefly surveys the evidence of early prehistory and discusses the meaning of the Iron Age sites. Part II examines the correlation between literary and archaeological evidence for the Śaṅgam period in Tamiḻ Nāḍu and discusses some trends of civilizational development. Part III surveys the evidence of early civilization in the other three South Indian states. Part IV lists certain coastal sites and Part V presents my conclusions.

PART I: PREHISTORIC ARCHAEOLOGY

Early Stone Age

The distribution of the earliest stone tools—large, unhafted "hand axes" and cleavers dating from half a million or so years ago—shows a diffusion pattern which was followed in every subsequent phase of peninsular Indian cultural evolution. They follow the route from Gujarāt and Mahārāshṭra to the Deccan and the cul-de-sac of South India. Throughout prehistory the mixed deciduous and scrub forest and grassland of the Deccan was a favorable habitat. No hand axes have been found along the western littoral or in the alluvial soils of the eastern side, which must have had selva vegetation cover.

While these earliest tools have been picked up at scores of places over the interior of the peninsula, attempts to classify them typologically have not led very far.[1] There are a few stratified excavated sites with some faunal associations. A three-phase sequence is common in the river valleys of the Deccan and Orissa which have been comparatively studied by H. D. Sankalia. Kurnool in Āndhra is a typical site.[2] A lower laterite deposit presumably representing a humid phase is devoid of evidence of early man; in the succeeding stratum, laid down when the climate was drier and the plains were open, hand axes appear. In the laterite soils superimposed on this there are again no tools, and the precipitation caused river gravels to form. In the succeeding, drier phase advanced hand axes and somewhat smaller tools appear, and this assemblage is called the Middle Stone Age tool industry. On the surface of the site are microlithic tools representative of the Late Stone Age. This three-stage sequence of Early, Middle, and Late Stone Ages is more or less applicable to all India, and Indian archaeologists prefer this terminology to that worked out for other parts of the world. This three-stage sequence is found around Madras too, as at Vaḍamadurai, where hand axes may appear even below the lower laterite, and at Attirampākkam; at Guḍiyam Cave in Chingleput District the hiatus between the three phases is indistinct or absent, suggesting continuous habitation.[3]

Indian archaeologists have engaged in considerable debate about the chronology represented by these climatic and typological phases and their correlation with climatic phases of the Narmadā Valley, where faunal remains in quantity have been discovered in river gravels. This was debated in a symposium in 1964 edited by V. N. Misra, as well as the even more problematic question of the relationship between the prehistory of the peninsula and the phases of the Pleistocene glaciation in the Himalayas. A very early pebble tool industry in the western Himalayas and Panjāb, called the Soan, possibly merged with the hand ax industry in western India before the latter reached South India.[4]

The need now is for stratigraphic excavation of a number of Early Stone Age sites, correlation of Deccan geological features with river terraces and ocean levels, evaluation of faunal remains, and firm dating by radioactive isotopes. The goal would be to find links between the Madrasian hand ax tradition and hand ax cultures of the Near East and Africa, where they appear earliest. Another goal would be to find hominid fossil remains dating well back in the Pleistocene, none of which have so far been noticed in South Asia.

Middle Stone Age

Guḍiyam Cave in Tamil̠ Nāḍu suggests typological evolution because the earlier hand axes and cleavers merge into the smaller flakes, points, and blades of the Middle Stone Age. These were apparently produced as wood-working instruments. In Mahārāshṭra and Karṇāṭaka these tools are made of fine-grain stone such as jasper, but farther south in the peninsula quartz continued to be used.[5]

Possibly this tool tradition, dating probably from the last millennia of the Pleistocene, represents an intrusive culture analogous to the Mousterian of the Near East, Central Asia, and Europe, which is associated with Neanderthal man in those regions. Though Indian archaeologists have investigated many sites, they have not yet been rewarded with firm dating evidence and skeletal material for the Middle Stone Age.

Late Stone Age

Now we see for the first time elements which have gone into the composition of modern South Indian culture. In most sites the appearance of the Late Stone Age (more or less equivalent to what elsewhere might be called Mesolithic), characterized by small tools called microliths, heralds a rather abrupt cultural change and may represent intrusive influences. Microliths might have been used from the fifth millennium B.C. if not considerably earlier, and they continued in use after the invention of pottery and even into the Iron Age.

The Deccan was still a favored region, and in such sites as Beḷḷāry and Brāhmagiri[6] microliths are found just below the level containing evidence of food production and cattle keeping, which may be dated here about 2300 B.C. Now for the first time we have evidence of habitation along the humid west coast, at Kōzhikōḍ in Kēraḷa, Goā, and Bombay. Also, on the southeast coast of Tamil̠ Nāḍu there was a flourishing microlithic industry on sand dunes, locally known as *tēri*, which had become fixed with tools embedded in them. The artifacts include short blades, backed blades, a few discoids, lunates, and other geometric stones which were hafted and used as knives or gouges, transverse arrowheads, and almond-shaped bifacial points. Their makers knew how to pressure-flake stone tools, and also had the bow and arrow. These sites perhaps date from 4000 B.C. if not considerably earlier.[7] Similar tools are found in Śrī Lankā.[8]

Population increased during the Late Stone Age; there are sites over most of the Deccan and Central India. In Āndhra, on knolls overlooking the Godāvarī, over a hundred sites have been spotted. Some excavations have yielded several thousand microlithic tools; at other sites it is evident that several acres were occupied. The site of Birbhānpur in western West

Bengal has a stratum containing early forms of microliths extending over a square mile, from which over 5400 artifacts were recovered in two excavated trenches and on the eroded surface.[7] This implies not only greater population, which was possible because of the advanced hunting techniques of the Late Stone Age, but also increasingly complex social structure and cooperative effort in hunting and gathering.

Only recently has Indian archaeology moved from the study of the typology of these tools to understanding the total ecological and cultural picture. Having the bow and arrow and probably the domesticated dog, these people were efficient hunters. Fishing was also important in the case of such habitation sites as the *tēri*, Kōzhikōḍ, and the islands of Bombay harbor. At a site called Kṛṣṇa Bridge, the Allchins discovered Late Stone Age tools at a river crossing that was in use in all subsequent phases of culture including even the railroad era.[10] The Late Stone Age people could cross bodies of water, no doubt by using coracles and rafts such as are still to be seen in remote parts of South India. Almost certainly, fish nets, baskets, and mats would have been fashioned.

Drawings on cave walls in central India, Āndhra, and Śrī Lankā depict scenes of hunting peoples and suggest, for instance, that there were dance rituals associated with hunting.[11] It is probable that belief in the soul, rebirth, mana, menstrual and death pollution, feeling of empathy with other living things, elementary forms of *pūja*, the sanctity of many present sacred spots, fundaments of kinship systems, and other aspects of early cultures which became elaborated and formalized in historic times, all have their roots in the advanced hunting cultures of the Late Stone Age.

Among the best sources is Bridget Allchin's *The Stone-Tipped Arrow*, a comparative study of past and present advanced hunters in Africa, India, Southeast Asia, and Australia. The Seligmanns, while studying the Väddās of Śrī Lankā in 1911, excavated a cave in the eastern part of the island then inhabited by Väddās, which yielded Late Stone Age artifacts typical of the island. Valuable ethnographic records produced in past decades of the small South Indian hunting groups such as the Kāḍar and Chenchus[12] provide further insights into the social systems and ethos that might have prevailed over South India prior to 2000 B.C.

Neolithic and Chalcolithic

Food production techniques diffused from Iran to northern Afghanistan in the seventh and sixth millennia B.C. and extended throughout the hills west of the Indus plain in the fourth millennium, soon becoming adapted to the plains and giving rise to the Indus Civilization by 2400 B.C. A second Neolithic culture complex spread into India from Southeast Asia bringing such plants as the banana, coconut, areca nut, sago palm, and yam.

Though this reached central India—accompanied by the ensconcement of the Muṇḍa languages there—archaeological evidence of its impact on South India is lacking. In spite of diligent search, Indian archaeologists have not found any evidence of an indigenous Neolithic development in the subcontinent apart from that stimulated by these two food-producing culture complexes (except for a minor Neolithic culture in the western Himalayas).

Contemporary with the Indus Civilization, food-producing cultures extended down the Deccan and by about 2300 B.C. had begun to adapt to the ecological conditions of the inland parts of the peninsula. Two good studies of these early Neolithic cultures are Nagaraja Rao's *Stone Age Hill Dwellers of Tekkalakota* and F. R. Allchin's *Neolithic Cattle-Keepers of South India.* The latter book is an excellent example of how folklore, festivals, and economics of present peoples can be correlated with archaeological evidence, and it compares early cattle-keeping cultures in India and Europe.

In *The Birth of Indian Civilization* the Allchins have divided the early Neolithic of the Deccan (also called Chalcolithic because people used bits of copper) into three phases. The first is found mainly in the Deccan plateau and is datable 2300 to 1800 B.C. It was a cattle-keeping economy with little cultivation. Cattle were kept in huge pens in which dung accumulated to a depth of several feet, to be fired in a ritual which presumably had the function of warding off disease. Allchin excavated several of these dung-ash heaps, especially at Uṭnūr, Ganesh Majumdar excavated one at Kupgal, and A. Sundara has recently discovered thirteen more in northern Karṇāṭaka.

A second phase, from 2000 or 1800 to 1400 B.C., was fully agricultural, with an economy based on millets, pulses, and oilseeds. This phase had links with, or derived from, the early Neolithic cultures of Mahārāshṭra and the northern Deccan, uncovered by Sankalia and his students at such sites as Nevāsā, Prakāsh, Daimābād, Chandoli, Nāsik, Jorwe, Maheshwaṛ, and Nāgdā.[13] While these are beyond the area of our interest here, we should note that these and some of the Deccan sites have evidence of the influence of the Late Indus Civilization levels of Gujarāt and the succeeding Lustrous Red ware phase, with tall vessels perforated all over, spouted vessels, terracotta figurines, copper, and bronze.

Siṅganapaḷḷi in Kurnool District in Āndhra was a settlement of this type, a prosperous agricultural community which excavations showed to have extended over three or four hectares. The pottery showed evidence of the post-Indus painted pottery tradition.[14] Other important sites include Māski, Piklihāl, Hallur, Uṭnūr, Tekkalakōṭa, Śanganakallu, Kupgal, Brāhmagiri, Chandravaḷḷi, T. Narsipūr, and Pattupāḍu.[15] Some of these, such as Wheeler's excavation of Brāhmagiri and B. K. Thapar's of Māski, have been well published. There is no doubt that the peasant economy of the Deccan today—dry farming of millets and grams—derives from these inhabitants nearly four millennia ago, and in fact change in village life seems to have been marginal.

The third Neolithic phase occurs at a number of these sites and, according to Allchin, extends geographically even to Kēsarapaḷḷi in Kṛṣṇa District in Āndhra and to Gaurimēḍu and Maṅgamāl at Pondicherry.[16] A site of an early level of this phase is Paiyampaḷḷi on the Madras-Bangalore road, dated by carbon-14 to 1390 ± 200 B.C.[17] Typically this horizon contained pointed-butt stone axes and blades of jasper, agate, and chert, and in some sites there is copper. At Paiyampaḷḷi people lived in stone-lined dwelling pits covered with roofs supported by posts; floors were of rammed earth plastered with ash-mixed earth. Green gram, horse gram, and rāgi were the crops, while bovids, sheep, pigs, and fowl were kept. These Neolithic villagers must have had ideas of rebirth, for in several sites they buried the dead, especially children, in urns recognizable as representing pregnant women with globular bellies and breasts; bodies were interred under house floors or nearby outside. Pointed butt axes are found in parts of the Āndhra and Tamil̠ Nāḍu plains regions as well as on the Deccan, and the cumulative eivdence suggests that in the second half of the second millennium B.C. the settled Neolithic way of life had diffused to most areas in South India except Kēraḷa, where forests were too thick to be controlled with Neolithic tools.

Iron Age

The Iron Age in peninsular India, as in the north, is now known to have begun somewhat earlier than was formerly believed. At Haḷḷūr in Karṇāṭaka it has been dated as early as 1000 B.C.,[18] but carbon-14 data from more sites are needed before such a date can be firmly established. In general it spread widely by the middle of the millennium. In Deccan sites such as Māski and Brāhmagiri the Iron Age comes up to the Sātavāhana historical level, and at Haliṅgali it is dated as late as 80 ± 100 B.C. In Tamil̠ Nāḍu at Paiyampaḷḷi Level II, which was associated with enormous deposits of iron slag, has been dated to about 300 B.C.[19] People lived in circular houses, had gold ornaments and bangles and beads of glass, and constructed megalithic funerary monuments. Pottery consisted of ordinary red and brown wares, the Black and Red ware, and in the later levels Russet-coated Painted ware. This culture merges into the Śaṅgam period; the introduction of iron weapons and the horse seems to have been a key factor in its diffusion.

A few sites around Kōlār in southern Karṇāṭaka have been excavated. Banahaḷḷi is the largest Iron Age settlement found, extending 100 by 300 meters and containing a large number of polished stone axes, chisels, digging stick scythes, hoes, and grinders. The pottery included a pale gray ware and the Black and Red ware. Both here and at a nearby site, Doḍa Kaḍattūr, people lived in rock shelters, while at the latter site they also dug dwelling pits, some of which contained burned rice husks and ashes. At Keṇḍatti similar artifacts were found, in addition to iron slag. Both the pale gray ware and the Black and Red ware have been found in the ancient gold mines of the Champion Reefs at Kōlār, indicating the antiquity of these mines.[20]

Most archaeological attention at Iron Age sites has been devoted to burials, which are often associated with megaliths in the form of large stone slabs placed in various formations as menhirs, dolmenoid cists, or circles of stones, sometimes marked by stone cairns. Such monuments can be seen overlooking the little cultivable valleys of the Nīlagiri and Paḻaṉi Hills as well as over the Deccan where stone abounds. Stone alignments and sarcophagus burials are found over northern Tamiḻ Nāḍu (over two hundred sites in Chingleput District alone). In almost every sizeable settlement in the fertile parts of southern Tamiḻ Nāḍu, *tāḻi* (pot) burials have been uncovered, suggesting that this region was well populated. In Kēraḷa there is a considerable range of distinctive but related monuments, such as large umbrella-shaped stone structures and burial chambers excavated in laterite.

A wide variety of iron implements occurs in these megalithic burial complexes, together with lamps, etched conch shells, and the inevitable Black and Red ware. At Āticcannallūr on a bluff overlooking the lower Tāmbaraparaṇi, a number of burials were excavated in the 1920s, some of them interred in *tāḻi*. These artifacts are on display in the Madras Government Museum. Among the iron artifacts found in such burials are knives, tanged daggers, barbed arrowheads, adzes, sickles, wedge blades, double-edged midrib swords with hilts, hooks, horse bits, chisels, bangles, nails, frying pans, ladles with long handles, and tripod pot stands. It is notable that there is a fair degree of uniformity in Iron Age burial goods throughout the south.

Iron Age or megalithic burials have been investigated and reported on by a number of archaeologists: B. K. Thapar, N. R. Banerji and K. V. Soundararajan, J. M. Casal, M. Seshadri, B. K. Gururaja Rao, Y. D. Sharma, G. N. Das, K. S. Ramachandran, and others, who have developed a number of theories about them. For instance, Wheeler finds similarities between the stone cist burials of South India and those of the Near East and Europe, particularly the feature of the porthole-like apertures in the cist slabs, but points out that the South Indian ones are well over a millennium later than those in Europe.[21] K. S. Ramachandran thinks the South Indian burial megaliths are different from those of northeastern India and also from those of north central India, but the latter might be related to those occasionally found in Baluchistan and Sindh. D. H. Gordon suggests that Iron Age cultural influences came to South India by sea. I would suggest that the distinctive subterranean burial chambers dug out of the laterite in Kēraḷa might support the view that influences from the Near East came by sea in the South Indian Iron Age, but we can hardly attribute the whole culture phase to that. Y. D. Sharma, however, places the Kēraḷa burial monuments squarely in the South Indian megalithic tradition. G. N. Das thinks the megaliths of the Nīlagiris were built by ancestors of the Toḍas. K. R. Srinivasan finds several of the South Indian burial types referred to in Śaṅgam literature.

Fürer-Haimendorf has suggested that the builders of the South Indian megalithic monuments were of a different cultural tradition than those who produced the burial monuments of northeastern India, and those in the south must have been speakers of Dravidian languages. The whole subject has been reviewed by N. R. Banerjee in "The Megalithic Problem of India" and put in wider historical context in his *Iron Age in India.*

Though the tradition of constructing burial monuments of megaliths is perhaps traceable to Baluchistan and the Near East, we cannot isolate this particular feature as regards South India but must regard it as part of the Iron Age complex. Large stone slabs could have been easily detached in the Deccan and the southern hills by heating and then cooling with water. These were naturally used for burials even as they have been used in historic and recent times for constructing roomlike shrines in Karṇāṭaka. What is perhaps of more interest is the diffusion of Black and Red ware and particular types of Iron Age tools over the south in the second half of the first millennium B.C.

But the most important change to come over South India in late prehistoric times was the diffusion of irrigated rice agriculture. When did this occur? The question is important because rice provided the economic basis for the development of more complex social patterns. It is the symbiotic relationship evolved between man and his cattle and the land that has made possible dense population, full-scale plow peasant economy, and civilization. Archaeological evidence is skimpy at present. The earliest date for rice so far is 2000 B.C. in Gujarāt. It is found in some of the Neolithic sites of Mahārāshṭra and Karṇāṭaka but need not have been irrigated. Irrigated rice cultivation probably did not become widespread over the middle Gaṅgā region and Bengal before the early centuries of the first millennium B.C.—though it may have been present much earlier—and Allchin thinks it was a feature of the rise of civilization along the Gaṅgā and that it spread through the peninsula during the Iron Age.[22]

An excavation recently conducted by the Tamil̲ Nāḍu State Department of Archaeology, at Kor̲kai on the southern coast in the Tāmbaraparaṇi alluvial delta, has yielded a carbon-14 date of 785$\pm$ 95 B.C.[23] This came from a hearth at the lowest excavated level, and no cultural artifacts were associated with this level. Further excavations are in progress. It is reasonable to assume that in the first half of the millennium irrigated rice cultivation spread through Bengal and the coasts of Orissa, Āndhra, and Tamil̲ Nāḍu, reaching the extreme south and crossing to Śrī Lankā where there are prehistoric irrigation works and some Iron Age burials. Irrigated rice cultivation made possible a way of life somewhat different from that of the Deccan, which was dependent primarily upon millets, grams, pulses, oilseeds, and cotton because over most of it only dry farming is possible.

Dravidian Languages

What can we infer archaeologically about the diffusion of Dravidian languages throughout the south? The possibilities are (1) that they evolved from the speech of early South Indian tribal hunters, (2) that they diffused with the early cattle-keeping phase of the Neolithic, (3) that they diffused with the full-scale Neolithic village way of life emanating from the Deccan, (4) that they diffused along with irrigated rice cultivation, (5) that they were brought by Iron Age intruders, and (6) that they came by sea.

The final hypothesis seems ruled out for lack of sufficient evidence, and the initial one seems ruled out by Dravidian historical linguistics. What the pre-Dravidian tribal languages might have been is totally unknown and never will be known. At the very latest the upper limit for the spread of these languages is the third century B.C., before the earliest Tamil̲ inscriptions in Brāhmī script, while in Āndhra Telugu diffused before the time of the Sātavāhanas, who were not the agents of its spread.

As for the lower limit, it seems to me that we cannot assume it to be indefinite, for the spread of early Tamil̲-Malayāḷam, Kannaḍa, and Telugu each came to occupy a vast region rather uniformly. It almost seems necessary to assume that each was imposed, either by a more efficient cultural system, or a political-military system, or both. Now among the possibilities enumerated above, the early cattle-keeping Neolithic is recognized as having been limited geographically. The subsequent Deccan Neolithic was also ecologically adapted to the central part of the peninsula, and V. D. Krishnaswamy's survey of the Neolithic pattern shows clearly that this was "a local industry developed on the soil" with a nuclear area in Beḷḷāry;[24] its pointed-butt stone axes did not reach the Āndhra deltas nor the west coast, though some have been picked up in Tamil̲ Nāḍu. It also seems unlikely that a language covering as large an area as does Telugu would have remained unfragmented from 1500 B.C. or so to historic times without some kind of unifying factors. Even more convincing is the fact that the Telugu-Kannaḍa boundary bisects the nuclear zone of this Deccan Neolithic. It is also unlikely that the spread of irrigated rice cultivation in itself caused the diffusion of these languages, which as a group seem to have had their focus on the Deccan. Tamiḻ is close to Old Kannaḍa; Telugu and Gōṇḍi broke off somewhat earlier on one side of the Deccan and Tuḷu on the other, while the central Indian Dravidian tribal languages moved northeastward, as their own traditions testify.

Iron Age burials in the south are everywhere characterized by black and red pottery, ranging from Śrī Lankā back to Mahārāshṭra, and Banerjee rightly points out that this links up with a similar pottery in Rājasthān from the Bāṇas culture, a copper-using culture which flourished about 2000 B.C. and was contemporary with part of the Indus Civilization. B. B. Lal has written a provocative paper on the scratch marks on pottery, particularly comparing those on the South Indian Iron Age ware with those on vessels in northwestern South Asia during and after the Indus Civilization, and he also relates these marks to the Indus Civilization script. Other artifacts of the South Indian Iron Age are also traceable to the northwest, such as perforated jars, spouted bowls, and bead types, while the Russet-coated Painted ware diffused from the northern Deccan into Āndhra and Tamiḻ Nāḍu. The kinship system characteristic of South India exists in Mahārāshṭra, Gujarāt, and parts of Rājasthān and has been only partially modified by the kinship system of the North Indian plains, according to Irawati Karve's survey.[25] This is a compelling reason to believe that Indo-Aryan speech has been imposed on former Dravidian-speaking peoples in western India.

Archaeologically and culturally, therefore, it would appear that the Iron Age people of the south were Dravidian speakers—and not only that, but it seems that they brought these languages and that the speech from which modern Dravidian languages evolved became established in the south much later than has been supposed. The Iron Age in the Doāb region was characterized by Painted Gray ware, datable to 1050 to 450 B.C. This ware represented the culture of the *Mahābhārata* period and did not become established in Gujarāt. But the successors of the transplanted Indus Civilization in Gujarāt plus the copper-using Bāṇas culture of Rājasthān were apparently stimulated by the iron-using Indo-Aryan speaking culture of the Doāb. I believe that the pressure of these iron-using peoples on Gujarāt is reflected in the accounts in the *Mahābhārata* of various peoples moving southward after the war and that Indo-Aryan speech may not have become established in Gujarāt until well into the first millennium B.C. The Neolithic-Chalcolithic in Mahārāshṭra seems to persist up to about 700 B.C., as Banerjee points out, though there is some evidence that iron appeared in Karṇāṭaka two or three centuries earlier.

Most of the rest of the south felt the full impact of megalithic iron-using culture only from about the middle of the millennium, and megaliths were apparently built into the Śaṇgam period. From the density of Iron Age burials it seems that population density reached a new plane. It would appear that the major Dravidian languages, each covering so wide an area, became established only with this culture phase.

The evidence is that the Iron Age culture diffused through the south with a militaristic people. They were apparently invincible because they had iron weapons and the horse. In Karṇāṭaka ancient militaristic traditions are certified by the profusion of hero stones and by well-developed traditions of physical competition such as wrestling and boulder-lifting. In Tamil̲ Nāḍu the *pur̲am* category of Śaṅgam literature idealizes militarism, the horse, iron arrowheads, and spears; after a battle sacrifices were made to Kor̲r̲avai, goddess of war, while soldiers danced among the bloody carnage of the battlefield.[26] Victorious armies indiscriminately set fire to whole villages and standing crops, ruined the fields, polluted the drinking water, and left the land to bandits.[27] Such a militaristic tradition, using the iron tools and weapons listed above, plus the rather uniform diffusion of Iron Age material culture and the larger population supported by rice, best explains the extension of a single language such as Telugu or Tamil̲ over so wide an area.

My assumption that the major Dravidian languages spread over the south only about 500 B.C. does not preclude the existence of earlier Dravidian languages—only that there was no earlier culture strong enough to produce such widespread languages. It makes little sense to speak of "Dravidians" in a historical sense at least, for while people in Sindh and Gujarāt might have once spoken Dravidian languages those in the far south might not have done so. I would agree with Andrée Sjoberg that the Dravidian entity in South India is an amalgam of rather divergent peoples and cultures. I would also agree with her that we cannot justifiably speak of any Dravidian civilization in South India in the period under discussion.

PART II: CORRELATION OF ARCHAEOLOGICAL AND LITERARY EVIDENCE FOR THE ŚAṄGAM PERIOD

If Iron Age culture in the south was not civilization when was a grade of cultural evolution that can be called civilization achieved? Literary scholars claim that the Śaṅgam period, the first three centuries A.D., represents civilization in Tamil̲ Nāḍu and Kērala̲, but what of the archaeological evidence?

We shall define civilization as a grade reached by the well-known "primary civilizations" in other parts of the world. It is generally characterized by urbanization usually supported by a fully developed peasant economy specializing in cereals, permanent or monumental buildings, diversified economy, elaborately structured society, formalized religion, the state, and usually writing. We shall see whether the archaeological evidence supports the literary evidence on these points and then ask a further question: Was there a catalyst which stimulated the transition from the Iron Age to the culture of the Śaṅgam period?

The Agricultural Basis: Rice

There is no doubt that the early Tamiḻ kingdoms were located in rice-producing regions: Cōḻas on the Kāvēri, Pāṇḍiyas on the Tāmbaraparaṇi and Vaigai, and Cēras on the Kēraḷa coast. Food production could therefore have supported something more than bare subsistence economy. The literature says that tanks and agricultural facilities were destroyed in warfare.[28]

At the site of Kāvērippaṭṭiṉam on the Kāvēri estuary there is a well-built sluice with rounded walls to funnel the water. This particular structure has not been carbon-14 dated, but nearby was a punch-marked silver coin and Rouletted ware so it was probably contemporary with the Śaṅgam period.[29] Nearby was a brick platform (the "dock," described below) having posts firmly dated to the third century B.C. The Kāvēri delta was producing rice by that date. (The site of Dhāranikōṭa in Guntūr District, Āndhra, is located on similar alluvial soil and has a similar chronology; it is described below.) The Koṟkai excavation suggests an even earlier date for the Tāmbaraparaṇi delta, so that the very early Pāṇḍiyan towns said in legend to have existed there could have been provided with sufficient quantities of locally produced rice. Small sections of many ancient bunds can be seen, rising up to twelve feet above the rice fields. It might be worthwhile to use them to trace the ancient meanderings of the river in the delta in order to locate ancient towns and ports.

Northwestern Śrī Lankā, around Māntai, has elaborate irrigation works of early origin. They were first studied by H. Parker, an irrigation engineer, in 1909. It is clear that some of the structures, such as the Giant's Tank with a bund eleven miles long, were constructed before the historical period, which began in the mid-third century B.C. Water supply was regulated by valve gates. These tanks are associated with what P. Deraniyagala calls the Tabbova-Maradanmaduva culture, characterized by numerous terracotta phalli and other fertility symbols, which are generally found associated with the irrigation facilities and must have been in some cases smashed near the tanks during festivals. Inland from Puttalam there is a complex of megalithic burials, while several *tāḻi* burials have recently been discovered. The rice production of this region supported the two earliest capitals of the island: Tambapaṇṇi (at Māntai on the northeast coast) and Anurādhapura. Probably these irrigation works were part of the Iron Age culture of the island, and though it provided the agricultural base to support incipient urbanization, the latter was not achieved until a new stage of history was set in motion with appearance of the intrusive elements which gave rise to Sinhala civilization.

Urbanization

Śaṅgam literature is elusive on the nature of urban places, and obviously the bulk of the population lived in typical Iron Age villages. The chief description is the well-known one in *Maturaikkāñci*. Considerable information about early towns can be garnered from Greek sources contemporary with the Śaṇgam period; there are over a hundred named towns or political or trade centers mentioned in Śaṅgam literature, Ptolemy's map, and the other Greek sources.[30] Ptolemy lists six coastal places in Tamiḻ Nāḍu to which he appends the word "emporium," meaning an important trade center. Three of these, Muciṟi, Koṟkai, and Kāvērippaṭṭiṇam, are known from Śaṅgam literature to have been respectively the chief ports of the Cēras, Pāṇḍiyas, and Cōḻas. Two others in South India he calls "metropolis," six he calls "mart," two others "city," and five more "town." He also names fifty-eight "inland cities" as well as several other identifiable royal or chiefly seats. Another city, called either Perimula or Perimuda, is tantalizingly called "the greatest emporium of trade in India."[31] From the description given I believe it was on the Vaigai delta near Rāmēśvaram.

Medieval Tamiḻ legends refer to a city called South Madurai or Old Madurai and also to a walled city called Kapāḍapuram, both around the Tāmbaraparaṇi delta. On the basis of evidence given elsewhere I believe that these did exist on the South Indian coast opposite Śrī Lankā in the fourth and third centuries B.C.[32]

Indian archaeologists have dug at a number of the towns mentioned in literary sources, but the results have been meager. At Kāvēripaṭṭiṉam a few structures and some pottery were found, but not the city, which must be buried somewhere under the rice fields and has so far eluded electronic devices designed to detect walls under the soil.[33] At Uṟaiyūr, a Cōḻa capital on the middle Kāvēri well known from the literature, an excavation was conducted by the University of Madras. Level I, which represents the Śaṅgam period, yielded Black and Red ware, Russet-coated Painted ware (both traceable to the Deccan), plus Rouletted and supposedly Arretine ware (of Roman inspiration), besides ordinary red and black pottery. There were shell and paste beads, terracotta gamesmen, bone points, and potsherds inscribed with Brāhmī script. Graffiti marks included symbols interpreted as the sun, moon, fish, trident, pentagonal star, square, arrow, and zig-zag lines. In Level II the Black and Red ware phased out and is probably datable from the late Śaṅgam period to about the sixth century.[34] But the Cōḻa capital has not been found.

The results of excavations at other sites presumed to have been cities in the Śaṅgam period can be quickly summarized. At Ākkāḍu village in Tanjāvūr District, suggested to have been the "Arkatos" of Ptolemy and the second capital of the early Cōḻas, exploration yielded the usual pottery types and some urns,[35] but proper excavation is needed. Ālagarai on the north bank of the Kāvēri in Tiruchirāppaḷḷi District is not known to have been mentioned in the literature as a city, but its location is favorable and there is some evidence of brick structures. Period I had the Black and Red ware and Russet-coated Painted ware, some characteristic dish-on-stand pieces, and the usual beads, bangles, and earrings of terracotta, shell, and glass.[36] The excavation at Tirukkampuliyūr nearby yielded similar results.[37] At Kāñcipuram, excavated by the University of Madras, results at lower levels were disappointing and did not even yield Russet-coated Painted ware. But there are some locally made imitations of Roman amphorae (wine jars) and some interesting terracotta figurines.[38] If this was a city of the Śaṅgam period, excavators have not struck the right location. At Pērūr near Coimbatore, Black and Red ware was found at the lowest level, together with a probable grain silo, and Russet-coated Painted ware appeared just above.[39] Work around Madurai at Kūḍal and Old Madurai nearby was also given up for lack of results.[40] The ancient port sites of Koṟkai and Toṇḍi in the south and Koḍuṅgalūr in Kēraḷa (described below) did not yield any evidence of real cities.

Only in Śrī Lankā at Anurādhapura (described below) did excavation yield substantial quantities of artifacts, partially supporting the literary tradition that it was a city in the third century B.C. having a wall three-quarters of a mile on each side enclosing numerous religious and official structures. Pliny in the first century says that a city named "Palaesimindus" in southern Śrī Lankā had a population of two hundred thousand and that the island had five hundred towns.[41]

We might acknowledge, then, that the many places referred to in the Greek geographies as "town" and "city" were not worthy to be so called, and that the capitals of the Tamiḻ kings were unimpressive. Alternatively, we can infer that they were built with wood. In any case the excavations conducted in regard to what is claimed as the golden age of Tamiḻ history consist mostly of small-scale exploratory trenches. We hope that some time in the future it might be possible to excavate under the sacred and populous parts of such cities as Madurai and Kāñcipuram.

Permanent Buildings

There are allusions in Śaṅgam literature to substantial buildings. Though we may take lightly the references that say town walls "touch the sky," we do know from *Maturaikkāñci* 351–356 that houses were built over the town gates. *Perumpāṇārṟuppaḍai* 319–324 and 446–451 describes a port town with high-storied buildings, large warehouses, and a tall lighthouse reached by climbing a ladder. *Naṟṟiṇai* 45 refers to a venerable town having shops along streets where many carts stood, while *Neḍunalvāḍai* 29–30 mentions a prosperous old town having streets broad like a river.

The forts of the Śaṅgam period were built of burned bricks covered with a reddish clay and usually consisted of an inner and an outer wall, each having a gate. They were surrounded by deep moats, containing crocodiles, which invaders had to cross by boat. The walls were as tall as the moat was deep, and on top were observation posts. Where possible, forts were located on hillocks or mountains whose sides were cut, sometimes enclosing large areas.[42]

The archaeological evidence is skimpy. To my knowledge, forts on hillocks have not been examined to elucidate the chronology of their construction. Brick structures were built in the Śaṅgam period, however. We have referred to the courses of bricks with embedded posts at Kāvērippaṭṭiṉam datable to the third century B.C. and the few bricks found in the Ālagarai excavation in Tiruchirāppaḷḷi District. At Koṟkai on the Tāmbaraparaṇi delta I have seen bricks which are about the size of those of Kāvērippaṭṭiṉam. The most impressive brick and lime mortar structures known are in Wheeler's Arikamēḍu excavation. A little progress has been made in establishing a relative chronology based on brick sizes.

Elsewhere in the south the vast Buddhist complexes in Āndhra preceding and contemporary with the Śaṇgam period in Tamiḻ Nāḍu leave no doubt about engineering ability nor about skill in stone sculpture—though stone sculpture in Tamiḻ Nāḍu preceding medieval centuries is represented only by a few fragments. In Āndhra there is a circular brick structure at Dhāranikōṭa which is datable to the first century. Even earlier at Bhaṭṭiprōḷu near the coast the brick stupa is relatively impressive; Rea's dating of it to the early second century B.C. probably still holds good. The brick stupas at Banavāsi in Karṇāṭaka are probably of Mauryan date. The excavation at Anurādhapura in Śrī Lankā, noted below, suggests that substantial construction of mud and wood preceded the large brick structures that appeared from the second and first centuries B.C.

Wood has been used to construct palaces and temples in Kēraḷa up to modern times, and Karunaratne has described how wood has always been the chief material of indigenous Śrī Lankā architecture in spite of some very impressive brick structures. Careful excavation will be required to elucidate more information about the early architecture of Tamiḻ Nāḍu.

Extensive Trade

We read in *Maturaikkāñci* that constant traffic flowed through city gates, while in the bazaar there were dealers in conch bangles, gold, salt, textiles, copper wares, perfumes, and sandal paste. Ox carts went in trains, and caravans of merchants were escorted.[43] Sea trade was important. *Paṭṭiṉappālai* 116–137 tells how goods brought to the Cōḻa port were piled up as if "without limit" and customs officers "busily stamped each bundle with the king's tiger seal and threw it aside." Fishers and coastal traders called Paratavar imported horses, sandalwood, and some kind of white stone; they traded in pearls, right-whorled conches, conch bangles, gems, tamarind, salt, and fish. Horses and other riches came from the north.[44] We read too that great ocean ships sliced through the waves bringing fine products to the Pāṇḍiyan shore. The well-known passage in *Puṟanāṉūṟu* 343. 1–10 tells how high-piled sacks of pepper were taken by Yavanas (Romans or other Westerners) in exchange for gold, while *Patiṟṟuppattu* 55. 3–6 says the Cēra king had warehouses ready for valuables coming by ship. From the Greek geography *Periplus* we know that the Cēra port of Muciṟi imported spikenard from the Gaṅgā, while silk, tortoise shell, and betel leaf came from distant Southeast Asia. Also imported were gold, copper, tin, lead, brass, coral, glass, pearls, ivory, and gems. At the Cōḻa port there were merchant colonies speaking different languages.[45] *Cilappatikāram* 14. 104–12 tells how ships sailed directly from Southeast Asia to the Cōḻa coast with special woods, silk, sandal, camphor, and spices; though this is a work of early medieval centuries, we might suppose, given the excavation of Roman ports on the Cōḻa coast and the list of goods mentioned in the *Periplus* as imported from Southeast Asia, that ships sailed directly across in the Śaṅgam period. We know too that Indonesians sailed to the Persian Gulf and the east coast of Africa in the early centuries of the Christian era and must have touched South India. But archaeology has not yet turned up objects identifiable as having come from across the sea, with the exception of Roman coins and pottery.

The study of numismatics will continue to throw much light on ancient trade patterns. Wheeler has shown what can be done by his review of the distribution and dating of Roman coins. Exact dates have been set for the beginning and end of Roman trade, which begins in the first part of the first century. The finds of coins mark out a trade route from the Kēraḷa coast through the Palghat Gap across the peninsula to the Roman trading stations on the east coast.[46]

Indian scholars have paid more attention to the distribution of punch-marked silver bar coins such as were used all over India from Mauryan times on. Many hoards and thousands of individual specimens have been found. A hoard of 193 coins turned up in Erode Taluk, 49 in Kalliḍakkurichi Taluk, and 83 in Pollāchi Taluk; the museums in Trivandrum and Madras have large collections of them, but most are surface finds. The punch marks on them need to be studied in detail, arranged in a relative chronology, and related to those on similar coins in North India and Śrī Lankā. Though they might have been minted by guilds, it appears that some, at least, were issued by kings, as we see below.

Though archaeological evidence is slight, we are assured by the literary references to trade and by the numismatic evidence that parts of South India by the Śaṅgam period had moved considerably beyond subsistence economy and that trade intensity could have supported what we might term civilization.

Division of Labor and Complex Society

The various Śaṅgam literary works mention diverse occupations: kings, chieftains, scholars, sacrificial priests, *purohita*, poets, warriors, customs agents, shippers, foreign merchants, horse importers, blacksmiths, carpenters, potters, salt makers, pearl divers, caravan drivers, guards, tailors, fishers, dancers, drummers, plow farmers, shepherds, hunters, weavers, leatherworkers, and robbers. So far archaeology has not produced evidence of well-developed handicrafts such as this list suggests. But for such a variety of occupations to be patronized there must have been an elite element leading an essentially urban way of life.

Named peoples may be considered as tribes, geographical or occupational castes, or ruling lineages: Kaḍambar, Vēḷir, Ōliyar, Aruvāḷar, Maṟavar, Āyar, Kōcar, Ōviyar, Paratavar, Paḷaiyar, Vēḷāḷar, Nāgar, and others. These functioned essentially as castes; both Paḷaiyar and Paratavar were living in Koṟkai under the Pāṇḍiyas. But caste as a structural system was not as rigidly hierarchical as it was to become in later medieval centuries.

N. Subrahmanian in his discussion of social life[47] mentions the *Tolkāppiyam* list of four categories: Andaṇar (Brahmans), Araśar (kings), Vaiśiyar (traders), and Vēḷāḷar (farmers), while it ignores most of the other names of peoples. These references in the *Tolkāppiyam* obviously show influence of the Sanskritic social ideal. In the Śaṅgam period the idea of ritual pollution was present, and some castes had their own hamlets. One problem with Subrahmanian's analysis is that he does not often distinguish the evidence of Śaṅgam literature from that of the epics which are medieval in date. K. Kailasapathy's work is most useful for understanding the function of bards in the context of the royal court and what kinds of heroes were idealized.

As for archaeological corroboration, the Brāhmī inscriptions on caves around Madurai and elsewhere mention people having the following occupations: lapidary, charioteer, gold merchant, cloth merchant, copra merchant, iron merchant, salt seller, and toddy seller.[48] In addition we know there were Jaina and Buddhist monks. The merchants had accumulated wealth sufficient to excavate caves for the ascetics. If this was true in the second century B.C., we can suppose that society would have been quite occupationally diversified in the Madurai of the Śaṅgam period.

Large-scale lateral excavation is required to elucidate the ancient social structure, and so far this has been done only in Āndhra at Amarāvatī and Nāgājarkoṇḍa. At the latter site, dated third and fourth centuries A.D., H. Sarkar has been able, by careful observation of the layout of the Buddhist structures, to distinguish five types and then to infer the existence of several particular Buddhist sects. Some of the construction was funded by merchants.

In Śrī Lankā the most promising site for large-scale lateral excavation would be Anurādhapura, though to date excavation has consisted mostly of trenches. The city is described in chapter 10 of the *Mahāvaṁsa* and may be datable to 300 B.C. or before. It is said to have had a wall containing the royal precincts, a place for Yonas (Yavanas, perhaps people from northwestern India claiming links with the Greek-derived post-Alexandrian kingdoms), and four residential sections. Outside its gates were chapels or hermitages of Jainas, Ājīvikas, Brāhmaṇas, and ascetics of heretical sects. Apart from the city was a separate village for Caṇḍālas (funerary functionaries and sweepers) and beyond that a line of huts for huntsmen. One would like to know if such social complexity could be archaeologically demonstrated for any city in Tamil̠ Nāḍu during the Śaṅgam period.

Formal Religions

In the Śaṅgam period there were Brahmans who supported the royal lineages, priestly Brahmans, Brahmans who studied the four Vedas,[49] and also "nonsacrificing" Brahmans who cut conch shells.[50] Subrahmanian has discussed the Pārppār or Andaṇar, Brahmans of the Śaṅgam literature who lived apart in their own clean *cēri*.[51]

There was a town on the Kērala coast which Ptolemy called "Bramagara" and another around Cape Comorin called "Brakme" where the "Brakhmai Magai" lived.[52] These have not been located, and the sacred spots such as Cape Comorin, Mount Mahendra, Tirucendūr, and Tiruppati have not been excavated. There is no specific archaeological evidence of how local deities or religious symbols were incorporated into the Great Tradition, nor of the processes of universalization, which we know from the literature occurred as part of civilizational development. There are, however, the rock-cut caves donated for the use of ascetics, such as the one at Tirupparankuṉṟam outside Madurai which has three rock platforms designed for use as beds. Some of these caves were used by Jaina ascetics, and possibly some by members of other sects.

The State

The fusion of "tribes" into incipient states was going on before and during the Śaṅgam period, much as it had in the plains of the north half a millennium earlier. Cēra kings fought numerous battles on the sea and incorporated all the territory from northern Śrī Lankā up to Tuḷuva, amply described in the *Pattuppāṭṭu*. Pāṇḍiyas took the Coimbatore region from the Paḻaiyar and the cape region from the indigenous Āys. Most of the states had their capitals inland with subsidiary capitals on the coast: for the Pāṇḍiyas, Madurai and Koṟkai; for the Cēras, Karūr and Toṇḍi; for the Cōḻas, Uṟaiyūr and Kāvērippaṭṭiṉam; for northern Śrī Lankā, Anurādhapura and Māntai; later on for the Kaḍambas, Banavāsi and Vākai; and for the Pallavas, Kāñcipuram and Māhabalipuram.

Monarchy was supported with numerous institutions such as royal sacrifices, fictitious ancestry such as that linking the Pāṇḍiyas to the *Mahābhārata* heroes, and feudatory chiefs. Their rule was validated by Brahmans and flattered by poets. They gave munificent gifts such as elephants, chariots, gold, and gems, and perhaps also lands and villages.

There is at least some archaeological evidence to show that the state controlled some aspects of the economy. The Cēra kingdom arose precisely where the Roman and other coin hoards are located in Kēraḷa, and it apparently extended across the Palghat Gap following the trans-peninsular trade. It is interesting to observe that all the Roman coins to be seen at the Trichūr museum have a deep slash across the Roman emperor's face. As for the Cōḻas, they certainly controlled the several ports along their coasts from which Roman artifacts have been excavated, and we have noted the literary reference to the king's customs agents levying import duty, then stamping the goods with the king's tiger seal. The Pāṇḍiyan king controlled the pearl fishery in the Gulf of Maṉṉār, as the *Periplus* says and as Megasthenes implied about 300 B.C.[53] Imitations of Roman coins have been found in Paṇḍiyan territory, presumably made by the state.

A hoard of silver punch-marked coins numbering 1128 was found in Bōḍināyakkaṉūr. They appear to be almost new, without the multiple punch-marks generally found on worn coins which were apparently stamped when they moved from one territory to another. B. Ramachandran thinks these were a Pāṇḍiyan issue because each has on the reverse the Pāṇḍiyan fish symbol. They are struck to a standard, a local one which was not a widespread unit of weight. Another hoard found at Māmbalam, Madras, numbered 770, and found with it was a solitary Roman coin of Augustus, placing the hoard in the early Śaṅgam period. These were more worn, with a number of punch-marks on most of them. The silver had been diluted by twenty-five percent copper, and considering wear, they were generally struck to a standard.[54] Even if these were produced by guilds rather than the state they give us an idea of the level of social and economic organization.

Writing

The well-developed literary forms of the first to third centuries A.D. had their roots in the Tamiḻ Brāhmī of the second century B.C. Short donative inscriptions in this script are found above the caves excavated for ascetics clustered around Madurai, with some in Tirunelvēli and Tiruchirāppaḷḷi Districts. These are exceedingly important for understanding early South India because they push history back two or three centuries prior to the Śaṅgam period.

The linguistic aspects of these inscriptions have been studied by Mahalingam, Zvelebil, and others. Iravatham Mahadevan claims that at least three of the later ones refer to monarchs ruling during the Śaṅgam period.[55]

I am quite sure we must look to Śrī Lankā to understand the origin of the Tamil Brāhmī script, which is like the North Indian and Śrī Lankā Brāhmī except that is has several modifications designed to suit Tamiḻ phonemics. Whereas there are some sixty of these inscriptions in Tamiḻ Nāḍu, there are vastly more in Śrī Lankā, dating from the third century B.C. Paranavitana's recent edition of the early Brāhmī ones alone contains over one thousand inscriptions! Also the Śrī Lankā inscriptions mention the first Tamiḻs known by name from any source; six of them had built a platform for meditation and had taken Prākrit names.[56] A merchant from Īlam (Śrī Lankā) donated the Tirupparankuṉṟam cave outside Madurai. The names of persons in the early Tamiḻ Nāḍu inscriptions are mostly Tamiḻ names comparable to those of Śaṅgam literature.

The epigraphic styles of all the early categories of Brāhmī script in India have been compared by A. H. Dani. He feels that the script of Śrī Lankā and Tamil Nāḍu is closely related to the early script of Gujarāt, which is correct, and that those of the south are not earlier than the first or second century A.D.,[57] and in this he is wrong, for at least six of the very earliest Brāhmī inscriptions in Śrī Lankā mention persons known to have been contemporary with Aśoka and King Devānampiya,[58] so that script was used in the third century B.C. W. S. Karunaratne of the Śrī Lankā Department of Archaeology thinks Brāhmī script was used in the island even before the formal acceptance of Buddhism, for by the third century B.C. it had already become adapted phonetically to Śrī Lankā Prākrit,[59] and the chronicles tell us that Brāhmaṇas, Jainas, Ājīvikas, and proponents of other sects were in the island before Buddhism was officially adopted.

On grounds of the style of script alone, the third or second centuries B.C. can be taken as the time when Madurai became a religious and something of a literary center. It was a town having an elite merchant class or royalty capable of patronizing the Buddhist and Jaina monks for whom the caves were prepared. Whereas the cave inscriptions of that period are almost entirely Tamiḻ, the scratched Brāhmī writings on potsherds from Arikamēḍu and a few other sites of the Śaṅgam period do contain some Prākrit words and names, and even some phonetic change influenced by Prākrit. Iravatham Mahadevan therefore distinguishes these two as the earlier and the later Tamiḻ Brāhmī forms.

Trends of Acculturation

It is clear that in the Iron Age the Tamiḻ region was well populated, but we can hardly speak of civilization in that period. It is also clear that certain aspects of the civilization that began to evolve in the second century B.C. and culminated by the third century A.D. were derived from outside South India. Among these aspects are: Brāhmī script; ascetic orders; the giving of caves with donors' names inscribed; Prākrit linguistic influence; Brahmanical deities; the notion of producing a grammar such as the *Tolkāppiyam* and some of the ideas it contains such as the fourfold segmentation of society; mythology and nomenclature of the *Mahābhārata* such as Pāṇḍiya, Madurai (Mathurā), and Paratavar (Bhārata);[60] the issuing of silver punch-marked bar coins and stamping of successive symbols on them; and probably the use of burned bricks and the idealization of four-square capital cities. These elements along with horses and other items were imported from the north. What sparked the development of early civilization in the south? What were the agents of acculturation?

While inland sites so far excavated have yielded poor results, work on the coasts has shown Roman evidence at a number of sites (see Part IV), and rouletted ware and imitations of it, of Roman inspiration, found its way to many places inland in the peninsula.

But I believe we shall be misled if we attribute too much importance to Roman influence. First, the foundations of civilization in Tamiḻ Nāḍu were laid two or three centuries before the time of Roman trade. Second, no Roman influence can be detected in the subsequent cultural history of

Tamil̠ Nāḍu, about the only influence persisting into medieval times being the motif of an oil lamp held in the cupped hands of a figurine, which does go back to the Śaṅgam period[61] and is of Roman origin.

A second alternative is to look for cultural stimulus by sea from Southeast Asia. Though all evidence points to urbanization in India earlier than in Southeast Asia, several scholars have thought that the movement of Malays about the time of Christ from Borneo and adjacent islands to Madagascar, and their trade links with the Persian Gulf and the Azanian coast of Africa, would have left some imprint on peninsular India. It is possible that single and double outriggers are a Southeast Asian invention, and some spices mentioned in the Tamil̠ epics such as cloves and nutmeg are of Southeast Asian origin. But W. G. Solheim, a specialist in Southeast Asian archaeology, spent several weeks in Śrī Lankā in 1970 working with the Department of Archaeology and looking specifically for such influences; he found nothing. Excavation in South India has similarly drawn a blank on this point.

A third alternative is to look northward for influences that might have diffused down the peninsula, for there is sufficient evidence of Mauryan influence in Karṇāṭaka and Āndhra. But there is no evidence of early civilization between the gold-bearing zones of Karṇāṭaka and Madurai. Likewise the tract between the Godāvarī and the Kāvēri has little to offer as regards early civilization.

We turn, therefore, to Śrī Lankā as the source of inspiration of much that was incorporated into the early civilization of Tamil̠ Nāḍu. Archaeology in the island is of some assistance. Excavations at Anurādhapura show microlithic tools of late hunters, and above is a level containing Black and Red ware characteristic of the Iron Age and also a beaten pottery. There is Rouletted ware characteristic of the first century and finally a black polished ware datable to about the fifth century. Carbon-14 dates are awaited.[62] The excavation shows a settlement not inconsistent with the detailed description of Anurādhapura given in the *Mahāvaṁsa*, having outlines three quarters of a mile on each side enclosed by a wall with four gates and surrounded by a moat. Brick structures were found, but they were not impressive, while apparently considerable wood was used in construction. Between the first century B.C. and the second century A.D. larger structures were built, as described in the chronicles, including *dāgäba* (stupas). When the city fell to the Tamil̠ invader Eḷāra in the second century A.D. it was strongly fortified.[63]

Tirukētīśvaram (Māntai in Śaṅgam literature, Tambapaṇṇi in the Śrī Lankā chronicles) has been explored archaeologically several times. The site is on the northwest coast and appears to be rich in medieval evidence of Chinese and Arab trade; it also has Roman ware. I think it was the first capital of the Sinhala-speakers in the island. It is now being excavated by R. H. De Silva, and we await his report. Another old site is Vävuniya, connected with early large-scale irrigation works. There is a stone wall, with some boulders ten feet in diameter, running from coast to coast about fifteen miles north of Anurādhapura, evidently an early political boundary but as yet undated.[64]

The early history of Śrī Lankā in the fifth to third centuries B.C. certainly points to Gujarāt and to western India in general. Some of the literary, etymological, and archaeological evidence has been summarized by H. C. Ray. While the chronicles attribute civilization in the island to influences coming from the Bengal side, in fact this aspect of the history of the island began only in the third century B.C. with the introduction of Buddhism. Ports on India's northwest coast such as Prabhāspāṭān, Bharukaccha, and Sopāra are known from both literature and archaeology to have been centers of shipping from the earliest historical times, and probably this tradition continued there from the Indus Civilization. Probably these ports, along with Gujarāt as a whole, were inhabited by Dravidian-speakers prior to the diffusion of Indo-Aryan in the first half of the first millennium B.C., an offshoot of which is the old Prākrit of Śrī Lankā. The early trade between Gujarāt and Śrī Lankā would not have left South India unaffected, and in fact I believe it was the chief stimulus in the evolution of civilization in the Tamil region, which arose on the southern coast opposite Śrī Lankā and parallel with the civilization of that island.[65]

Dr. S. Paranavitana, former Director of Archaeology in Śrī Lankā, has written two remarkable essays duplicated by the Department of Archaeology entitled "An Account of Alexander the Great and Greek Culture in a Universal History Written in the Reign of Mahāsena" and "Newly Discovered Historical Documents Relating to Ceylon, India, and Southeast Asia." He claims to have discovered faint interlinear inscriptions on medieval inscribed stones which narrate parts of a "universal history" written by a Śrī Lankā scholar who had lived in Panjāb and had learned Greek, Latin, Śaka, Sogdian, Persian, and Tocharian. The histories are soberly written, mention all the best-known early Greek figures, and describe Greek history, philosophy, and drama. These works cut through the early Buddhist overlay of the chronicles of the island and confirm that early civilizing elements reaching it emanated by sea from Sindh and Gujarāt. This discovery has the most profound importance for our understanding of the development of civilization in Tamiḻ Nāḍu—if these records are authentic. Some Śrī Lankā scholars deny that such interlinear inscriptions exist.[66] Paranavitana is now issuing the original texts as he claims to have found them, and resolution of this matter is awaited with interest.[67]

Paranavitana's *Inscriptions of Ceylon*, volume I, *Early Brāhmī Inscriptions* collects the numerous publications he previously issued of the earliest inscriptions and has valuable additional notes. The mention of Tamiḻs in a number of these has not been noticed by most South Indian historians. It seems clear to me that Brāhmī script spread from Śrī Lankā to southern Tamiḻ Nāḍu and then northward, for the inscriptions in Tirunelvēli and Madurai Districts are earlier than those in the Kāvēri and Coimbatore areas. This suggests that literacy, and indeed incipient civilization in general, spread from the southern Tamiḻ coast northward—and this is supported by the medieval legends of sunken Old Madurai and Kapāḍpuram on the Tāmbaraparani delta opposite Śrī Lankā.

Were the agents of acculturation in the south primarily religious practitioners (as might be suggested by the Jaina and Buddhist rock-cut caves), princely expatriates (as given in the Śrī Lankā chronicles), or merchants? This question has also been asked by historians of Southeast Asia regarding the implantation of Indian civilization there. I believe that merchants first came to the far south for pearls, gems, and conches considerably before the Mauryan period, that they brought the first Brāhmī script, and that in their wake came monks and Brahmans. The earliest Brāhmī inscriptions in Śrī Lankā specifically mention many merchants, including Tamiḻ horse importers. The early Brāhmī inscriptions around Madurai are on caves donated by persons including seven categories of merchants. Obviously they patronized the ascetics. The Brāhmī inscriptions on potsherds, including the twenty or so found at Arikamēḍu, are largely names indicating ownership. Probably the western Prākrit that took root in Śrī Lankā and made some impact upon Tamiḻ Nāḍu was the linguistic vehicle of wide trade patterns. Careful excavation at more coastal sites such as those mentioned in Part IV will be required to substantiate this hypothesis.

Part III: Early Civilization in Karṇataka, Āndhra, and Kēraḷa

Karṇāṭaka

Wheeler's well-known excavations at Brāhmagiri and Chandravaḷḷi show Iron Age culture on which was superimposed Sātavāhana material. Five Roman and many Sātāvahana coins show that this period extended from the first to third centuries A.D., contemporary with the Śaṅgam period for Tamiḻ Nāḍu. Pottery is wheel-turned and of high quality. The most characteristic type is Russet-coated ware, in which rectilinear decorations in white are painted under a russet wash; it is found in contemporary sites in Āndhra and Tamiḻ Nāḍu. In these sites, Rouletted ware dates from the same period and shows direct or indirect Roman contact. The site of Māski, described in great detail by Thapar, contains a similar horizon, including high-quality shell bangles, terracotta figurines, iron, copper, burned bricks, punch-marked coins, and one sherd of Northern Black pottery.

What is needed now is a site with evidence of Mauryan influence between the Neolithic or Iron Age levels and the Sātavāhana material. In the excavated sites, the megalithic Iron Age culture persisted to the beginning of the Āndhra period. But it is well known that there are six Aśokan inscriptions in Karṇāṭaka (three at Brāhmagiri, one each at Koppāl and Śanganakallu near Beḷḷāry, and one at Siddhāpura forty-five miles east of Māski; the latter mentions Suvaṇṇagiri, "gold mountain," as the seat of a viceroy of Aśoka). The ancient Tamiḻs knew of the Mauryas of Karṇāṭaka[68] and also had heard of the wealth of the Nandas at Paṭaliputra. The Kadamba kings of Karṇāṭaka claimed descent from the Nandas. It is possible that the alleged retirement of Candragupta Maurya in Śravaṇa Beḷgoḷa was not the earliest contact between the northern kingdoms and the gold mine region of Karṇāṭaka.

All six Aśokan inscriptions in Karṇāṭaka are on or near gold mines. Mining engineers have informed me that there is not a gold reef outcropping that was not worked in ancient times utilizing both open pit and shaft mines. Numbers of these have yielded querns and rubbers used for crushing the ore, and hand-made as well as wheel-made pottery. Some of the ancient mines were 300 feet deep, and one was 600 feet. In this mine, timber supports from 250 feet below the surface have been carbon-14 dated roughly A.D. 60 and 150, so it is probable that it was worked for a long time before the first century.[69] In the mines of Kōlār, Neolithic gray ware and also Black and Red ware have been recovered. What is needed is archaeological examination of the earliest mines and excavation of sites near them to discover Mauryan and pre-Mauryan influence in the region.

At Banavāsi I discovered two stupas which may provide archaeological evidence of Mauryan civilization in Karṇāṭaka. Both were located outside the town not far from the river. The largest had been half removed by the Public Works Department; it had been built in at least two stages. The *Māhavaṁsa* records that Aśoka sent a missionary to Banavāsi, and in the first century B.C. a contingent of monks from there came to the dedication of a stupa at Anurādhapura. In Gulbarga District another stupa was recently discovered, with sculptures, pillars, bricks, and pottery. Prākrit inscriptions were in Brāhmī script of about the second century A.D.[70] It is also reported that there are early Buddhist remains at Candrapura, upstream from Goā. Excavation at Banavāsi and other Buddhist sites may yield the desired evidence of the extensions of Mauryan civilization into Karṇāṭaka.

I believe that there was sea trade along the west coast long before the

Mauryan period and that in fact Solomon's navy obtained gold, silver, ivory, apes, peacocks, iron, tin, and lead from the Karṇāṭaka coast.[71] The Koṇkaṇī language of Goā is also intrusive and seems to be derived from a base resembling early Gujarātī; it might have been brought to that port area by sea. Such coastal sites as Kaḍavāḍa (Karwar), Gokarṇa, Kumta, and Honnāvara need careful examination. To date there has not been one excavation of early historic times on the whole west coast of India between Bombay and Cape Comorin.

Āndhra

Āndhra was known to the Mauryas, for there are two Aśokan inscriptions in Kurnool District. It might also have been affected by North Indian civilization earlier, but one is at a loss to know where to look for archaeological evidence of it. Coins of the Sātavāhanas who dominated the region around the time of Christ show the extent of their rule.

The best-known archaeology in Āndhra has been at Buddhist sites such as Nāgārjunakoṇḍa and Amarāvatī. These have been studied with the view of understanding Buddhism rather than finding out the total range of occupation or chronology. At Nāgārjunakoṇḍa the whole valley is now flooded, but fortunately it was all explored and important sites were excavated before the dam was completed; artifacts are now housed in a new museum, on a mesa once occupied by an Ikṣvāku fort, which is now reached by boat. There was evidence the valley was occupied in all periods of the Stone Age, and more than thirty Buddhist monasteries and establishments were excavated.[72] Amarāvatī is well known for its stupa and exquisite early Buddhist sculpture.[73] This site has been neglected since its art objects were studied in the 1950s, but it deserves stratigraphic excavation to elucidate the origins of early Buddhist civilization in Āndhra. It seems to go back to the second century B.C.

Two early historic sites in the deltas have been stratigraphically excavated. At Kēsarapaḷḷi in Kṛṣṇa District, the lowest levels were flooded and unfortunately could not be excavated. Above the Chalcolithic and Iron Age horizons was one with Rouletted ware, contemporary with the Sātavāhanas, and above this was a level with no Rouletted ware but brick structures.

At Dhāranikōṭa, Guntūr District, there is construction dating from about 200 B.C.; Northern Black pottery was found. There were several structural phases, of which all but the last were related to what is claimed to be an embankment and wharf abutting on a navigation channel. In Phase I the channel was cut into a natural laterite ridge, and in Phase II a large wooden wharf was built, with which glass and Black and Red ware is associated. Phase III had a brick wharf along the river, with a mud embankment, and Rouletted ware. In IV there was a brick revetment on both sides of the channel, and a new gray ware appeared. In V the embankment was raised and a retaining wall of laterite blocks was constructed. In VI the embankment was repaired, then abandoned, and in VII it was converted into a defensive wall associated with post-Iṣkvāku artifacts.[74] Other sites, such as Jambuladinne and Miṭṭapaḷḷi in Kurnool District, are said to have yielded Russet-coated ware, but these sites are not well reported.

There are numerous other potential sites in the Āndhra deltas which have not been touched. There is an interesting stupa at Bhaṭṭiprōḷu, twenty-five miles inland and four miles south of the Kṛṣṇa but formerly on the river. The core of it was excavated and described by Rea in 1894. It had been built in four stages, and it was estimated from epigraphy that the earliest was datable to 200 B.C. The four relic caskets contained a total of sixty-two pearls, besides gold and gems. Local legends connect this stupa with Áśoka's missionary movement.

Masulipaṭām was an important port at the time of the *Periplus*, which refers to it as Maisolia and says it manufactured and exported immense quantities of fine muslins. Ptolemy lists about eleven ports along the Āndhra coast; Pliny says the Andarae have thirty walled towns, and he describes their army.[75] Śrīkākuḷam, nineteen miles to the west of Masulipaṭām, is said in local tradition to have been a port connected with the earliest Āndhra kings and it was destroyed by the shifting river; nearby are other sites of possible early historic interest.[76] The extent of Sātavāhana rule in Āndhra can be judged from the distribution of their coins; among these Rapson listed nineteen "ship coins" showing vessels with one or two masts and double rigging.[77]

One would like to know whether there was any extensive urbanization or civilization in the Āndhra deltas before the appearance of Buddhism and whether this religion with its institutions was introduced by sea as a result of east coast trade, diffusing upstream in Āndhra.

Kēraḷa

Ptolemy and other Greeks mention more than fifteen towns along the Kēraḷa coast, while Śaṅgam literature refers to half a dozen more. The main port is known as Muciṟi in Śaṅgam literature and as Muziris to the Greeks. A subsidiary capital, Toṇḍi, is perhaps identifiable with Poṉṉāni to the north. From the Greek records we can recognize Vaikkarai, Nīlakanta, and the Netrāvati mouth (Mangalore) as ancient port towns. Pantar in the south of Kēraḷa and Pūḻi (probably around Tuḷuva) were ports of the Śaṅgam period but have not been identified.

One would like to know the antiquity of Brahmanism in Kēraḷa, which must have been intrusive by the Śaṅgam period according to the above-mentioned two towns named after Brahmans. Judaism and Christianity also came by sea to Kēraḷa either in the first century or within three centuries thereafter, followed later by a fourth religion, Islam. It is probable that the cultural history of Kēraḷa was dominated by coastal contact even in prehistoric times, but archaeology is required to supplement legends such as those of the intrusion of the Nambūtiri Brahmans by sea and the Paraśurāma and Agastya legends.

Krishnaswamy Iyengar has identified the Cēra capital of Vañci with Muciṟi and says this is modern Koḍuṅgalūr (Cranganore); he thinks that Karūr was just south of it (though others identify it as the Karūr near Salem in Tamiḻ Nāḍu). In any case, Koḍuṅgalūr was an important historic port until Cochin surpassed it. The erstwhile Government of Cochin conducted a small excavation at Koḍuṅgalūr, and although the published report is useless,[78] the artifacts are on view in the Trichūr museum. There is a gray pottery with a beaten striated surface, large urns characteristic of the Iron Age, Rouletted ware, and some plates of fine gray ware that might have been imported. There was a high-necked sprinkler, iron spikes, rings, copper rods, and nails. The excavation bared parts of rooms and drains of laterite blocks. There were also Arab and Chinese wares. These artifacts could range from the first to the tenth centuries. Recently the Southern Circle of the Department of Archaeology did undertake another small excavation nearby at a site called Cēramān Parambu, which Krishnaswamy Iyengar thought was an early one. Artifacts found were the same as in the previous excavation, but below a level datable to the seventh century there was only sand.[79] So we are still left to rely on the literary and numismatic evidence.

The trade mentioned in the Śaṅgam and Greek literature is evidenced by the Roman coins. In addition several hoards of punch-marked bar coins have been discovered from central Kēraḷa,[80] the focal region which also had trade connections with Tamiḻ Nāḍu. Aside from the small Koḍuṅgalūr excavations, there has not been one stratigraphic dig on the whole coast of Kēraḷa or Karṇāṭaka and surely this is among the most glaring gaps in South Indian early history.

Part IV: Coastal Sites of Tamiḻ Nāḍu

Excavated Coastal Sites

Best known of the excavated coastal sites is Arikamēḍu, two miles south of Pondicherry. The site was investigated by several Frenchmen, described by Pattabiraman and then by Casal, and finally reexcavated and described in detail by Wheeler. The site was dated on the basis of Arretine ware from Italy to the middle of the first century, and it passed its zenith by the end of that century (though dating on the basis of this pottery style alone has been questioned). It also had Roman amphorae, Roman as well as locally made Rouletted ware, and a Roman gem. There were substantial brick structures: a wall 150 feet long, brick tanks, and a brick drainage system, besides numbers of other structural fragments. Apparently Romans used the port to import Southeast Asian goods directly without utilizing Indian intermediaries.

Nāṭṭamēḍu is a similar site fifteen miles to the south, near Karaikkāḍu, excavated by K. V. Raman.[81] There were more than a dozen complete amphorae (some with residue of resin from the wine) and some Rouletted ware. Glass beads were made on the spot (as at Arikamēḍu). The materials are on display at the Tamil̲ Nāḍu Department of Archaeology.

Kāñcipuram, though not on the coast, was close to two probable ancient ports (see below). As mentioned, the small excavation carried out there has not been published, but a noteworthy feature of the site is that locally made amphorae were found side by side with imported Roman ones.

We now have amphorae from four sites on the eastern coast of Tamil̲ Nāḍu and Roman coins from three others and from two more sites in northern Śrī Lankā (Kantarōḍai and Tirukētīśvaram).

Kāvērippaṭṭin̲am is known to almost all Tamil̲s because of its mention in the epics, where it is called Pukār; the setting of the opening of the *Cilappatikāram* is there, its heroine the daughter of a rich merchant of the city. But it was a port in Śaṅgam times too, for Ptolemy, who calls it Khaberis, refers to it as an "emporium" and it is mentioned as a port in the *Akkita Jākata*. Today only a small hamlet occupies the spot, and what is left of the Kāvēri there is only a minor trickle. Several locations have been excavated, but the city itself has eluded discovery.[82]

Veḷḷaiyan̲-iruppu ("white man's settlement") is a location near Kāvēri-paṭṭin̲am where structures of the ninth to twelfth centuries were found. When it acquired that name is not known.

Van̲agiri, another nearby location, has the previously mentioned brick inlet channel with sluice gate. Here a punch-marked coin was found in the same level, and nearby was black Rouletted ware of local manufacture. The structure shows that irrigation facilities were carefully built.

Pallavan̲ēśvaram, also nearby, has a large brick structure which is thought to have been a Buddhist monastery because a figure of Buddha was found; it is perhaps datable to the fourth or fifth century.

Kiḷaiyūr is the most important location at Kāvērippaṭṭin̲am. Here a structure called a dock was uncovered (by S. R. Rao, who called the Lothāl tank a dock). I am not so sure that it was a dock, for it consists of only three to seven courses of bricks with a lengthwise channel or drain—

a small structure or the fragment of one. The bricks are the largest found in South India, some seventeen and others twenty-three inches long. Remnants of eight large posts were visible when it was excavated. The posts were obviously large enough to hold up a superstructure of considerable weight; it is unlikely that such large posts would have been planted to tie up boats, and the structure is too small to have served as a dock for large cargo vessels. Moreover, because the bases of the posts had been preserved, they must have remained in wet soil since they were set. This location has yielded a punch-marked coin. It is the date of this brick structure that is important: the middle of the third century B.C., coincident with Buddhist expansion and more frequent ship traffic along the east coast of India.

Koṟkai, a port of the Śaṅgam period, is now a small village on the Tāmbaraparaṇi delta five miles inland and two miles west of the river. It is referred to a score of times in Śaṅgam literature and also in the Tamiḻ epics. It was a pearl market and the seat of the Pāṇḍiyan vice-royalty. It was first excavated by Caldwell in 1876 and I twice explored the region in 1965 (see below). It was excavated in 1968–1969 by the Tamiḻ Nāḍu Department of Archaeology under R. Nagaswamy. Five locations were excavated, and three cultural phases were identified. Period I is characterized by urn burials, Black and Red ware, a black ware, a coarse red ware, shell bangles, carnelian beads, and bone ornaments. Period II is Pāṇḍiyan and has red wares, slipped wares, brown wares, sawed conches, and terracotta beads. Period III is post-Pāṇḍiyan, with coarse red and black wares. The site yielded several ring wells or soakage pits and part of a brick structure; nine potsherds bearing Brāhmī letters were found but the words are fragmentary, probably names. Large quantities of pearl oyster shells were uncovered, for this was a pearl market as the texts say. But the most important result of this excavation is the carbon-14 date, obtained from charcoal of a hearth in the lowest excavated stratum. The excavation here was a small pit 2.69 meters down, and no artifacts were associated. The date is 795 ± 95 B.C.[83]

Potential Coastal Sites

In 1965 I traversed the Tamiḻ Nāḍu coast from north to south, visiting most of the previously mentioned sites and noting in addition the following which I deem worthy of further exploration or excavation.

Kāñcipuram, though not on the coast, was reached by Roman influence as we have seen. It is thirty miles from Mahābalipuram, which may have been its port. Further stratigraphic excavation needs to be done there. Hsüan-tsang records that he saw there a stupa built by Āsokarāja. A Chinese record from the end of the second century B.C. says that the

Chinese got pearls, glass, rare stone, and rhinoceros there, and gave in return silks and gold.[84] A Chinese coin of the same time was found in Chandravaḷḷi.

Mahābalipuram has so far been studied primarily for its Pallava antiquities, but attention should now be turned to excavation. It must have been a natural port for Kāñcipuram, for it has a long backwater separated from the ocean by a rocky knoll used formerly for both defense and lookout. The site may have been Ptolemy's Melange (Māvilankai), said to have been an emporium. It is also perhaps identifiable with the port of Nīrpāyaṟṟurai mentioned in *Perumpāṇāṟṟuppaḍai.*[85] There seem to be pre-Pallava ruins there, and in places the sand is red with brick dust.

The Pālāṟu mouth has large bricks, ring wells, and other materials. Recently this area was explored by the Tamiḻ Nāḍu Department of Archaeology, though it was not excavated. Near the suburb of Vayalūr on the river mouth there were large bricks, imported Rouletted ware, an amphora fragment, forty large conical storage jars, and beads.[86] It may be that Kāñcipuram had access to the sea through the Pālāṟu, a tributary of which passes near that city.

Marakāṇam, on a large inlet north of Pondicherry, appears to have been a harbor which is now filled in with salt beds. It may have been the Sopatma of the *Periplus* and therefore the Ēyil of *Cirupāṇāṟṟuppaḍai*; three other towns mentioned in that poem are perhaps identifiable nearby.[87]

The mouth of the Veḷḷāṟu also appears to be a likely site; it was an Arab ship-building port, and quantities of pottery are lying about outside the two modern towns of Kaḍalūr and Porto Novo, but the antiquity of the site has not been established.

On the Kāveri delta eight miles east of Kāvērippaṭṭiṉam is a place called Karaiyappāl. I am informed by K. V. Raman that fishermen say they see structures under the water here, which is shallow, and that sculptures have been brought up. The epics state that Kāvērippaṭṭiṉam was deluged. But then most coastal cities are said in legend to have been deluged, and it is also rumored that structures can be seen in the sea off Mahābalipuram, so we cannot count on such reports being reliable.

Nāgappaṭṭiṉam was an important port at the height of the Cōḻa kingdom (tenth to twelfth centuries) and traded with Southeast Asia. The name suggests connection with Nāgas such as are mentioned as a coastal kingdom in the epics. At Sikkal seven miles to the west, the Tamiḻ Nāḍu Department of Archaeology picked up some Black and Red ware and urn pieces, while at Tirumalairāyaṉpaṭṭiṉam, eight miles to the north, the same ware was found on a canal bank.[88]

Toṉḍi on Palk Bay was certainly an ancient port mentioned in Śaṅgam literature (to be distinguished from the Toṇḍi in Kērala and also the Toṇḍi in Southeast Asia). The place called Agarlu in the *Periplus* was thereabouts, I believe, and not at Uṟaiyūr; it exported pearls and muslins. A magnetometer survey here did not lead to the discovery of any subsurface structures. I ascertained from local residents that several punch-marked coins have been found.

Dhanuṣkōḍi and the whole Vaigai estuary need exploration, and though I did not find any ancient sites there, I believe the estuary had ancient towns such as Perimula ("great promontory"?), called by Pliny "the greatest emporium of trade in India." The end of the peninsula, called Kōḍi, was one of the earliest points of the south known in the north (mentioned in *Arthaśāstra* ii.11.2) and was used by the Greeks as a fixed point for navigation.[89] Pāśikā, also mentioned in the *Arthaśāstra* as a source of pearls, I believe to have been there. The sanctity of Rāmēśvaram is undoubtedly linked in origin with the importance of the Vaigai delta in trade. But the sequence of the shifting of the river between Palk Bay to the Gulf of Maṉṉār has to be worked out.

Muttupēṭṭai, west of the delta, is a village on an old channel of the Vaigai, which used to flow southward into the Gulf of Maṉṉār. It was a pearl market, as its name indicates. Interesting medieval ruins near the village contain abundant Arab and Chinese pottery. The antiquity of the site is not known.

At Koṟkai I ascertained several facts before it was recently excavated, and the archaeological potential is considerable. For instance, villagers found a pointed-butt stone ax, the southernmost one so far found, which probably supports the carbon-14 date for pre-Iron Age occupation of the site and early agriculture. Large bricks were seen at one location, and the villagers had picked up punch-marked coins, besides Roman coins, Pāṇḍiyan imitations of Roman coins, and medieval coins from Southeast Asia. There is a ruined structure, locally called a "palace," of uncertain but probably early medieval date. The soil is thick with plain red or black potsherds down to and below the water level. Fortunately, further excavation is in progress at this place.

On a mound near the "chemical factory" a few miles southwest of Koṟkai I discovered ancient pottery lamps, ring wells, and large bricks. This mound overlooks an ancient river bed now used for rice cultivation, and near it are some sacred spots. The mound seems to be largely an artificial one and perhaps was the site of a port.

Kāyal (Paḻaiya Kāyal, Old Kāyal) was an early medieval port, south of the Tāmbaraparaṇi mouth. It was later superseded by the Muslim port of Putukāyal (New Kāyal), which Marco Polo visited. Its age is unknown but it may be ancient, for there are early Buddhist antiquities nearby in a thorn-tree patch at Cūraṉkāḍu.

Tirucendūr south of the Tāmbaraparaṇi delta has a well-known temple on the beach. The deity there is Murukaṉ, said in myths to protect the Pāṇḍiyas from incursions from the sea. The site is probably the same as the Centil of *Tirumurukāṟṟuppaḍai* and is certainly one of the earliest Pāṇḍiyan sacred spots. Somewhere in the vicinity, if not at Tirucendūr, was the early Pāṇḍiyan capital of Kapāḍapuram, and also on the coast in the same region was South Madurai. These are supposed to have been the first two Pāṇḍiyan capitals and the sites of the first two literary academies; I believe there is historical substance to the legends.[90]

Kaṉṉiyākumari (Cape Comorin) is mentioned as early as Eratosthenes and was one of the points in the south known earliest to North India, while the Greeks used it as a fixed point for navigation.[91] Ptolemy lists it among the ports, though one fails to see today where a port could have been located. Its name indicates that it has always been the sacred place of a feminine deity, and it may also have had near it the ancient and sacred Paḥruḷi river. Excavation at the cape would almost certainly be rewarding.

Part V: Conclusions

Historically the following conclusions are most important. First, Dravidian languages most likely spread through much of the south only with the Iron Age, roughly 500 B.C. Second, a grade of cultural evolution we can call civilization was achieved between 200 B.C. and A.D. 300, even though particular features such as literature, monumental brick construction, or coin hoards did not appear evenly in all the nuclear centers of the south. And third, the appearance of early civilization in the Tamiḻ area was sparked by sea trade and by the development of civilization in Śrī Lankā.

As regards archaeological research, the following conclusions are most important. First, more excavation is required of Iron Age habitation sites (as apart from funerary remains) off the Deccan, a beginning in premedieval archaeology along the west coast strip must be made, and a series of potential sites along the Tamiḻ Nāḍu coast needs further investigation. Second, scholars of South India would do well to make more use of the abundant early Śrī Lankā material to establish trends and chronologies applicable to South India. And third, results of many excavations have not been fully published and the materials are not available for organized research.

NOTES

1. See the classification attempts by Soundara Rajan (1968) and Deraniyagala (1971, p. 47ff.).
2. Sankalia (1962), pp. 30–31. Other relevant works bearing on peninsular India are G. C. Mohapatra's *The Stone Age Cultures of Orissa* (Poona, 1962)

and V. N. Misra's "Paleolithic Cultures of Western Rajputana," *Bull. Deccan College Research Inst.* 24 (1963–1964).

3. *IAR* (1962–1963), p. 12; (1963–1964), p. 19.
4. See the various papers and debates in V. N. Misra and M. S. Mate.
5. Allchin (1968), p. 77.
6. Wheeler (1948).
7. Zeuner; the dating of these sites on the basis of raised beaches is now considered questionable.
8. Deraniyagala (1971), p. 47ff.
9. B. B. Lal, "Birbhanpur, a Microlithic Site in the Damodar Valley, West Bengal," *AI* 14, (1958).
10. F. R. and B. Allchin (1962).
11. See notes on rock drawings in Chittor, Andhra, of dancing, in *IAR* (1963–1964), p. 1; in Raisen District of Madhya Pradesh of boar, bison, rhino, stag, elephant, singly and in rows, in *IAR* (1963–1964), p. 14; A. P. Khatri, "Rock Paintings of Adamgarh (Central India) and Their Age," *Anthropos* 49, (1964), pp. 759–769; Nagaraja Rao (1965), pp. 90–103; Deraniyagala (1971), pp. 38–39.
12. U. R. Ehrenfels, *The Kadar of Cochin* (Madras, 1952); C. von Fürer-Haimendorf, *The Chenchus: Jungle Folk of the Deccan*; L. A. Krishna Iyer, *Social History of Kerala. vol. I: The Pre-Dravidians* (Madras, 1968).
13. As these are not in South India we are not citing the many references pertaining to these and similar sites; for a summary, see Sankalia (1962) and the annual issues of *IAR* under "Maharashtra."
14. *IAR* (1967–1968), pp. 3–5.
15. See Allchin on Piklihāl and Uṭnūr; Nagaraja Rao on Tekkalakōṭa; Subbarao on Sanganakallu; Majumdar on Kupgal; and the issues of *IAR* under "Mysore" and "Andhra Pradesh."
16. Allchin (1968), pp. 163–70, 199.
17. *IAR* (1964–1965), pp. 22–23; (1967–1968), pp. 26–30.
18. Allchin (1968), p. 230.
19. *IAR* (1967–1968), pp. 26–30.
20. *IAR* (1967–1968), pp. 37–39.
21. Wheeler (1959), pp. 150–169.
22. Allchin (1968), p. 265.
23. Nagaswamy (1970), p. 52; personal observation.
24. Krishnaswamy, p. 50.
25. Irawati Karve, *Kinship Organization in India*, 3rd ed. (Bombay, 1968). Mrs. Karve has delineated Mahārāshṭra, Gujarāt, and part of Rājasthān as a third kinship zone, distinct from those of the northern plains and the south. Though Indo-Aryan speech has been superimposed, older practices such as cross-cousin marriage and a girl going to her natal home for the birth of her first child have been retained; there is also no mandatory village exogamy as is found in the northern plains.
26. *Patiṟṟuppattu* 57; see also Subrahmanian, pp. 163, 167, 252.
27. *Maturaikkāñci* 126; *Puṟanāṉūṟu* 15; Subrahmanian, p. 165.
28. *Patiṟṟuppattu* 25, 26, 33.
29. *IAR* (1963–1964), pp. 20–21; (1964–1965), p. 24.
30. Ptolemy, Strabo, Pliny, and the *Periplus*, relevant portions of which are reproduced in translation in R. C. Majumdar.

31. Pliny vi.21. 23; Aelian xv.8.
32. Maloney (1968), pp. 99–105; (1970), pp. 612–614; also (1971).
33. Information personally obtained fron Nagaswamy and other archaeologists in Madras.
34. *IAR* (1964–1965), p. 25; (1967–1968), p. 30.
35. *IAR* (1964–1965), p. 23.
36. *IAR* (1963–1964), pp. 20–21.
37. *IAR* (1962–1963), p. 14.
38. Information personally obtained in Madras.
39. Information personally obtained in Madras.
40. Information personally obtained in Madras and Madurai.
41. Pliny vi. 22. 24.
42. Subrahmanian, pp. 160–162.
43. *Kuṟuntokai* 390; *Akanāṉūṟu* 89.
44. *Perumpāṇāṟṟuppaḍai* 319–324.
45. *Maturaikkāñci* 75–78.
46. Wheeler (1954).
47. Subrahmanian, pp. 258–261.
48. Iravatham Mahadevan (1970), p. 14.
49. *Patiṟṟuppattu* 63.1 and *patikam*; *Puṟanāṉūṟu* 357, 358.
50. *Akanāṉūṟu* 24.1–4.
51. Subrahmanian, pp. 262–277.
52. Ptolemy vii. 1. 8 and 74.
53. *Periplus* para. 58; Megasthenes in Arrian in R. C. Majumdar, pp. 222–223.
54. B. Ramachandran.
55. Iravatham Mahadevan (1970), pp. 3–4.
56. Paranavitana (1940).
57. Dani, pp. 72–73, 66–68, 216–219, 225.
58. Paranavitana and Godukumbura, pp. 210, 217, 218, 220, 231–232.
59. Personal communication.
60. Maloney (1969).
61. *Neḍunalvāḍai* 101–103.
62. Information obtained in Anurādhapura based on H. W. Codrington's excavation.
63. Ellawala, pp. 123–124.
64. Based on exploration of the Śrī Lankā Department of Archaeology.
65. Maloney (1968 and 1970).
66. Silva and Fernando.
67. In addition to the two above-mentioned printed lectures, see S. Paranavitana, *Ceylon and Malaysia* (Colombo, 1966) and also *Greeks and Mauryas* (Colombo, 1967). I discussed these controversial finds with him in 1965, 1970, and 1971, and feel inclined to reserve further judgment pending full publication of the texts.
68. *Akanāṉūṟu* 251.
69. Information derived from gold mining engineers and from artifacts taken from the mines; see also Allchin (1962).
70. *IAR* (1967–1968), pp. 37–38.
71. Maloney (1968), pp. 227–233.
72. Soundara Rajan (1958); H. Sarkar.
73. A. Ghosh and H. Sarkar; C. Sivaramamurti.

74. *IAR* (1963–1964), pp. 2–4; (1964–1965), pp. 2–3.
75. Pliny vi.21.22.
76. Rea, pp. 39–40.
77. Rapson, pp. 22–23, plate 5.
78. *Annual Report of the Archaeological Department*, Cochin State (1947), pp. 1–3.
79. Information obtained from K. V. Raman and other archaeologists.
80. H. G. Unnithan.
81. Information obtained from the excavator.
82. *IAR* (1962–1963), pp. 2–4; personal observation, with information from the Tamiḻ Nāḍu Department of Archaeology.
83. Information obtained from the excavators; see also Nagaswamy.
84. Duyvendak, pp. 9–10.
85. *Perumpāṇaṟṟuppaḍai* 219 and commentary, pp. 89–90.
86. Nagaswamy and other archaeologists.
87. Vēnkaṭacāmi has plotted the location of several towns mentioned in this poem.
88. *IAR* (1964–1965), p. 24.
89. Ptolemy i.13.1–9; vii.1.96.
90. Maloney (1968), pp. 99–105; (1970), pp. 612–614; also (1971).
91. Eratosthenes in Strabo xv.1.14.

BIBLIOGRAPHY

General Works on Indian Archaeology

Allchin, B. *The Stone-tipped Arrow*. London: Phoenix House, 1966.
Allchin, B. and R. *The Birth of Indian Civilization*. Baltimore: Penguin, 1968.
Ancient India, Bulletin of the Archaeological Survey of India. Delhi, annual (abbreviated here as *AI*).
Banerjee, N. R. *The Iron Age in India*. Delhi, 1965.
Bühler, G. *Indian Paleography*. English ed. New Delhi, 1960.
Dani, A. H. *Indian Paleography*. Oxford: Oxford University Press, 1963.
Duyvendak, J. *China's Discovery of Africa*. London, 1949.
Gordon, D. H. *The Prehistoric Background of Indian Civilization*. Bombay, 1958.
Indian Archaeology—A Review. New Delhi, annual (abbreviated here as *IAR*).
Lal, B. B. "A Picture Emerges—An Assessment of the Carbon-14 Datings of the Protohistoric Cultures of the Indo-Pakistan Subcontinent." *IA* 18 and 19, 1962–1963.
Misra, V. N. and Mate, M. S. *Indian Prehistory: 1964*. Poona, 1965.
Sankalia, H. D. *Prehistory and Protohistory in India and Pakistan*. Bombay, 1962.
Sen, D. and Ghosh, A. K. *Studies in Prehistory*. Calcutta, 1966.
Wheeler, M. *Rome Beyond the Imperial Frontiers*. London: Bell, 1954.
———. *Early India and Pakistan*. London: Thames and Hudson, 1959.

South Indian Archaeology

Allchin, F. R. "The Stone Alignments of Southern Hyderabad." *Man* LVI, no. 150, 1956.
———. "The Neolithic Stone Industry of the North Karnataka Region." *Bull. School of Oriental and African Studies* XIX, no. 2, 1957.
———. "Poor Men's *thālīs*: a Deccan Potter's Technique." *Bull. School of Oriental and African Studies* XXII, no. 2, 1959.

———. *Utnūr Excavations*. Andhra Pradesh Archaeological Series, no. 5, Hyderabad, 1961.
———. *Piklihal Excavations*. Hyderabad, 1961.
———. "Upon the Antiquity and Methods of Gold Mining in Ancient India." *J. Econ. Soc. History of the Orient* 5, 1962.
———. *Neolithic Cattle-Keepers of Southern India*. Cambridge: Cambridge University Press, 1963.
Allchin, F. R. and B. "The Archaeology of a River Crossing," in T. N. Madan, *Indian Anthropology*. Bombay, 1962.
Andhra Pradesh Archaeological Series. Hyderabad.
Annual Report of the Archaeological Department. Cochin, 1947 and 1948.
Banerjee, N. R. "The Megalithic Problem of India," in D. Sen and A. K. Ghosh, *Studies in Prehistory*. Calcutta, 1966.
Banerji, N. R. and Soundararajan, K. V. "Sanur 1950 and 1952." *AI* 15, 1959.
Casal, J.-M. *Fouilles de Virampatnam-Arikamedu*. Paris, 1949.
———. *Site urbain et sites funéraires des environs de Pondichérry*. Paris, 1956.
Damilica, Journal of the Tamil Nadu Department of Archaeology. Madras (from 1970).
Das, G. N. "The Funerary Monuments of the Nilgiris." *Bull. Deccan College Research Inst.* 18, 1957.
Elliot, W. *Numismata Orientalia: Coins of Southern India*. London, 1866.
Filliozat, J. "Intercourse of India with the Roman Empire during the Opening Centuries of the Christian Era." *J. Indian History* XXVIII, pt. 1, 1950.
Fürer-Haimendorf, C. von. "New Aspects of the Dravidian Problem." *Tamil Culture* II, no. 2, 1953.
Ghosh, A. and Sarkar, H. "Beginnings of Sculptural Art in South-east India: A Stele from Amaravati." *AI* 20 and 21, 1964–1965.
Gopalachari, K. *Early History of the Andhra Country*. Madras, 1941.
Gururaja Rao, B. K. "Megalithic Culture in Tiruchirapalli District." *Prof. K. A. Nilakanta Sastri Felicitation Volume*. Madras, 1971.
Hornell, J. "The Utilization of Coral and Shells for Lime-burning in the Madras Presidency." *Fisheries Bull.* VIII, 1914–1915.
Hyderabad Archaeological Series. Hyderabad.
Iravatham Mahadevan. *Corpus of the Tamil-Brahmi Inscriptions*. Seminar on Inscriptions. Madras, 1966.
———. "Tamil-Brahmi Inscriptions." Lecture printed by Tamil Nadu State Dept. of Archaeology. Madras, 1970.
Journal of Tamil Studies II, no. 1. "Special Number on the Decipherment of the Mohenjodaro Script." Madras, 1970.
Kailasapathy, K. *Tamil Heroic Poetry*. Oxford: Oxford University Press, 1968.
Krishnan, M. A. (ed.). *Gold Mining in India*. Bangalore, 1963.
Krishnaswami, V. D. "The Neolithic Pattern of India." *AI* 16, 1960.
Krishnaswamy Iyengar, S. *Cēran Vañci*. Madras, 1956.
Mahalingam, T. V. *South Indian Paleography*. Madras, 1968.
Majumdar, G. and Rajaguru, S. *Ashmound Excavations at Kupgal*. Poona, 1966.
Maloney, C. *The Effect of Early Coastal Sea Traffic on the Development of Civilization in South India*. Ph. D. dissertation, University of Pennsylvania, 1968.
———. "The Paratavar: 2000 Years of Culture Dynamics of a Tamil Caste." *Man in India* 48, no. 3, 1969.
———. "The Beginnings of Civilization in South India." *J. Asian Studies* XXIX, no. 3, 1970.

———. "Dynastic Drift: A Process of Cultural Universalization." *Prof. K. A. Nilakanta Sastri Felicitation Volume*. Madras, 1971.
Nagabhushana Rao, S. "Middle Stone Age Industry at Asifabad." *Bull. Deccan College Research Inst.* 24, 1963–1964.
Nagaraja Rao, M. S. "Recent Exploration in the Tungabhadra Basin—The Chalcolithic Phase." *Bull. Deccan College Research Inst.* 23, 1962–1963.
———. *The Stone Age Hill Dwellers of Tekkalakota*. Poona, 1965.
———. "Survival of Certain Neolithic Elements among the Boyas of Tekkalakota." *Anthropos* 60, 1965, pp. 482–486.
Nagaswamy, R. "Architecture in Tamilnad." *J. Tamil Studies* 1, no. 1, 1969.
———. "Exploration and Excavation." *Damilica* 1, 1970.
Pattabiraman, P. Z. *Les Fouilles d'Arikamédou*. Pondicherry, 1946.
Ramachandran, B. "Study of Weight Standards of Silver Punch-marked Coins of Mambalam and Bodinayakannur Hoards." *Trans. Arch. Soc. S. India*, 1957–1958.
Ramachandran, K. S. "Megalithic Zones in India." *Prof. K. A. Nilakanta Sastri Felicitation Volume*. Madras, 1971.
Rapson, E. *Catalogue of the Coins of the Andhra Dynasty*. London, 1908.
Rea, A. *South Indian Buddhist Antiquities*. Archaeological Survey of India, 1894.
Sahney, V. *The Iron Age in South India*. Ph.D. dissertation, University of Pennsylvania, 1965.
Saletore, B. "Ptolemy and Western India." *J. Indian History* XL, pt. 1, 1962.
Sankalia, H. D. "The Beginning of Civilization in South India." *J. Tamil Studies* 1, no. 2. 1969.
Sarkar, H. "Some Aspects of the Buddhist Monuments at Nagarjunakonda." *AI* 16, 1960.
Seshadri, M. *Report on the Jadigenahalli Megalithic Excavations*. Mysore, 1960.
Sewell, R. "Roman Coins Found in India." *JRAS*, 1904, pp. 593–598.
Sharma, Y. D. "Rock-cut Caves in Cochin." *AI* 12, 1956.
Sivaramamurti, C. *Amaravati Sculptures in the Madras Government Museum*. Madras, 1956.
Sjoberg, A. "Who Are the Dravidians?" in A. Sjoberg (ed.), *Symposium on Dravidian Civilization*. New York: Jenkins, 1971.
Soundara Rajan, K. V. "Stone Age Industries near Giddalur, District Kurnool." *AI* 8, 1952.
———. "Studies in the Stone Age of Nagarjunakonda and Its Neighbourhood." *AI* 14, 1958.
———. "Determinant Factors in the Early History of Tamilnad." *J. Indian History*, 1967 (III) and 1968 (I).
Srinivasan, K. R. "Megalithic Burials and Urn Fields in South India in the Light of Tamil Literature and Tradition." *AI* 2, 1946.
———. "Megalithic Monuments of South India." *Trans. Arch. Soc. S. India*, 1958–1959.
Subbarao, B. *Stone Age Cultures of Bellary*. Poona, 1948.
Subrahmanian, N. *Sangam Polity*. Bombay, 1966.
Sundara, A. "New Discoveries of Ash-mounds in North Karnataka: Their Implications." *Prof. K. A. Nilakanta Sastri Felicitation Volume*. Madras, 1971.
Thapar, B. K. "Porkalam 1948: Excavation of a Megalithic Urn-burial." *AI* 8, 1952.
———. "Maski 1954: A Chalcolithic Site of the Southern Decan." *AI* 13, 1957.

Transactions of the Archaeological Society of South India. Madras, annual; especially Silver Jubilee Volume, 1962.
Vēnkatacāmi, Mayil Cīni. "Ciruppāṇaṉ Ceṉṟa Peruvaḻi." *Tamil Culture*, 1961.
Wheeler, E. R. M. "Arikamedu: An Indo-Roman Trading Station on the East Coast of India." *AI* 2, 1946.
———. "Brahmagiri and Chandravalli 1947: Megalithic and Other Cultures in Mysore State." *AI* 4, 1947–1948.
Yazdani, B. *The Early History of the Deccan.* Oxford: Oxford University Press, 1960.
Zeuner, F. and Allchin, B. "The Microlithic Sites of Tinnevelly District, Madras State." *AI* 12, 1956.
Zuckermann, S. *The Adichanallur Skulls.* Madras, 1930.
Zvelebil, K. "The Brahmi Hybrid Tamil Inscriptions." *Archiv Orientalni* 32, 1964.

Relevant Items Concerning Śrī Lankā

Allchin, B. "The Late Stone Age in Ceylon." *J. Royal Anthro. Inst.* 88, 1958.
Ancient Ceylon, Journal of the Archaeological Survey of Ceylon. Colombo, annual (from 1971).
Brohier, R. L. *Ancient Irrigation Works in Ceylon.* Colombo, 1935.
Ceylon Administration Reports (Archaeology). Colombo, annual.
Deraniyagala, P. "Some Aspects of the Prehistory of Ceylon." *Spolia Zeylanica*, 1944–1946.
———. "Some New Records of the Tabbova-Maradanmaduva Culture of Ceylon." *Spolia Zeylanica*, 1961.
Deraniyagala, S. "Prehistoric Ceylon—A Summary in 1968." *Ancient Ceylon* 1, 1971.
———. "Stone Implements from a Balangoda Culture Site in Ceylon—Bellan Bandi Palassa." *Ancient Ceylon* 1, 1971.
Ellawala, H. *Social History of Early Ceylon.* Colombo, 1969.
Gunasekera, U., Prematilleke, P., and Silva, R. "A Corpus of Pottery Forms Found in Ceylon." *Ancient Ceylon* 1, 1971.
Karunaratne, L. K. "Architecture in Wood." *Ancient Ceylon* 1, 1971.
Paranavitana, S. "Tamil Householders' Terrace, Anurādhapura." *JRAS—Ceylon Branch*, 1940.
———. "An Account of Alexander the Great and Greek Culture in a Universal History Written in the Reign of Mahāsena." Lecture reprint. Colombo, 1964.
———. "Newly Discovered Historical Documents Relating to Ceylon, India, and Southeast Asia." Lecture reprint. Colombo, 1964.
———. *Ceylon and Malaysia.* Colombo, 1966.
———. *Inscriptions of Ceylon*, vol. I: *Early Brāhmī Inscriptions.* Colombo, 1970.
Paranavitana, S., and Godukumbura, C. E. (eds.). *Epigraphia Zeylanica* V (Brāhmī inscriptions). Colombo, 1963.
Parker H. *Ancient Ceylon.* London, 1909.
Pieris, P. E. "Nagadipa and Buddhist Remains in Jaffna." *JRAS—Ceylon Branch*, 1917.
Ray, H. C. (ed.). *History of Ceylon* I, pt. 1. Colombo, 1959.
Seligmann, C.G. and B. Z. *The Veddas.* Oosterhout: Anthropological Publications, 1969 (first ed. 1911).
Silva, R. and Fernando, D. "The Use of Photogrammetry in the Deciphering of Inscriptions with Special Reference to Ceylon." *Ancient Ceylon* 1, 1971.

Literary Sources

The Kauṭilīya Arthaśāstra, trans. R. P. Kangle. Bombay, 1965.
The Mahāvaṁsa, ed. and trans. W. Geiger. London: Luzac for the Pali Text Society, 1964.
All the Greek sources mentioned are translated in R. C. Majumdar (ed.), *Classical Accounts of India*. Calcutta, 1960.
All the ancient Tamiḻ sources mentioned are published with commentaries (in Tamiḻ) by the Śaiva Siddhanta Publishing Society, Madras.

Ancient Tamil Literature: Its Scholarly Past and Future

GEORGE L. HART III
University of Wisconsin

Among the most important sources for the study of ancient India are the Tamil anthologies and other representatives of the earliest Tamil literature. The six earliest anthologies can be reliably dated back to the second and third centuries A.D., while the *Kalittokai*, the *Paripāṭal*, and the *Pattup-pāṭṭu* are a little later.[1] The *Tolkāppiyam*, a prescriptive grammar and system of poetics, has often been considered to be even older than the earliest anthologies but has now been shown to describe paleographic features which do not enter the language until the fifth century A.D.[2] Other works which are probably pre-Pallavan are the eighteen minor works (*Patiṉeṇ-kīlkkaṇakku*), the *Cilappatikāram*, and the *Maṇimēkalai*, all of which were probably written about the fifth and sixth centuries A.D. All the anthologies are rich in the details of everyday life which are neglected in most Sanskrit literature. It is no exaggeration to say that they furnish a better view of the daily life of the ordinary Tamilian of their period than is available for any other period or area of premodern India. It would be difficult to make too much of this fact. Current Indian histories consist far too much of unimaginative rehearsals of dynasties and generals; moreover, the source material for most ancient Indian history has been Sanskrit literature, which, while overwhelming in quantity, ignores for the most part the great majority of the population, who were neither Brahmans nor nobles. As a result, those customs and patterns of daily life with which we are acquainted are not representative of the majority of the people of ancient India. A reading of any of Nilakanta Sastri's books discloses many facts concerning the daily life and culture of the Brahmans of South India, who were never more than a tiny (though important) minority, but it reveals an almost total lack of information concerning other segments of the South Indian population, even those high non-Brahman castes in whose hands the power has almost always been held. Ancient Tamil literature, on the other hand, was written by high-class poets who followed the model of the oral poetry of the Pāṇaṉs and Paṟaiyaṉs, men of the lowest castes, and is devoid of both high-class and Brahmanical bias. For this reason, it gives a more accurate picture of the social life and customs of the area to which it belongs than does any other classical literature of India.

Not only does ancient Tamil literature furnish an accurate picture of widely disparate social classes; it also describes the social condition of Tamilnad much as it was before the Aryans arrived in the south. In other words, it reveals what at least one part of pre-Aryan India was like. It is true that Nilakanta Sastri and others have suggested that early Tamil literature is indebted to Sanskrit and that it shows a hybrid society in which Aryan and non-Aryan elements cannot be separated. In fact, however, there is relatively little which the most ancient Tamil owes to Aryan influence. Words of Sanskritic origin are quite few, comprising less than two percent of the *Murukāṟṟuppaṭai* and one percent of the *Pattuppāṭṭu*,[3] itself later than the earliest works. This shows that Tamil literature developed at a time when Sanskrit did not have the boundless prestige it had attained when the other South Indian languages, which from the beginning are full of Sanskrit words, developed literatures. It follows that Sanskrit, and the northern culture for which it was the vehicle, had not penetrated into Tamilnad to a degree sufficient to supplant indigenous customs at the time when Tamil literature developed in the first centuries A.D. As regards customs, it is true that Brahmans were present in South India by the time of the Tamil anthologies and that they had some influence; and it is a fact that Buddhism and Jainism had been present in Tamilnad for a few hundred years; yet almost all the customs described in ancient Tamil are wholly alien to Aryan India of the time. Those elements which are Aryan, such as the three fires, are generally associated with Brahmans. When the anthologies were written, Brahmans were not yet used in indigenous temples and their presence was not demanded at marriages (a function they assumed as early as the *Cilappatikāram*),[4] both of which facts show that they were relatively recent arrivals.

The availability of a literature describing Tamil society at a time when it was still unaffected by Aryan elements makes it possible to trace the origin of many customs and conventions which made their way into North India and eventually became pan-Indian. Especially significant is the insight which ancient Tamil provides into the development of Indian religion. The religion of the early Tamils was an animistic one in which divine forces were conceived of as immanent within actual objects and as potentially harmful. These divine forces, called *aṇaṅku,* were for the most part not personified as gods; hence early Tamil literature is almost wholly lacking in mythology (another fact which shows how unaffected it is by Aryan elements, as later Tamil borrowed and developed the mythology of North India). This power had to be rigidly controlled. As a result, religious rites were carried out by the lowest castes: the Paṟaiyaṉs, the Pāṇaṉs, the Tuṭiyaṉs, and the Vēlaṉs (here caste translates *jāti,* Tamil *kuṭi*; it is indigenous to South India and has nothing to do with *varṇa,* an Aryan system which has never been present in Tamilnad). There is evidence that the low status of these castes and their religious duties, which made them handlers of dangerous power, are intimately connected. These castes had the job of lighting the cremation fire and of worshiping the memorial stone, which was thought actually to be inhabited by the spirit of a dead hero. The Vēlaṉ, who is even today found among the Paṟaiyaṉs of Kerala, would dance ecstatically as he was possessed by Murugan, an indigenous god. The Paṟaiyaṉ, the Pāṇaṉ, and the Tuṭiyaṉ would each play a special instrument which was thought to be inhabited by sacred power and which was used for various ritual purposes. The pollution which is attached to the low castes is thus a legacy of indigenous Dravidian religion. It should be pointed out, however, that it has been influenced by Brahmanism. With the advent of the Brahmans as the new sacerdotal order, religious elements not identified with the Brahmans kept their dangerous properties while elements which the Brahmans espoused (many of which were indigenous) were set up opposite to them and were considered to be pure.[5] Extreme measures were taken to insulate these elements from the dangerous powers, and so pollution in its modern sense came into being. It is not for purely theological reasons that Rāmānuja makes one of the most important qualities of God *nirmalatvam,* untaintedness.

Ancient Dravidian religion also elucidates the origin of many pan-Indian customs which have to do with women.[6] In early Tamil, sacred power (*aṇaṅku*) clings to a woman and, as long as it is under control, lends to her life and to that of her husband auspiciousness and sacred correctness. But it is a power which must be kept firmly under control, lest it wreak havoc. Thus women must carefully observe chastity; they must restrain themselves in all situations, having "chastity increased by patience, with sharp teeth which their tongues fear if they talk loudly." At the dangerous times associated with birth and death, a woman must practice strong asceticism. When she is menstruous, she must stay outside the house and cannot touch dishes, while for a period of several days after childbirth (called *puṉiṟu*) she is impure and cannot see her husband. After the death of her husband, she is especially dangerous and must shave her head, cake it with mud, sleep on a bed of stones, and eat lily seeds instead of rice. It is interesting to note that the tonsure of widows appears first in Sanskrit in the *Skandapurāṇa* in the ninth century A.D. If a widow is chaste and young, she is so infected with magic power that she must take her own life, her condition being such that "her youthfulness makes her sweet life tremble even though she is alone for a few seconds in the vast guarded palace of her husband where the eye of the drum [*muḻavu*] never sleeps" (*Puṟam* 247). It is possible to trace the importation of virtually all these customs related to woman's chastity into Aryan India.[7]

Ancient Tamil illumines several other elements of Indian civilization. Caste, for example, is found in the anthologies. There it is clear that caste is indigenous to South India and did not depend for its development on the *varṇa* system which was later superimposed on it (and which never had more than superficial importance for the caste systems of South India). It appears that the caste system was somewhat less elaborately developed at the time of the anthologies than it was later, though it is difficult to tell exactly since any information gleaned with regard to caste is incidental to the poetry. It is clear that each caste possessed a magical fitness to do certain work, especially those low castes whose occupations involved close association with and control of *aṇaṅku*, sacred power. Thus there are at least three discrete castes whose main function is to sing and play instruments: each caste plays a different type of drum and has certain instruments which are peculiar to it.

Other customs found in early Tamil include *pūjā* with flowers; temple worship; drawing designs in front of houses (*kōlam* or *raṅgāvali*); the king as the locus of sacred power (the early Tamil king is far more like the Indian king of classical Sanskrit than is the Vedic one); ecstatic worship of gods; use of the parasol by king; use of grass and dung as insulators from dangerous magic forces; and the performance of funerals by outcastes. Other customs died out but still provide insight into Indian culture: the erection of a memorial stone (*naṭukal*) in which the spirit of a dead hero was thought to reside; the establishment of a royal tutelary tree (*kaṭi maram*) which symbolized the king's connection with heaven and whose hewing down was the first task of an enemy; the worshiping with blood and liquor of a royal drum (*muracu*, whence Sanskrit *muraja*) made from the skin of a bull which defeated another bull and from the wood of an enemy tutelary tree; the use of various drums to evoke the sacred in battle (such drums are sometimes called the agency by which the battle is won); the sacrifice performed after battle in which skulls were used as pots, filled with blood, stirred with severed arms, cooked up by a barren woman, and offered in a ceremony modeled after the marriage ritual; and *vaṭakkiruttal*, a ceremony in which a slighted king starved himself to death together with those of his retinue and friends who would join him. The description of these and other customs and the assessment of their importance is one of the most critical tasks of Tamil scholars.

The significance of early Tamil for the history of Indian literature is perhaps even greater than its importance for other fields. According to the Allchins, there was for a long period before the birth of Christ an extremely conservative and homogeneous culture in the Deccan which produced the megaliths found there today.[8] It was this culture which gave rise to Tamil civilization. In the north, this Deccan culture merged with Aryan culture in Maharashtra to produce a civilization which today is perhaps the most complete synthesis of Aryan and Dravidian in India. Both these offshoots of the original Deccan culture produced important literatures in the early centuries of the Christian era: Tamilnad gave rise to the poetry under discussion here, while Maharashtra produced the *Sattasaī* of Hāla, representative of a large body of popular poetry, the great bulk of which has been lost. I have shown in my dissertation that ancient Tamil and Maharashtrian literature are closely related.[9] They share a common metrical system, a common technique of rhyme, a common technique of suggestion, and hundreds of themes and conventions. With the exception of a few conventions, none of these shared elements appears in Indo-Aryan literature prior to the *Sattasaī*. Beginning with Kālidāsa, however, whose date is after the first half of the fourth century A.D.,[10] conventions shared by Tamil and Māhārāṣṭrī appear prominently in Sanskrit, together with their common technique of suggestion. It is in fact no exaggeration to say that Kālidāsa has synthesized in a most felicitous manner elements from the two great literary traditions of India, Dravidian and Aryan. The reason for this synthesis is that he relied heavily for his conventions and techniques on Māhārāṣṭrī Prakrit literature, of which the *Sattasaī* is a part. This fact has long been suspected, but it has been possible to prove it by isolating elements which appear first in Māhārāṣṭrī and Tamil and then showing that Kālidāsa has used them. There are some themes which appear in early Tamil that are found as early as the *Mahābhārata* and the *Rāmāyaṇa* in Sanskrit. Through a detailed consideration of their use in both traditions, I have shown that these must have been used originally in the Deccan culture and must have entered North India with other Dravidian elements and words which become prominent in the Sanskrit epics. It is thus evident that a comparative study of ancient Tamil and Indo-Aryan literature can throw light on important areas of the history of Indian literature which until now have been dark. The development of *kāvya*, for example, is an area on which Winternitz, Macdonell, and Keith confess they cannot say anything beyond speculation. Yet a consideration of Tamil literature discloses clearly the main lines of that development. With further comparative investigation of ancient Tamil and Indo-Aryan, we may hope that more areas of ancient Indian literary history may be clarified. For example, much of the *Kalittokai* is written in dialogue form; it is possible that this form is related to Sanskrit drama.

Already much can be said of the history of Tamil literature. Moreover, since many themes present in ancient Tamil entered classical Sanskrit and then became pan-Indian, such a study is important for the history of all Indian literature. In spite of the assertions of Kailasapathy, the poems of the anthologies can be shown to be sophisticated literary compositions, not oral poetry of the sort described by Lord in his *Singer of Tales*.[11] They are analogous to early Greek lyric poems, which, while they had their roots in an oral tradition, were themselves literary compositions. The Tamil poems were composed by a class of men called *pulavaṉ*, who included in their ranks Brahmans (perhaps ten percent),[12] kings, the highest non-Brahman castes, and a few women. There is some evidence that men of low birth could not be *pulavaṉ*,[13] but the poems of the *pulavaṉ* were often composed in imitation of songs sung by Pāṇaṉs, Kiṇaiyaṉs (also called Paṟaiyaṉs), and Tuṭiyaṉs, all of whom belonged to low castes and made their living wandering from the court of one king to another and singing of the king's greatness, hoping to be rewarded (an occupation they shared with the *pulavaṉ*). These Pāṇaṉs, Kiṇaiyaṉs, and Tuṭiyaṉs were without question oral poets; it is because the poems of the *pulavaṉ* were imitations of their oral compositions that they contain the many oral elements described by Kailasapathy in his book. The *pulavaṉ* must been an institution produced by the spread of literacy across Tamilnad several centuries before the anthologies; for had they been older, so many of their poems would not be imitations of the poetry of the Pāṇaṉs and others. The Pāṇaṉs, the Kiṇaiyaṉs, and the Tuṭiyaṉs formed three separate castes at the bottom of the social structure. Their function was chiefly ritualistic, connected with the magic power thought to be present in the instruments they played, as has been indicated above. It is for this reason that the separation between them and the *pulavaṉ* was complete. It is almost certain that in the earlier Deccan culture, from which Tamil civilization sprang, there existed the equivalent of these low groups, whose duty was also to play musical instruments, to sing, and to invoke the sacred.[14] It must have been they who were chiefly responsible for the oral literature of the Deccan civilization, which was the basis for both early Tamil literature and early Maharashtrian poetry. It is possible that these institutions can be traced even further: there were in epic times in North India various classes of bards, evidently oral, called Sūtas, Māgadhas, and Bandins. These shared at least one function of the Tamil bards: they would wake the king in the morning. They were, however, of relatively high caste (Sūtas are supposed to be produced by the union of a Brahman man and a Kṣatriya woman). Nor is there any evidence that these northern bards played drums with ritual function.

There was also in ancient Tamilnad a class of dancing women who were courtesans (*parattaiyar*).[15] Their exact role in that society remains to be worked out, but they appear to have had some ritual function, for which reason they lived in a separate part of the city and ultimately came to be associated with temples. It it likely that important information concerning the later pan-Indian institution of Devadāsīs and the development of Indian dance can be discovered by the study of their role in early Tamil.

It is a commonplace that all literatures have their roots in religion. In early Tamil literature there is a dual focus: the king in *puṟam* or "exterior" poems, which deal with life outside the family, and love between man and woman in *akam* or "interior" poems, which deal with life seen from inside the family. This corresponds exactly to the two chief loci of the sacred in that society. It was chiefly to develop the proper sacred power of the king that the Pāṇaṉs and others were supposed to praise him and to beat drums in his presence. On the other hand, the sacred importance of love between man and woman for the early Tamils is shown by all the ritual restrictions imposed on woman and by the emphasis on chastity. Most themes of ancient Tamil fit well into this system. In love poems, for example, it is often described how the heroine's parents mistake the love she has for her lover for possession by the god Murugan. Here the poet stresses the sacred nature of the heroine's feeling. Before the hero can marry his beloved, he must often go on a journey to bring back wealth (usually gold) from a foreign land. In making this journey, he travels through parched land (called *pālai*) in the summer, undergoing many perilous experiences. It is easy to see in this journey the theme of initiation, which involves crossing through the land of death in order to become fit for manhood and experience of the sacred, in this case taking a wife. While this theme is present also in the *Sattasaī* and in Sanskrit, it is not there specified that the journey takes place as a condition for marriage. Thus in Aryan literatures the theme has been "desacralized," that is, deprived of its religious significance. Another pan-Indian literary theme whose history is revealed by a study of early Tamil is that of the *abhisārikā*, the lady who goes out at night, often through the rain, to visit her lover. In Tamil, it is the man who comes at night to visit his beloved, who, being unmarried, is guarded by her parents. In some poems, the heroine comes a little way to a rendezvous near her house, often through the rain. The Tamil poems which describe this theme leave no doubt that she is the prototype of the *abhisārikā*.[16] In Tamil, the theme is full of religious significance, showing man and woman who are destined to be married meeting at a mysterious time and attaining a sacred state in their union. In Indo-Aryan, the religious significance of this theme has been lost, being replaced by pure eroticism. There are other pan-Indian literary themes whose original significance is revealed through an examination of early Tamil. Certainly the investigation of this area is one of the most important tasks which need to be undertaken by students of Indian literature.

The history of classical Indian music has yet to be written. Some have seen its origin in the melodies of the *Sāmaveda*; yet from evidence adduced by Sambamoorthy, who has written most prolifically in English on Carnatic music, the tie between classical music and the *Sāmaveda* must be weak indeed if it in fact exists.[17] Certainly the *Sāmaveda* has nothing resembling ragas or talas. On the other hand, early Tamil music is known to have had both these components of Indian music; moreover, all important musical elements mentioned in early Tamil have Tamil, not Sanskrit, names. The word *paṇ*, which means raga, must go very far back, for it has been used to name the Pāṇaṉ, which, besides being the name of the clan that plays the lute in ancient Tamil, is the name of a low caste in Prakrit. To this may be compared the situation in Tamil astrology, which was imported from the north and where most names used in the anthologies are *tadbhava* of Sanskrit equivalents. In fact, there are a few terms of evident Dravidian origin used in Sanskrit musical treatises: *Kurañjī*, the name of a raga (Tamil *kuṟiñci*);[18] *kambala*, the name of a *jāti*, (Tamil *kampalai*, the sound of a lute);[19] and *utpalī* and *nīlotpalī*, the names of ragas (Tamil *neytal*, which like *utpala* and *nilotpala* means a blue waterlily and is the name of a Tamil raga).[20] Many instruments used in Carnatic music appear in ancient Tamil with Tamil names. The *muḻavu*, evidently the same as the *mṛdanga* and like that instrument rubbed with mud on its skin, was used in concerts, as was the *kuḻal*, a bamboo flute. Many instruments used in classical Indian music have Dravidian names: the *ḍamaru*, the *paṇava*, the *muraja*, and the *muralī*. A convention of the anthologies compares various natural phenomena to a concert, the wind blowing through holes in waving bamboo being likened to the sound of the flute and other natural sounds being compared to other musical instruments. In Indo-Aryan, exactly the same simile appears first in Kālidāsa. Further, it is evident that the music and dance of the Tamils formed an important element in their religion, certain ritual classes being determined by the drum or instrument they played. Music is mentioned much more often in the anthologies than it is in earlier Aryan texts such as the *Mahābhārata* or *Rāmāyana* (and far more often than in Vedic literature). In light of these considerations, it seems likely to me that Indian music owes even more to the early Deccan culture of which Tamil civilization was an offshoot than does Indian literature. But such a likelihood need not remain in the realm of speculation: there are ample sources to determine just what the contributions of Dravidian music were, when those contributions appeared in Aryan sources, and how they were combined with originally Aryan elements.

The earliest extant Tamil grammar book and treatise on poetics is the *Tolkāppiyam*. There can be little doubt that where its treatment of grammar is the same as or similar to treatment in Sanskrit, it is Tamil which has been the borrower.[21] Work needs to be done, however, to determine just what Sanskrit sources were used. Hartmut Scharfe has recently been engaged in just such research, and he has found that Jaina grammatical material was used by Tolkāppiyar; his final results have not yet been published. We may hope that such determination will give us a better idea of which grammarians were studied in ancient India and which Aryan books were brought into Tamilnad. It may be that we have attributed to Pāṇini a more important place among ancient Indian grammarians than he actually occupied.

In poetics also the *Tolkāppiyam* contains significant parallels with Aryan works. For example, the seven *meyppāṭu* are identical to the *sthāyibhāva* listed in the *Nāṭyaśāstra* and later Sanskrit works.[22] Is it possible that their source may be Dravidian and thus that the *rasa* theory, the very cornerstone of Sanskrit aesthetics, may be Dravidian? Such a possibility seems unlikely to me. I have shown that those elements of Dravidian poetry which entered Aryan literature did so from the early Deccan culture and were originally passed on in an oral tradition. The theory of *meyppāṭu*, or *sthāyibhāva*, is on the other hand a sophisticated one which would seem to be a literary development. It is far more likely that Tolkāppiyar, who used some northern texts for his grammatical sections, borrowed also from Aryan aesthetic texts than that some early Tamil text found its way into North India and was imitated. It should be pointed out too that the *meyppāṭu* are not really an essential part of Tamil aesthetics; knowledge of them is quite unnecessary to enable one to analyze satisfactorily an early Tamil poem. On the other hand, knowledge of such original Tamil elements as the five tracts is essential for the proper analysis of any *akam* poem. In any case, further research is necessary to determine from what sources Tolkāppiyar borrowed poetic elements, particularly those which he took from Aryan sources. Knowledge of the beginnings of Indian aesthetics is still incomplete; it is quite possible that such research, besides giving insight into the history of Tamil literature, might contribute significantly to our knowledge of the beginnings of North Indian aesthetics.

In addition to such comparative research on the *Tolkāppiyam*, work should be done to determine whether all parts of that work are indeed as late as the section of the *eḻuttatikāram* which Mahadevan has attributed by paleographic data to the fifth century A.D.,[23] or whether this section is an interpolation and the rest or parts of the *Tolkāppiyam* are earlier. Such a determination can be made by a study of the language of the *Tolkāppiyam*. A comparison of the poetic theories contained in the *Tolkāppiyam* with the poems they purport to describe would also be valuable.

In my dissertation, I made a study of the astrology used by the ancient Tamils and showed that it was imported from North India:[24] not only is the system identical to that found very early in Aryan literature, but the names of many months and constellations are northern as well, some of them going as far back as *Ṛgveda*. Occasionally there appear astrological beliefs, distinguished by their lack of systematization, which may reflect the original system of Tamil astrology. The new system must have been imported at a time far anterior to the ancient Tamil poems, for it is already well established in them and is used to determine the dates of festivals and marriages. Moreover, most of the northern names have been radically changed to accord with Tamil pronunciation, invariably not in accordance with the rules laid down in the *Tolkāppiyam* for making *tadbhava* of Sanskrit words. This fact suggests that their importation goes back to a period when such rules did not exist; indeed, so changed are their forms that it seems impossible that they could have been imitations made by literate men. At least one month, Āvaṇi, is found in its Tamil form in Kanarese as well, and it is possible that this means that northern astrology appeared in South India even before these two languages split apart (though the Kanarese form may have simply been borrowed at a later date). It should be possible by a comparative study of astrology in the various Dravidian traditions to determine approximately at what time the northern system was imported and to discover whether in fact such importation took place in the period of Tamil-Kanarese unity.

Of all things revealed by early Tamil literature, it is dynasty history which has been most studied. Ironically, this is, I believe, one of the least significant of the many things the poems have to contribute to our knowledge of ancient India. In the realm of history itself, far more important than the names of a few kings are the facts the poems provide concerning the political organization of the times. Recently Burton Stein in a brilliant article has traced three "episodes" of integration of the agrarian order of South India between the ninth and the nineteenth centuries.[25] The first of these is the Pallava-Chola period, during which the nuclear areas of South India were dominated by the Brahman and the high-caste landlords, to whom the warriors were subordinate. Such nuclear areas had only the lightest links to the great warrior families of Kanchi and Tanjore, their chief duty being the payment of taxes. In the fourteenth and fifteenth centuries, the Brahman-landlord[26] hegemony of the nuclear areas broke down, according to Stein because of a new need for self-defense caused by the intrusion of Muslim warriors. The control of the nuclear areas passed to warriors who could command enough troops to control them. Thus Stein writes, "Warriors whose private jurisdiction had been forged by the warriors themselves were recognized by and submitted to the overlordship of the great warriors of Vijayanagar."[27] The third episode resulted from the coming of the Europeans and need not be considered here. Stein states, "During the 9th century, we find the first solid evidence of an agrarian system, the dominant characteristics of which persist for the next thousand years. The nature of the agrarian order prior to this time is obscure."[28] This statement shows that Stein is unfamiliar with early Tamil literature, though in fairness to him it must be stated that no other historian has used that literature to describe the political organization of pre-Pallavan times. The early Tamil poems describe clearly the agricultural organization which preceded the Pallava-Chola period. The land was divided between *meṉpulam*, which was paddy land, and *vaṉpulam*, mountainous or forested territory on which only such crops as millet could be grown. Lands were further subdivided into mountainous (*kuriñci*), forested (*mullai*), ocean (*neytal*), and riverine (*marutam*) tracts. Most kings and chieftains had control of only one kind of land, and the poets often describe the different tracts ruled by a particularly great monarch in order to praise him and to show that he ruled a greater area than was common.[29] The riverine tracts, on which paddy is grown, are less prominent than in the periods which Stein has described, but it is clear that the strongest kings governed such areas.

The period of early Tamil literature is analogous to the warlike Vijayanagar period. The country was divided between small kings (called *kuṟunilamaṉṉar*), most of whom controlled one nuclear area. The poems describe dramatically how such small kings would be reduced to the worst poverty when there was famine in their area. For example, *Puṟam* 127 describes how a king would give to bards even if he got only a little rice, while in *Puṟam* 327 a chieftain is reduced to giving all his tiny millet yield to creditors and then to borrowing enough to eat. Often, if a chieftain does not have enough to give to bards and other suppliants, he orders his soldiers to go out on a looting expedition. For example, in *Puṟam* 180 the poet says of a king, "He does not possess wealth to give away every day; nor is it his nature to refuse saying, 'There is nothing.' . . . When I ask him [for wealth], he . . . calls the strong-armed blacksmith of his city and says, 'Shape a long spear with a straight blade' [so that the bard can join his army and share in the booty]." Even at this early period, Tamilnad had three chief kings, the Chera, the Chola, and the Pandya monarchs. It appears, however, that as in the later periods described by Stein, the absolute authority of these kings extended only within a small area constituting the capital city and the land surrounding it. To increase their wealth and, what is more important, their glory, these monarchs would demand tribute from the warrior kings of other nuclear areas.[30] For example, in *Puṟam* 51 the poet says of the Pandyan monarch, "If you oppose [and defeat another king] and demand tribute, kings who give, saying, 'Take!' are without trembling. But pitiful, pitiful are those who lose your mercy! Like the white insects [flying] from red mounds laboriously made by tiny termites, living for one day is confusion for them!" Stein claims that in the Vijayanagar period, traditions of personal loyalty such as were found in feudal Europe were absent.[31] Perhaps so, but it is clear that such traditions were present in the period of the anthologies. In *Puṟam* 139, for example, the poet, addressing his patron, tells him to give at once, for he might have to die at any time for his king. In *Puṟam* 287, it is clear that a king would reward his warriors by giving them conquered lands. Thus part of the power of the greater Tamil kings at least in this period was derived from their ability to enlist warriors of nuclear areas whose rulers were in vassalage to them. In one poem, the poet approaches a Brahman to whom a king has granted land and begs him to give (*Puṟam* 166). It is noteworthy that here the Brahman is treated as a king would be: he has personal authority over his area, and the poet glorifies him personally to cause him to give. This poem makes it clear that the system of collective Brahman-landlord hegemony of nuclear areas had not yet begun in the period of the Tamil anthologies.

The political conditions described in the anthologies provide a reason, I believe, for the decision of the Pallava kings to attempt to pass the control of the nuclear areas to Brahmans and landlords. The power of the Guptas, who had actually controlled most of North India, must have impressed them greatly. They must have seen that traditional South Indian organization gave them no opportunity to acquire such power. Rather, control of nuclear areas would have to be passed to groups which were nonmilitaristic and had a vested interest in the kind of stability which a powerful king could provide. It is easy to see that the Brahmans were one such group: they were universally respected as Hinduism was coming to be more and more adopted by the common people; and they represented an alien element among the extremely militaristic native aristocracy. The difference between the Brahmans and the native warriors is well defined in *Puṟam* 362, where the poet, addressing a group of Brahmans, describes a gathered army: "Listen to the voice of attack, its might as hard to oppose as Death, Brahmans! It has nothing to do with the four Vedas, for it is not concerned with kindness. It has nothing to do with *dharma* [Tamil *aṟam*], since it is concerned with gain [*poruḷ*, the equivalent of Sanskrit *artha*]."

The Brahmans, however, were not the only ones who stood to gain by a stable government. When one king conquered another, he would plunder his rival's lands, taking everything of value and, at least sometimes, spoiling the crops and ruining the fields. He would often award the conquered lands to his generals or his allies. Clearly it was the landholders who suffered most in this process. It seems likely, moreover, that as the area under cultivation in Tamilnad increased and as the chieftains of riverine tracts became more powerful than their counterparts in uncultivated tracts, the number and power of landholders increased. The Pallava kings must have allied themselves with such landholders, somehow passing control of nuclear areas to them. In this regard, the means by which the Pallavas and the landholders succeeded in overcoming what must have been the formidable opposition of the warrior overlords to their schemes need to be investigated. It seems almost certain that the Brahmans played only a small role in this process and that it was not until Chola times that the Brahmans really became prominent as controllers of nuclear areas. It was natural, however, for the Pallavas to follow the Gupta example and to represent themselves as upholders of orthodox Hinduism in order to dramatize the break with the old system and the new nature of their rule, and for this reason the important place of the Brahmans is stressed in Pallava source material.

Thus we see that a careful investigation of the political organization described in the anthologies can clarify a great many points of South Indian history. In the short analysis undertaken above, for example, we see that the form to which the society reverted after the Cholas during the Vijayanagar period was a natural one which had occurred before. The question is raised how much the organization depicted by Stein during the Pallava-Chola period was a result of the careful suppression of every potentially strong warrior. The reversion to warrior control of the nuclear units may simply have been the result of the inability of any monarch to keep such warriors in hand.

It may safely be said, then, that the potential scholarly value of Tamil literature is great indeed. What progress has been made in exploiting this literature? First, translations are few and inadequate. Ramanujan's *Interior Landscape*, translations of selected poems from the *Kuṟuntokai*,[32] is beautifully done but is not large enough to be of use in the extensive research which needs to be undertaken. Gros's *Le Paripāṭal*[33] is the one truly good, adequately annotated translation of a whole Tamil anthology which has appeared. It is in fact by far the best book on early Tamil which has appeared in a Western language; none who are interested in ancient Tamilnad should fail to read it. One hopes that both Ramanujan and Gros will translate more from the anthologies. Chelliah's *Pattuppāṭṭu*, while mostly accurate, is in an ornate Victorian style which detracts considerably from its usefulness; its notes, moreover, are quite inadequate, so that the reader who has not spent much time studying early Tamil is likely to find himself lost very often.[34] *The Golden Anthology of Ancient Tamil Literature*, published in three volumes by Kazhagam, is of little use even for its avowed purpose of providing a general introduction to ancient Tamil. The comments are of little help to the scholar, concerning themselves exclusively with questions of morals (and often giving an idealized and incorrect view), while the translations are in a thick sort of Indian English which cannot fail to put off the most sympathetic reader.[35] Of later works in translation, mention should be made of the *Tirukkuṟaḷ*, of which none of the translations is really adequate,[36] and of Pope's translation of the *Nālaṭiyar*,[37] which is excellent. The English version of Danielou's translation of the *Cilappatikāram* is beautiful in its language, giving a fine feeling for the poetry of the original, but it is completely inaccurate in its details and often provides incorrect and misleading translations.[38]

Given the scant number of translations from ancient Tamil, it is perhaps no wonder that the job of researching ancient Tamil literature has scarcely been begun. Those attempts which have been made have been uniformly poor. I shall adduce one example: the consideration of the historical significance of a single poem, *Puṟam* 335, by several writers. Kailasapathy says of this poem, "In a poem enumerating the names of excellent flowers, food, gods, and other things, a bard speaks of the Pāṇar as one of the four noble clans. In passing, it is interesting to note that another ancient clan—The Paṟaiyar, 'drummers,' enumerated under the category [sic] in the same poem—was also degraded in the caste hierarchy of latter times."[39] K. K. Pillai writes, "It is noteworthy that a poem in the *Puṟanāṉūṟu* says that there is no caste or tribe except the Tuṭiyar, Pāṇar, Paṟaiyar, and Kaṭampar. This is attempted to be explained as a reference only to the martial communities of the land. But it does not seem too much to consider them as the only four indigenous communities then uninfluenced by the later caste system."[40] Nilakanta Sastri writes, "One poem in the *Puṟanāṉūṟu* affirms that there are only four castes (*kuḍi*), viz., Tutiyaṉ, Pāṇaṉ, Paṟaiyaṉ, and Kaṭampaṉ, and only one god worthy of being worshiped with paddy strewn before him, namely the hero-stone recalling the fall of a brave warrior in battle. These castes and this worship were of very great antiquity, perhaps survivals from pre-Aryan times."[41] The poem itself is quite simple:

> If strength hard to subdue. . .
> . . . .
> Except for *kuravu*, *talavu*, *kuruntu*, and *mullai*
> there are no flowers.
> Except for black-stemmed *varaku* [a kind of millet],

large-eared *tinai* [a kind of millet],
the little creeper *kol*,
and *avarai* [beans] with round pods,
there is no food.
Except for the Tuṭiyan, the Pāṇan̲,
the Par̲aiyan̲, and the Kaṭampan̲,
there are no clans.
Except for stones worshiped
because [men] stood before hostile enemies
and blocked them
and killed elephants with high shining tusks
and died,
there are no gods worshiped
with offerings of paddy.

All the flowers and foods enumerated here are peculiar to less productive mountainous and forested land called *van̲pulam* in Tamil and differentiated from land on the more prosperous plains called *men̲pulam*, where paddy is cultivated. They all grow in the *mullai*, or forest, tract. Context demands that the four castes here mentioned be as lowly with respect to the prestigious groups of society as the *varaku, tin̲ai, kol*, and *avarai* are to the rice and other rich food of favored provinces. Thus Turaicami Pillai, the commentator on the Kazhagam edition,[42] must be correct when he suggests that the purpose of the poet here is to paint a desolate picture of *mullai*, the forested tract, a fact no doubt made clear in the lines which have been lost. All the English interpretations of this poem quoted above were written after the Kazhagam edition of the *Pur̲anān̲ūr̲u* appeared; yet their writers chose to ignore Turaicami Pillai's excellent commentary, which is in clear and lucid modern Tamil; rather these translations constructed interpretations which are fanciful and misleading. This example is quite sufficient, I believe, to show with how much caution the extant secondary sources for the study of ancient Tamil must be treated. Even the *Tamil Lexicon* is sometimes mistaken. For example, it identifies the wife of a *kinai* drummer (Kinaimakaḷ) with the Virali,[43] a woman whom I have shown can only be the wife of a Pāṇan̲, who is of entirely different caste than the *kinai* drummer. Similarly, the *Pre-Pallavan Tamil Index* by Subrahmanian, which is often useful, though it ignores many important words, often gives inadequate references, and is often inaccurate, says that the *kinai* player (or Par̲aiyan̲) was a Tuṭiyan̲, who in fact belonged to an entirely different caste.[44]

After the study of ancient Tamil literature itself, the most important discipline for the study of ancient Tamilnad is archaeology. A team of Russians under Knorozov has recently shown that the structure of the language written on seals recovered from Indus Valley sites is structurally identical with Dravidian languages while differing in structure from Sumerian, Elamite, Sanskrit, and Munda.[45] A team of Finns has recently come to similar conclusions in a more publicized but less scholarly article.[46] The Finns actually claim to have deciphered the writing on the seals, a claim belied by the facts that their analysis differs from the Russian translations of almost all suffixes and that their interpretation of various signs is almost pure speculation (with one or two exceptions) having inadequate confirmation from outside sources. They have promised to issue a large and well-documented book in the near future; we must hope that that publication provides more substantiation for their claims of decipherment than has appeared to date.

The hypothesis that the dwellers in the Indus valley were Dravidian is strengthened by facts elucidated by B. B. Lal in an article in *Ancient India* in which he shows that over ninety percent of the graffiti found on pottery in megalithic tombs in South India dating from the first millennium B.C. are identical to signs used in Indus Valley writing at least a thousand years earlier.[47] If in fact the megalithic peoples are a much-changed remnant of the Indus Valley dwellers and not merely the descendants of uncivilized copiers of their writing, we may expect ultimately to be able to trace their entire history through archaeology.

Some of the graffiti found on sherds from megalithic sites are no more than a few hundred years anterior to the anthologies. We know that it was the custom at the time of the anthologies to write the deeds of a hero on the memorial stone erected to him. It is possible that a thorough search would turn up such memorial stones, some of which may be inscribed with writing derived from the Indus Valley script. In any case, the early Tamil poems give us hopes of discovering many more specimens of Tamil writing from that era than have been unturned.

One of the most difficult problems which archaeologists must undertake to resolve in South India is the date of the establishment of cities there and the direction from which the impetus for their establishment came. Wheeler has suggested that the impetus came from the Ganges Valley;[48] yet without many excavations on the sites of ancient cities, such a suggestion is little more than speculation.

The bewildering array of burial customs in ancient South India has often been mentioned. Before the introduction of cremation, we find megalithic burial and excarnation with subsequent interment in urns. Some have seen this as a sign of two different cultural traditions.[49] The anthologies seem also to show a society divided into two different parts: on the one hand, there are the *uyarntōr*, or "high ones," spoken of in the *Tolkāppiyam*, who are warriors and leaders of society and whose death is often commemorated by memorial stones; on the other hand, there are the *iḻintōr*, or "low ones,"[50] represented by the *kinai* and *tuṭi* drummers, the Pāṇaṉ, the Vēlaṉ, washermen, leather workers, and others. It is conceivable that the "high ones" are descendants of Dravidian-speaking invaders from the north who erected megaliths to their dead, while the "low ones" were an indigenous race who interred their dead in pots. Yet there are strong objections to this theory: early Tamil is very similar to proto-Dravidian, a fact which would indicate that its speakers did not assimilate speakers of another language, since such assimilation generally causes a language to change rapidly. Moreover, it appears in several poems of the *Puṟanāṉūṟu* that warriors may be buried in a pot[51] and thus that that method of burial was not confined to the lower strata of society. In any case, we may expect that our ignorance regarding the ethnic composition of the ancient Tamils will be enlightened by archaeological research carried out in the next few decades.

In some areas, a careful study of ancient Tamil would be of use to archaeologists. In *The Iron Age of India*, Bannerjee points out that megalithic graves often contain the bones of several individuals and suggests that "obviously there was a time-lag between erection of the tomb and the actual interment so that as many as could be accommodated at a single ceremony were interred at a time and the burial sealed once and for all."[52] The early Tamil poems describe how those close to a king would starve themselves to death with him when he chose to die in the rite of *vaṭakkiruttal*.[53] Marco Polo describes how, in the kingdom of Maabar (evidently the Pandyan country), "knights" who attend the king throw themselves on his cremation fire and so take their lives.[54] The Jesuit Carneiro, writing in the sixteenth century, says in a letter that on the death of a king in southern India, it was customary for his retainers to run amok in order to avenge his death or to die in the attempt.[55] In light of this information, it seems to me quite likely that the megalithic graves may contain the bones of the king and of his retainers, who died with him like their counterparts in ancient Egypt. It has already been remarked that suttee was almost certainly indigenous to Tamilnad. Westermarck has shown that the practice was motivated by the belief that the dead man's spirit haunts his wife, filling her with dangerous magic power and obliging her either to practice asceticism or to kill herself.[56] In ancient Tamil society, there were two main foci of the sacred: marriage and the king. It stands to reason that if the forces unleashed on a man's wife when he died were deemed strong enough to cause her to take her life, the same should be true for a king, and that when he died, his followers should have been considered to be so affected by ominous forces that they too would have to take their lives. It should be possible for archaeologists to prove or disprove this hypothesis.

Anthropologists too stand to gain greatly by a study of ancient Tamil. There customs of many groups are described which can still be found today. For example, the *kinai* drum player would hold in his hand a staff called *piṟappuṇarttuṅkōl* (a rod that determines birth, that is, what has arisen and what will arise), which would enable him to tell the future. Today in Kerala, there is a caste called Kuravans, one of whose functions is to prognosticate with staff in hand.[57] Vēlans, who are often described in ancient Tamil, are also found today in Kerala as a subcaste of the Paṟaiyaṉs. In fact, many of these groups are described in Tamil literature from all periods. It does not seem too much to hope that some day anthropologists will actually be able to trace the history of many Tamil castes. Unfortunately, most work done by anthropologists on modern Tamilnad has been devoted to the descendants of the *uyarntōr*, or "high ones." Much more study needs to be devoted to the low castes, who are, after all, just as important for a proper understanding of the customs of the area as their higher counterparts.

Thus we see that when the literature in early Tamil is translated, researchers in all areas of South Indian studies will have their horizons broadened considerably. Yet however good they are, translations will be inadequate, for they cannot convey significance of which the translator is unaware. To translate *Pāṇaṉ* by "minstrel," for example, is to ignore the fact that the Pāṇaṉ was of low status, of a separate caste, was often a servant, and was supposed to play the drum in wars. When indexing some of the anthologies for my dissertation, I included one category for all drums. I subsequently discovered that each of about ten drums had a distinct and important function and could be played only by one caste, facts which are overlooked in all research done to date that I know of. I am sure that there are other categories which I have unwittingly done away with in my translations and which remain to be discovered by future researchers. More important than this is the fact that we possess old, detailed commentaries on much of ancient Tamil literature. This ancillary literature is so large that no translation can take it all into account in annotations. Added to this are the fine modern editions of the Tamil classics, with excellent commentaries and, most important, with exhaustive indexes. There is simply no possibility that all this literature can be adequately rendered into English in the near future. At best, we may hope to possess fairly accurate translations of ancient Tamil which will be of use in developing general ideas of ancient Tamil society and literature. The material which exists only in Tamil will become more and more indispensable as research progresses.

What will the result of this research be on our ideas about South India? We shall realize, I believe, that the role of Aryan culture in Tamilnad has been overestimated. We shall see that all classes of South Indian Brahmans follow mostly Dravidian customs; that the "sanskritization" made so much of by some anthropologists is, in the case of Tamilnad at least, for the most part the adoption of Dravidian customs which have always belonged to the upper classes; and that where Aryan elements have entered into this process, they have been radically altered to fit Dravidian norms. For example, Brahmans today put stronger constraints on widows than do any other group; yet all these constraints can be shown to be Dravidian in origin, including continuous tonsure, which to my knowledge is today practiced only by Brahmans. Temple worship is likewise indigenous to South India. It is true that some of the original gods in the temples have been replaced by idols with Sanskrit names and that many rites performed in Brahmanical temples are imported from the north; but the treatment of temple idols as receptacles of immanent divine power and the place of the temple in the society go back to a time before the advent of the Aryans and are utterly foreign to the Vedas. It is also true that many stories in Tamil literature can be traced to North India. But the stories have invariably been modified to conform to Tamil ideals. In the *Kamparāmāyaṇa*, for example, Rāvaṇa is never allowed to touch Sītā, a change in keeping with southern notions of chastity. Indeed, Vālmīki's *Rāmāyaṇa* and Kampaṉ's *Rāmāyaṇa* are as different as Marlowe's *Faust* and Goethe's *Faust*; that is to say, beyond the fact that they adhere roughly to the same story, it is difficult to see anything which they have in common. Linga worship, which was imported from the north, was incorporated into the native religion; the phallic emblem being treated as the memorial stone was earlier. The tufts worn by Brahmans are found in ancient Tamil literature on warriors as well. Pollution itself, which is one of the most important factors in the working of sanskritization, appears to be a development of the ancient Dravidians' notion of being infected with immanent sacred power. Thus sanskritization in Tamilnad can be seen as a process not only of imitating the Brahmans but also of adopting practices which have always belonged to the "high ones." It is noteworthy that there are few Aryan customs followed by the Brahmans which have been imitated by non-Brahman castes in Tamilnad. Veḷḷāḷars do not undergo *upanayana* and do not wear the sacred thread;[58] nor do non-Brahman pūjāris light the sacred fires. It would in fact be as accurate to say that the Brahmans have undergone tamilization as to say that the non-Brahmans have been sanskritized. But both notions are simplistic and can only lead to confusion. Until we rid ourselves of the ideas of the supremacy of the Aryan in South India and also of the incorruptibility of the Tamil, we shall not understand the historical processes which have taken place.

The cause for our misconceptions can easily be explained. We have been able to trace the customs and beliefs of the Brahmans in all periods and areas of India through the large number of law books and other writings they have left us, but for the great majority of the Indian population we have had no such literature and so have remained ignorant of their role. In fact, while the influence of Aryan culture in South India has no doubt been large, it has not been the predominant cultural influence. Rather, the Brahmans have been slowly assimilated until today in Tamilnad few of their customs can be traced back to the Aryan culture from which they purport to come. But the Brahmans have always traced their customs, no matter what their source, to an idealized Aryan society. Thus while the high non-Brahman classes of Tamilnad and, I suspect, elsewhere in India have simply followed many customs they have always possessed, we have found those customs described in Brahmanical literature and falsely concluded that the indigenous inhabitants were adopting Aryan customs. And when the lower classes have adopted higher-class ideals to better their position, as they have done in every society, we have falsely seen that as involving only the imitation of Brahmans rather than the imitation of all the higher classes. We must come to see that, in the south at least, the Brahman has imitated the high-class non-Brahman as much as the non-Brahman has imitated the Brahman, and probably even more; for in the south the Brahman was a newcomer, and to be accepted in the society he had to adopt those values and customs which were espoused by the highest indigenous members of that society. These facts emerge from a study of ancient Tamil literature. We shall come ultimately to see, I believe, that Aryan culture in Tamilnad, while important, has not been the all-dominating influence it has been claimed to be. We shall begin to discover, as we grow familiar with ancient Tamil literature, an entirely new stream in Indian culture which will dispel many of the mysteries which have plagued Indologists while they have relied only on Aryan sources.

NOTES

1. See G. L. Hart, *Related Cultural and Literary Elements in Ancient Tamil and Indo-Aryan* (Ph.D. dissertation, Harvard University, 1969), p. 2.
2. Iravatham Mahadevan, "Tamil-Brahmi Inscriptions of the Sangam Age," in *Proceedings of the Second International Conference of Tamil Studies*, vol. I (Madras, 1971), p. 83. Use of the *puḷḷi* is described in the *Eḻuttatikāram* of the *Tolkāppiyam*.
3. J. V. Chelliah, *Pattupattu, Ten Tamil Idylls* (Madras: Kazhagam, 1962), p. 337. This estimate includes such words as *mīn* (DED 3999), *tāmarai* (DED 2583), and *muttu* (DED 4062), which are known to be of Dravidian origin. It should be pointed out that the *Murukāṟṟuppaṭai* is later than the bulk of the literature contained in the anthologies.

DED numbers refer to T. Burrow and M. B. Emeneau, *A Dravidian Etymological Dictionary* (Oxford: Clarendon Press, 1961).

4. Hart, *op. cit.*, pp. 36–37.
5. *Ibid.*, pp. 15ff.
6. *Ibid.*, pp. 119ff. All these customs are described fully and documented in my dissertation.
7. *Ibid.*, pp. 108ff.
8. B. and R. Allchin, *The Birth of Indian Civilization: India and Pakistan Before 500 B.C.* (Baltimore: Penguin, 1968), p. 232.
9. Hart, *op. cit.*, pp. 207ff.
10. M. Winternitz, *A History of Indian Literature*, vol. III, trans. H. Cohn (Calcutta, 1963), pp. 23ff.
11. A. B. Lord, *The Singer of Tales* (Cambridge, Mass.: Harvard University Press, 1964).
12. K. K. Pillay, "Aryan Influences in Tamilaham During the Sangam Epoch," *Tamil Culture* XII, no. 2 and 3 (1966), p. 164.
13. This is not the place to marshal all the evidence (which is extensive and, I believe, conclusive) that *pulavaṉ* were from the high classes, while the Pāṅaṉs and others were of low caste. Those who wish to investigate this important subject may consult my dissertation, pp. 119ff. See also *Puṟam* 170, 287, 289, 335; *Naṟṟiṇai* 77; *Kalittokai* 68.19, 95.10. Kailasapathy in *Tamil Heroic Poetry* (Oxford: Oxford University Press, 1968), p. 95, is quite mistaken when he states that the Pāṇaṉs were high (cf. pp. 43–47 of this essay).
14. Pāṇa is a low caste in Prakrit (DED 3351); even today there is a low caste of musicians called Pāṇas in Orissa. *Parn* means *paṟaiyaṉ* in Kota (both words being derived from *parai*, "drum"—see DED 3319). Malas, a low caste in Andhra, are community musicians.
15. Hart, *op. cit*, p. 151.
16. *Ibid.*, pp. 236ff.
17. P. Sambamoorthy, *South Indian Music*, 5 vol. (Madras, 1958–1963). Mr. Krishnamoorthy Athreya, a friend of mine who is passionately devoted to Carnatic music, informs me that ragas and talas can be found in a crude form in Tamil folk music.
18. Sārṅgadeva, *Saṃgītaratnākara*, vol. 2 (Madras, Tamilnadu: Adyar Library, 1959), p. 147.
19. *Ibid.*, p. 335.
20. *Ibid.*, p. 146.
21. For example, the system of seven cases (eight with the vocative) found in both the *Tolkāppiyam* and in Sanskrit grammatical works is obviously native to the Sanskrit tradition since it fits that language but is most unsuitable to Tamil.
22. *Nāṭyaśāstra, Gaekwad's Oriental Series* 36 (Baroda, 1956), I.p. 350; *Tolkāppiyam, Poruḷatikāram, Meyppāṭṭiyal.*
23. See note 2 above.
24. Hart, *op. cit*, pp. 76ff.
25. B. Stein, "Integration of the Agrarian System of South India," in *Land Control and Social Structure in Indian History*, ed. R. E. Frykenberg (Madison: University of Wisconsin Press, 1969), pp. 175–216.
26. Stein uses the unfortunate term *Sat-Sudra*, which means "good Śūdras," for these landlords. Such a term can only perpetuate the present Brahman-oriented view of South Indian history. The high-caste non-Brahmans of Tamilnad, who have always been the most powerful and most imitated group in South India, never considered themselves Śūdras; nor has the *varṇa* system ever

been applicable to South India. It would be no less misleading to adopt the non-Brahman prejudice and call the Brahmans "Northerners" instead of "Brahmans." The reader may note that Thurston in his *Castes and Tribes of South India*, 7 vol. (Madras, 1909) does not use the term *Sat-Sudra*, while he gives only three lines to *Śūdra*. In canto 22 of the *Cilappatikāram* and in the *Marapiyal* of the *Tolkāppiyam*, where the Tamil versions of the four *varṇa* are enumerated, none is applicable to a class remotely similar to Śūdras; nor have I ever come across the term *Śūdra* in reading Kampaṉ and other later Tamil authors.

27. Stein, *op. cit*, p. 191.
28. *Ibid.*, p. 179.
29. *Puram* 49, 58, 377, 384, 386, 395.
30. See *Puram* 22, 97, 156.
31. Stein, *op. cit.*, p. 190.
32. A. K. Ramanujan, *The Interior Landscape: Love Poems from a Classical Tamil Anthology* (Bloomington: Indiana University Press, 1967).
33. François Gros (tr.), *Le Paripāṭal* (Pondichery, 1968).
34. Chelliah, *op. cit.*
35. N. R. Balakrishna Mudaliyar, *The Golden Anthology of Ancient Tamil Literature*, 3 vols. (Madras, 1959). These translations are so remarkable that an example must be given: "A chandelier, shaped like a lovely damsel, is radiating luxurious light in the jewelled bed chamber [sic] of a beautiful towering seven-storied mansion. It rains cats and dogs. Rain water, like a cataract gushing down the confluence of eves, makes manifold music, dulcet to the ear." (I.55)
36. A. Chakravarti (tr.), *Tirukkuṟal* (Madras, 1953); F. W. Ellis (tr.), *Tirukkuṟal* (University of Madras, 1955); V. R. Ramachandra Dikshitar (tr.), *Tirukkuṟal* (Adyar, 1949); G. U. Pope, *The Sacred Kurral of Tiruvalluva Nāyanār* (London, 1886).
37. G. U. Pope, *The Naladiyar, or Four Hundred Quatrains in Tamil* (Oxford, 1893).
38. Ilango Adigal, *Shilappadikaram* (The Ankle Bracelet) (New York: New Directions, 1965). As an example of the inaccuracy of this work, I cite its version of the first verse of the epic:

> Blessed be the Moon!
> Blessed be the Moon that wraps the Earth
> in misty veils of cooling light,
> and looms, a royal parasol
> festooned with pollen-laden flowers,
> protecting us.

A correct translation of this verse is as follows:

> Bless we the moon, bless we the moon,
> for like the cooling white umbrella
> of the Chola king,
> whose garland is rich with pollen,
> it shows forth love
> to this vast world.

39. Kailasapathy, *op. cit.*, p. 95.
40. K. K. Pillay, "Landmarks in the History of Tamilnad," in *Proceedings of the Second International Conference of Tamil Studies*, vol. I (Madras, 1971), p. 18.
41. K. A. Nilakanta Sastri, *A History of South India from Prehistoric Times to the Fall of Vijayanagar*, 3rd ed. (Oxford: Oxford University Press, 1966), p.

131. Nilakanta Sastri has also missed the point of the memorial stones: they did not merely "recall the fall of a brave warrior in battle"; they were actually supposed to be inhabited by his spirit. Mention should be made here of the bibliography compiled by Xavier S. Thani Nayagam, *A Reference Guide to Tamil Studies: Books* (Kuala Lumpur: University of Malaya Press, 1966), which lists all books on subjects related to Tamil in Western languages up to 1966.

42. Auvai C. Turaicami Pillai (commentator), *Puṟanāṉūṟu,* 2 vols. (Madras: Kazhagam, 1964, 1962), vol. 2, pp. 267–268.

43. *Tamil Lexicon*, 6 vols. and suplement (University of Madras, 1936), p. 921.

44. N. Subrahmanian, *Pre-Pallavan Tamil Index* (University of Madras, 1966), pp. 274, 441.

45. Y. Knorozov (ed.), *Predvaritel'nye Soobshcheniya ob Issledovanii Protoindiĭskikh Tekstov* (Moscow, 1965).

46. A. Parpola, S. Koskenniemi, S. Parpola, and P. Aalto, *Decipherment of the Proto-Dravidian Inscriptions of the Indus Civilization* (Copenhagen, 1969).

47. B. B. Lal, "From the Megalithic to the Harappan: Tracing Back the Graffiti on the Pottery," *Ancient India* 6 (1960), pp. 1–24.

48. Sir Mortimer Wheeler, *Civilizations of the Indus Valley and Beyond* (London: McGraw-Hill, 1966), pp. 128ff. Wheeler adduces no evidence that the impetus for the cities of South India came from the Ganges Valley, though he does so for Central India. It seems to me unlikely that the south could have been as urbanized as it was by the time of the anthologies if the civilizing impetus came from as far afield as the Ganges Valley, especially since Wheeler states that that impetus did not reach Central India until at least the third century B.C. (*ibid.*, p. 130).

49. J. M. and G. Casal in *Site urbain et sites funéraires des environs de Pondichérry* (Paris, 1956), p. 43. These authors suggest that megalithic and urn burials were practiced respectively by invading Dravidians and indigenous people. They ascribe red and black ware, which is intrusive and soon disappeared, to the invaders, while they attribute red ware, which is found before, during, and after the period of red and black ware, to the original inhabitants. It seems to me that this theory is based on far too little archaeological work and that it thus represents little more than an educated guess. As I have indicated in this essay, there are strong objections to it.

50. See *Tolkāppiyam, Marapiyal*, 85, 94. There may be a middle class in addition, but it is never mentioned and does not appear to figure in any of the poems.

51. *Puṟam* 228, 238, 239.

52. N. R. Bannerjee, *The Iron Age in India* (Delhi, 1965), p. 213.

53. Hart, *op. cit.*, pp. 92ff.

54. Marco Polo, *The Travels of Marco Polo* (New York: Liveright, 1930), p. 287.

55. D. F. Lach, *India in the Eyes of Europe* (Chicago: Phoenix, 1965), p. 443.

56. E. Westermarck, *The History of Human Marriage*, 3 vols., 5th ed. (London: Macmillan, 1925), I.326.

57. Hart, *op. cit.*, pp. 152ff.

58. Some Chettiyars, however, do wear the sacred thread. This hardly constitutes wholesale imitation of Brahmans. A study of Tamil dialects is most revealing in this regard: non-Brahmans never imitate Brahman Tamil; rather, the dialect of the high-caste non-Brahmans is universally accepted as standard and is often used even by Brahmans.

The State and the Agrarian Order in Medieval South India: A Historiographical Critique

BURTON STEIN
University of Hawaii

I

South India is perhaps unique among the major regions of India in the degree to which it has come to possess a robust and impressive historiographical literature dealing with its early history. Looking back some forty years to the time when K. A. Nilakanta Sastri first published his work on the Cholas,[1] one would have had to agree with him that relatively little had been done on the southern peninsula by historians as compared with the attention given to the history of the Gangetic Valley. However, since that time, and thanks largely to Nilakanta Sastri himself, that has changed. Presently there exists a coherent and widely accepted view of South Indian history from the Pallava through the Vijayanagar periods. This view is both a tribute to and a product of scholars like R. G. Bhandarkar[2] and Nilakanta Sastri, who were trained in epigraphy and devoted to the canons of modern historical research as well as to much recent scholarship in the classical literature by Indians and by foreign scholars. But this view, though it changes in very minor respects with new research findings, has developed a conventional quality which resists alternative views. In this, South Indian historiography is not, of course, different from others in India and elsewhere. Once established, historiographical conventions cannot easily be changed by the displacement of accepted parts of that conventional historiography by partial interpretations which are new. Historiography tends to become systematic, and substantial changes cannot be easily assimilated without challenging the entire system.

Essayed here is the first step in the formulation of an alternative historiographical interpretation of political organization in South India during the medieval period. The historiographical critique presented is based upon research in the social and economic history of the period, and it does not involve significant new facts nor philosophical or ideological presuppositions different from those of most scholars who have worked on the period. Rather, this critique is the result of a growing conviction that the facts of political organization have not been interpreted plausibly and that there have been basic errors made in the interpretation of political evidence largely as a result of not considering the political system of the time within a systematic framework.

One test of the adequacy of any historical political system is the demonstration that what is taken as the political system is reasonably consonant with other aspects of the social system. When one is dealing with the Chola or the Vijayanagar states of medieval South India—political systems of considerable chronological and spatial scope—it is to be expected that political arrangements at all levels would be without contradictions. Contradictions in political principles and processes between the lowest level of political organization and the highest cannot be reconciled with such relatively long-lived states. Equally important, the political system at all levels must be reasonably consistent (or at least without contradiction) with respect to principles and processes in the social and cultural arrangements of the people ruled by such states. Here too, contradiction is an implausible concomitant of long-lived states. It is obvious, of course, that no historical states have been without the strains of conflicting forces, and an important part of political analysis is concerned with the means by which conflicting claims among parts of a political order or conflicts between the political order and the rest of a society are resolved. However, it is precisely in the difference between conflict within a single system of rules and contradiction between one and more rule systems that dynastic change or political periodization must be understood. Thus in medieval South India, which was spared massive foreign conquest, the only plausible way of explaining the careers of states—their beginnings and their ends—must be with reference to the development of irreducible and fatal flaws, or contradictions, within the political system or between the political system and the encompassing social system.

This systematic framework is lacking in the present interpretation of the medieval South Indian state. There is no effort in this conventional interpretation to demonstrate the manner in which the formal and concrete institution of the state is related to existing social arrangements and cultural features of South Indian society. It is argued in this prolegomenon of a reinterpretation of the medieval South Indian political system that the present conventional interpretation can be discredited primarily because the conception of the state in that view cannot be reconciled with what is known of the social and cultural elements of the medieval agrarian order of South India.

It is almost entirely on the side of the nature of the state that error exists. The agrarian system during the medieval period appears accurately perceived by most historians as one in which localized peasant agriculture based upon minor irrigation works in most, but not all, places dominated all other economic relationships. Industrial (that is, artisan) production and trade are seen as integral parts of the peasant agrarian economy. Urbanization is seen as relatively minor except, perhaps, in association with religious activities.

This relatively simple yet, I would submit, accurate perception of the economic order of the age is not the result of careful economic history; as little has been done in the economic aspects of South Indian history as elsewhere in early India. Such accuracy as exists seems rather to result from the fact that the basic evidence available to scholars is the same whether the interests of these scholars are in the fields of political, social, religious, or economic history. The same inscriptions upon which the political historian depends afford the best information to one concerned with economic relations. Consider, for example, that the great copper-plate inscriptions whose Sanskrit preambles (*praśasti*) provide the basic chronology of Chola history also provide the most detailed descriptions of village organization and land tenure. South Indian inscriptions which have been analyzed in periodicals like *Epigraphia Indica, Indian Antiquary*, and others for their political or religious interest provide as good a selection of records on the economy of the age as one might compile. There being no special class of economic or administrative documents which might shed light upon the medieval economy, as one finds in other places, every South Indian historian depends upon the same corpus of records. Despite themselves, most South Indian historians have in this way assimilated a reasonably good idea of general economic organization. But there are perhaps other reasons for the largely inadvertent accuracy about economic organization.

Ideological factors and what might be regarded as a "golden age" nostalgia have served to attribute high importance to what inscriptions describe of the localized, peasant economy of the time. Evidence of powerful, sophisticated local assemblies in the South Indian macroregion have been seized upon by nationalist historians in other parts of India as precocious examples of rural democracy. Even if, as in the case of Nilakanta Sastri, this claim was denied and ridiculed, he and others have found much to admire in these local institutions. Here groups of many kinds and at all levels could live harmoniously, even elegantly, in numerous rural localities where Brahmanical life and learning were sustained and thus gave to the age characteristics of which golden ages are made.[3] Despite the essential lack of interest in economic relationships, such factors inevitably led to an emphasis upon the locality ("local government") and "corporate groups" and thus to a basically sound view of the economy in which local and corporate elements attained overwhelming importance.

The historiography of the early South Indian state, lacking the salutary neglect of its associated economy, has been subject to serious distortion. Found in the literature on the Chola and other contemporary states are such expressions as the following:

> A Byzantine monarchy . . .[4]
>
> There is no definite evidence of the existence of a council of ministers or of the officers connected with the central government [yet] a numerous and powerful bureaucracy assisted the king in the tasks of administration.[5]
>
> Indian society did not commit to the care of the government anything more than the tasks of police and justice.[6]
>
> The elaborateness and correctness of [land] measurements are borne out by the minutest details regarding the division of land contained in the records. . . . Land as small in extent as 1/52,428,800,000 of a *vēli* [or 1/500,000th of a square foot!] was measured and assessed for revenue.[7]

It is conceded, of course, that the historical writings of other cultures could be picked over to yield equally inconsistent and bizarre statements. However, in few others are there inconsistencies, distortions, and ill-founded generalizations such as one finds in medieval South Indian historiography as it deals with the nature of the state. Inevitably, this affects the presumed relationship of the state with the economic order. I shall try to support this indictment by discussing what are clearly among the most impressive works on the Chola period of South India: those of Nilakanta Sastri, T.V. Mahalingam, and A. Appadorai.

In keeping with the compartmentalized mode of exposition of these and other writers on early South Indian history, discussions of the state and the economy as interacting aspects of a polity or a social system almost never occur. When, rarely, such discussion does occur, violence is done to what is known of both aspects. In the works of the writers mentioned above, discussion of the relationship of the state and the economy take somewhat different lines of development reflecting their diverse interest. Nilakanta Sastri, being concerned with a dynasty in *The Cōḷas*, for example, has a clear and defensible chronological framework. Half the monograph is straightforward, narrative, political history; the other half deals with administrative, social, and cultural aspects of the large territory associated with the Cholas for about four centuries. References to the relationship of the state and economy are oblique and suffer primarily from his perception of the Cholas state as a centralized, bureaucratized monarchy, a view which he did much to promote. His enthusiasm for the vitality of local, self-governing institutions, with which other of his works also deal, makes for contradictions which he either never recognized or never felt the need to reconcile. T. V. Mahalingam's *South Indian Polity* has recently been republished in a version which adds a few footnotes and a glossary and thus claims to be revised; but, in fact, it shows no sign of significant research over the past eighteen years since it was first published. Its chronological organization is utterly indefensible since it ranges from the classical or Sangam period to the middle of the seventeenth century with the implicit assumption that there were no changes of importance in any of the topics treated. Evidence from classical literature of uncertain date is juxtaposed with evidence from the Vijayanagar period and even some nineteenth-century evidence to support a point on some institution which is considered not to have changed in that vast age nor to have altered its relationship with other institutions.

Appadorai's work is the most pertinent for the question considered here. His important study of the economy from A.D. 1000 to 1500[8] is marred by a chronological scheme which bears no relationship to the subject in an explicit way but is implicitly based upon the presumed existence of strong, centralized states from the eleventh to the sixteenth centuries. Thus periodization for his economic material is based upon political factors the relevance of which to the economy is never queried. He accepts Nilakanta Sastri's view of a centralized, bureaucratized state without pausing to consider how irreconcilable the economic order he describes is with such a political model. Under the rubric of "conditions" Appadorai takes up discrete aspects of the economic system without ever regarding the economy as a system at any level. His brief chapter, in volume II, on the role of the state is among the least useful and most brief sections of this large work.

While granting the difficult nature of the evidence pertaining to the relationship between the state and the economy, these writers add further problems in their analyses. Each has implicitly assumed static and uniform conditions which appear to justify the use of evidence on points widely disparate in time and space based upon inscriptional evidence drawn from many places and times with scant regard to possibly variation. Moreover, each uses evidence anecdotally with the implication that it is statistically valid. Thus a particular datum from an inscription is often stated to "represent" or "illustrate" or "exemplify" general usage for all time and over all southern India, even though each of the writers concedes strong subregional variations. Finally, each, but especially Mahalingam and Appadorai, uses various classes of literary evidence to provide "evidence" of how things are supposed to be ("theory") and then corroborates or occasionally disputes these supposed phenomena by stray inscriptional evidence ("practice").

These critical comments upon the character of what all would agree are the best of the scholarship on the Cholas as well as upon the problem being examined here are meant only to provide a basis for considering that problem more clearly. It has been contended that while the perception of particular aspects of the economic order has been accurate on the whole, and obviously most comprehensively considered by Appadorai, the role and function of the state relative to the economy have been subject to basic distortions. This thesis can best be explicated by reviewing what has been written about the Chola state in terms of the levels of state organization, the functions carried out at these levels, and the institutions through which these functions were carried out.

In this discussion, the order in which the levels of state organization are usually examined is reversed: I turn first to the local level instead of considering the "central" governmental level first as do most writers. There are various reasons for this reversal. Though three levels are usually delineated—"central," "provincial," and "local"—there are but two for which there is much evidence, the first and the third.[9] "Provincial" organization until Vijayanagar times, except perhaps in Karnāṭaka, is extremely hazy even by the necessarily permissive standards which prevail in this field of history. Hence it is really only a matter of reversing a two-part order. Moreover, the most firm facts for the entire political system exist at the local level. Finally, I believe that by analyzing the functions and institutions of the political system at the local level initially, it can be shown that there was little scope for the kinds of political functions attributed to "central" state institutions by the conventional view.

Administration is the term usually adopted for discussion of the local level of medieval South Indian society. Thus "local government" is the category under which such diverse institutions as Brahman village assemblies (*sabhā*), locality assemblies (*nādu*), castes, and guilds are characteristically examined, even though none of these institutions can properly and formally be called "political" or "administrative." These institutions and others, such as the non-Brahman village assembly, *ūr*, are viewed as the effective units of local government invested with administrative functions by devolution or decentralization of the centralized, monarchical state. It is implied that "local government" could have been managed by the "central state" but for the deliberate restraint of Chola rulers.[10] Among the functions thus devolving upon such local bodies as those mentioned above were "control and regulation of land, management of irrigation works and temples, collection and remission of taxes, management of charities, serving as banks receiving deposits of money and lending, and supervising the cultivation of lands."[11] To these rather omnibus powers may be added the "administration of justice"[12] and the "maintainance of records."[13]

The conventional historiographical view at times recognizes that the local institutions allegedly charged with central administration were made up of groups whose corporate character and essential nature were prior to and existed apart from any state functions. No explicit argument is made that the *sabhā*, *ūr*, or *nādu* were "constituted" by the state for the purposes of carrying out administration, though something close to this seems to be meant by Mahalingam when he says: "The village communities were each an organism born out of the consciousness of its members of a kingship among them."[14] It is more usually recognized that local groupings and institutions owed their existence to functions other than the administration of "central" government regulations. It is further assumed that the political values of the age restrained the Cholas and other rulers from usurping the corporate authority of these bodies. Thus we have Nilakanta Sastri's formulation that these local institutions were permitted to enjoy autonomy as a means of preserving the character of the society as "a federation of groups," while yet maintaining a balance of functions between "an able bureaucracy and [these] active local assemblies which... fostered a live sense of citizenship and . . . a high standard of efficiency and purity, perhaps the highest ever attained by a Hindu state."[15] Where this balance was presumably most clearly seen was at the level of the village, considered the primary unit of society.

Inevitably, the village considered is the *brahmadēya* and its assembly, the *sabhā*, to which the term *village republic* is as frequently and as irrelevantly used by South Indian historians as those elsewhere in India.[16] A rather extravagant statement of the significance of the village is made by Nilakanta Sastri. He compares the South Indian village with the cities of Gaul in the Roman Empire, stating that the Chola villages of Coromandel, "the townships in the Cōḷa empire," were like the Gallic city as described by Fustel de Coulanges: "Doubtless it [the Chola village] was not a free state; it was at any rate a state."[17]

To this view of "local government" during Chola times certain queries must be posed. If it is true that the local institutions considered as "local government" were in existence before Chola times, or at least before the time of Rajaraja, from when Nilakanta Sastri correctly dates the mature Chola state, would not one expect considerable variation in such units from place to place and time to time? Mahalingam spoke of village communities "adapting themselves to changing conditions in the country,"[18] but because he does not explicitly analyze variation, it is impossible to know whether he meant "changing conditions" of time or of place or both. The impression conveyed in the writings referred to here is that there was a single style of local government. In reality, there must have been many kinds. What must have been considerable variation according to place at any time, and what must have been considerable variation in time, tends to be lost in the basically additive approach of a writer like Mahalingam. He conveys the impression, and apparently believes, that from the classical period, the undated evidence of which he frequently uses, to the seventeenth century, for which he is willing to accept the evidence of the nineteenth century, there were few changes. All the evidence together, from all parts of South India and through many centuries, is taken to represent functions of all or any *sabhā*, *ūr*, temples, or other local institutions.

In fact, there was considerable variation in the nature and function of local institutions in different parts of South India and at different times. If, as the conventional interpretation argues, the *sabhā* was an, if not *the*, important institution of local government, then the spatial distribution of these unique bodies must be significant. In certain parts of the Coromandel plain the density of these settlements was obviously much greater than in other parts. Being settlements with relatively large, nonproductive, and high-consumption populations, *brahmadēya* would have had to be located in fertile, irrigated tracts, and so they were. Apart from the major riverine basins, these institutions were found more thinly scattered over very large tracts of less productive land and thus, in political, economic, and any other terms, they were less influential.

Another query, already touched upon, is this: What is the "locality," the governance of which so occupies the historical writings on South India? Almost invariably, "locality" means village, and "village" means *brahmadēya*. The assumption has almost always been that non-Brahman, peasant settlements—which all agree were the overwhelming majority—were a somewhat less complex version of the Brahman village and often coexisted side by side with the latter.[19] This assumption is without a foundation in evidence, and it is incorrect to conceive of local society in South India as a congeries of self-governing villages, each of which, as Nilakanta Sastri seems to suggest, was complete in itself. Two aspects of the society of Chola times may be noted to indicate how false the village-centered assumption is. The first is the important role of those in control of *nādu* localities (*nāttār*) in the affairs of Brahman and non-Brahman villages; the other is the logic of irrigation management in many parts of the Coromandel plain.

The *nāttār* are the dominant peasant group in a locality, judging from their functions in many of the grants of land recorded in the Chola copper plates. The *nāttār* are identified as the chief executors of "orders" establishing newly created Brahman settlements, and they are intimately involved in the solemn demarcation of the lands comprising such settlements. In the Larger Leiden plates, there is confirmation of the importance of locality groups; representatives from over twenty neighboring villages were involved in granting lands to the new Brahman village of Anaimangalam.[20] In post-Chola times, the identity of dominant peasant groups of a locality tended to be preserved in a territorial element in the names of castes: for example, Tondaimandala Vellalas.

Underlying the social and economic prominence of the local landed groups comprising the *nāttār* was the maintenance of small-scale irrigation systems upon which much agriculture in the macroregion depended. In most parts of the Coromandel plain where irrigation was the basis of agriculture, the system employed was that of tanks fed by riverine channels and augmented by tank storage of monsoonal rains. The maintenance of local systems of irrigation depended upon cooperation and coordination among the dominant peasantry utilizing the system, who were thus bound together by specific economic interests usually reinforced by social and ceremonial ties. Thus the relevant locality which must be considered in Chola times and later was an ethnic and ecological one—the *nādu*. Here dominant agricultural groups were bound closely together either by having opened the tract to settled agriculture or by having achieved control over it by conquest. These groups gave the locality its identity. The village was a unit of convenience then as it has been in modern times. Essentially it was a residential site for peasant families and their various service groups with easy access to fields served by local irrigation systems.

Brahman villages, *brahmadēya*, were not simply residential units of convenience as were peasant villages. Brahman settlements differed from others in several ways. In origin, *brahmadēya* were prosperous peasant settlements granted to Brahmans for their support and their residence. Solemn ceremonies attended the grant of such villages, and the new village thus created was made independent of local peasant control to which it had previously been subject. This was a recognition of the special character of *brahmadēya* with their large population of Brahmans to serve the Vedic temples and schools and other Brahmanical institutions. Most large peasant villages in any locality were probably as pluralistic in social composition as *brahmadēya*, though the latter were accorded a degree of control in their settlements which was as considerable as the dominant peasantry had in the locality as a whole. In fact, it may be suggested that the creation and constitution of the *brahmadēya*, on which great attention has been focused by historians, inform us less about other villages—non-Brahman ones of various kinds—than they suggest about how the locality as a whole was controlled by its dominant landed groups.

These queries and comments on the nature of "local government," or more generally local society, do not diminish the significance attached to this level of society by historians. On the contrary, it makes that level even more important, for it emphasizes the competence of local institutions in early South Indian society to manage all aspects of local life in a wide variety of ethnic and ecological contexts. There can have been no single mold for local society, and the evidence indicates a high degree of diversity. This important fact has been neglected by scholars to date.

The conventional historical view does not dispute the significance of quite powerful, effective, and diverse local groups and institutions with an impressive capacity for control over local society. This is a proud heritage. However, there remains the fundamental question of how these nuclei of local societies of early South India were integrated into something called a "state." The usual approach is to ignore in the section entitled "the central government" what is conceded and admired in the section entitled "local government." Thus it is supposed that there was a central secretariat which directed a bureaucracy whose officials penetrated into local societies. This view is almost wholly manufactured from names of "officials," of which some were simply ancient titles of respect, like *ēnādi* and *mārāyan*, dating from classical times; others were honorifics, like *mūvēnda-vēlār* and *adigārgal*, dating from a later time; and only a few may have indicated a genuine functional office, like *sēnaipati*, or army leader. Terms for such a crucial department as taxation are painfully reconstructed from fragments which occur infrequently and do not, in any case, relate explicitly to "central" government officials.[21] Or the term *utam-kūttam* becomes "liaison officers between the king and the regular bureaucracy" on the strength of an inscription of the time of Kulottunga I which is construed to refer to the "land revenue department" of the *utam-kūttam*.[22] Instances of this sort are easily duplicated and urge the strong corrective of requiring that the proof of a central bureaucracy be not in the identification of what may have been officials but in the demonstration that such persons were actually officeholders in a functional system of centralized, administrative control. This has never been demonstrated for any South Indian state; it could not be.

When pressed on the question of what functions were carried out by the state as a centralized, bureaucratized institution, proponents of the conventional view speak of the king and the rhetoric of power associated with the kingly institution in inscriptional preambles and in shastras; they speak of justice and police or security functions of the king which required a system of officials; and, finally, they speak of the maintenance of an army and the administration of charitable works carried out by the Chola rulers, members of the royal family, and "officers" of the king. When further pressed, they concede that there is little empirical evidence to correspond with the *chakravartin* rhetoric of the medieval inscriptions and/or shastras, the languages of which are to be understood as metaphorical. If not super-kingship—"Byzantine monarchy"—then the conventional view is likely to shift to a position diametrically opposed and speak of limited police and justice as the prime functions of the state. These functions, too, can easily be shown to be local in character. There was no "king's law," and it is significant that the example which Nilakanta Sastri cites to illustrate the royal judicial process is an obviously didactic story from the *Periyapurā-nam* involving adjudication of the alleged slave status of a great Saivite saint with respect to his "master" Siva! Police functions in the sense of providing security from the depredations of war are belied by the frequency, frivolousness, or predatory character of warfare during the period. As Mahalingam suggests, kings of the day were often at war because that is what kings do and that is what biology—an aggressive instinct—commands of men.[23]

Of the putative functions of a central government, two have been given the most serious emphasis. The first is the redistribution of what are regarded as "state" resources among various special groups in society deemed especially worthy and enjoying high prestige. The second is the maintenance of a central or "royal" army for purposes of defense as well as predation. Charity and the army occupy substantial portions of the works of Nilakanta Sastri and Mahalingam. But was the "central government" necessary for these purposes? There is considerable evidence to suggest that it was not.

Charitable and welfare functions of the Chola state, according to the conventional view of South Indian historians, consisted of support to such Brahmanical institutions as temples, seminaries (*maṭha*), schools, and the most important locus of Brahman activities, the *brahmadēya.* After the thirteenth century, the Cholars joined others in the support of non-Brahman *maṭha* as well. In fact, however, there are few records involving direct grants by the Chola rulers, members of their families, or others close to them, and these grants are made to a few institutions only, ones which had a special relationship to the ruling family. One was the Tanjavur temple of Rajaraja I. Many grants of income from the land to temples, *maṭha*, and similar institutions were first purchased by the donor, including the royal donor. Where, as in the case of the Brihadīśvara temple of Tanjavur, the king was the principal supporter, it is instructive to notice that construction and maintenance costs were met not from the regular resources of a central treasury but from the loot of predatory conquest and labor commandeered from hundreds of villages in the delta region.[24] This is surely a demonstration of the powerful Chola overlordship in the Kaveri region; it is not, however, a demonstration, as often proposed, of the capacity and effectiveness of a bureaucratic central government. Moreover, it is clear that such institutions were subject to revenue demands. If these were demands for royal or central revenue and if the support of such institutions by the central state is considered a significant state function, then the logic is questionable. We are to understand that what was granted by the state with one hand was taken back with the other!

The maintenance of Chola armies and the requirements of warfare as central state functions requiring a bureaucratic structure constitute the ultimate defensive redoubt of the conventional view of the state and the economy. Substantial chapters are devoted to territorial security and the organization of royal armies. Where a military unit is identified, it is assumed to be part of a central military organization. Thus the many *vēḷaikkārar* military units of the period of Rajaraja are considered not only as the "king's own" but as soldiers who have vowed to sacrifice their lives, by suicide, if necessary.[25] The evidence upon which these conclusions about Chola armies are based is highly doubtful, and it is interesting to note that the early epigraphists Hultzsch, Krishna Sastri, and Venkayya held the view that the warriors called *vēḷaikkārar* were probably made up of men from various occupational groups temporarily engaged in military activities.[26] Gopinatha Rao, Nilakanta Sastri, and Mahalingam have, in recent years, transformed these soldiers into a centrally recruited and controlled force completely devoted to the ruler. The implication of the revised view is that the Chola state had a monopoly of coercive power which at once required an effective mobilization and centralization of resources through a bureaucracy and, simultaneously, provided the "central" government with a powerful instrument of coercion for that purpose—a large, royal, standing army. This proposition is indefensible and contrary to a considerable body of evidence that military power was distributed among many groups quite independent of the "centralized monarchy." We have substantial evidence that mercantile groups maintained a formidable military capability which was required by the extensive, itinerant trade network of of the age. Ayyāvoḷe inscriptions bear this out, as does the famous Polonnaruva inscription of Sri Lanka in the time of Vijayabahu (ca. 1120) in which the Tamil *iḍaṅgai vēḷaikkārar* are referred to in association with the trade organization of the *vaḷañjiyar*.[27] References to *kaikkōlar vēḷaikkārar* have suggested that artisans too were capable of maintaining armed units, though Nilakanta Sastri has questioned this.[28]

However, the major loci of military power were from those prosperous and populous tracts of agriculture throughout the Coromandel plain and parts of the interior uplands. The logic of resources—human and nonhuman—would make the dominant peasant population the major source of armed power. Local military authorities, local "chiefs," were conspicuous in the early Chola period, before Rajaraja I, and once again attained high visibility in the thirteenth century when the Chola overlordship weakened. During the period of the great Cholas, from Rajaraja I through the time of Kulottunga I, these local chiefs almost disappear from view as that view is provided by inscriptions. This may, of course, mean that as a class of local leaders these warriors were eliminated much as the "poligars" were reduced later by Tipu Sultan and the British. In a few cases there is evidence of this. However, it is much more likely that this level of leadership continued intact, but submerged beneath the surface of a society only partially revealed to us in the inscriptions of the age.

Given the corporate character and local orientation of peasant society at the time and given the evidence of nonpeasant military power (mercantile and artisan guilds), it is difficult to suppose that those in control of the land—leaders of peasant groups—could have been anything but significant militarily. Under the circumstances of widely distributed military power which the evidence of the Chola age provides, the supposed monopoly of military power by the state can only be rejected—and with that rejection the final presumed function of the centralized state.

II

Historical scholarship is no exception to the principle in ordered inquiry that it is clearly one thing to challenge a comprehensive, even if incorrect, view of an age, and quite another to cause it to be abandoned. If the conventional conception of the medieval South Indian state is to be challenged and perhaps displaced, an equally comprehensive interpretation will have to be offered, one which may explain better than the existing one those facts which we possess. At the outset, and partly in continuation of the critique above, it is argued that any formulation on the nature of the medieval South Indian state must incorporate a set of characteristics applicable to all or to most medieval Indian states.

Medieval Indian states, as formal and concrete systems, appear to have been characterized by the following salient attributes: they were custodial, tributary, locally based, and oriented to rural networks. By "custodial" is meant that the state did not arrogate to itself and attempt to monopolize the coercive functions and authority of other, essentially nonpolitical institutions in the society. Notably, the Indian ruler tended to leave to kinship, occupational, and religious groups the authority for social control of its members; he tended to leave to various territorial associations—villages and circles of villages—the same authority with respect to their constituent groups. Indeed, it was through such corporate and associational entities that the Indian ruler exercised such power as he might claim and possess, for it was on the recognition of a ruler by such bodies that his power depended. The Indian king was an overlord, not a manager; he demanded submission to his claim of superiority, rather than obedience to his orders; he did not distribute directives over the ruled.

The most important reason why the medieval Indian state was not a managerial state is that there was little for extralocal agencies to manage. Agrarian economies based upon large-scale irrigation works as in China and Mesopotamia required, or at least utilized, centralized and bureaucratized monarchies as the political instruments of management. While irrigation was of importance in Indian agriculture, it never, except perhaps in the Harappan culture, assumed the extensive and integrated forms which would have required hydraulic management. Control and storage of water consisted of minor, local works with but few exceptions; most cultivation, then as now, was carried on in a variety of "dry" ecotypes dependent upon monsoonal rains or mixed ecotype varieties involving some dry and wet agriculture based upon local tanks, wells, and minor riverine channels. No South Indian state, including Vijayanagar, had a department of irrigation. This appears to be true elsewhere in the subcontinent, for even the *Arthaśāstra* of Kautilya, which seems to have left no aspect of statecraft out of its imaginative purview, does not provide elaborately for the management of water.

If the mode of agriculture in southern as well as northern India provided no scope for the managerial state, industrial production and mercantile activities did not either. These activities were to a minor extent only concentrated in urban places, thus affording little scope for state control. Sacred, rather than economic or political, factors appear to have been responsible for many of the more persistent urban places in India, south and north. Without dense populations of rural folk bound to land enriched by elaborate irrigation works or large urban populations bound by interdependence to specific umlands, two essential elements of the managerial state were absent in India until the nineteenth century.

It is, of course, the custodial state which is implied in and extolled by the shastric tradition. The dharmic conception of kingship and rule in *nitiśāstra* from Kautilya onward affirms the role of the monarch as custodian. The institution of caste, as defined in *dharmaśāstra* and in reality, is viable only as each corporate ethnic entity, in hierarchical relations with others, supervises its own members. Such supervision is not simply permitted in shastra, it is enjoined. Unlike China, where the juridical parity of all families below the nobility was established from the time of Mencius and provided the basis for a civil law based upon the family, India recognized no homogeneous unit according to which state supervision and control could be exercised. It was a recognized responsibility of the Indian ruler to support those units in society which were charged with supervision and at most to adjudicate conflicts among them when other means of coping with conflict, for example through corporate groups or territorial associations, failed. Even such adjudicating functions appear to have been rare. Under these conditions, there is truth in the often repeated statement that in ancient and medieval Indian polity, "legislation" was not considered an appropriate function of the state and the ruler. Without legislation (that is, statutory directives expressive of the coercive authority of the state), there could be no effective management of resources or people by the ruler or state; only custodianship was possible.

The concomitant of custodianship with respect to the sharing of resources which might be claimed by the state was tribute. The distinction here between a taxation system and a tributary system is not categorical but dimensional. Medieval South Indian society knew many means of transferring a portion of agricultural production and a share of the goods and/or profit from their sale by artisans and merchants. Tribute payments require a continuous demonstration of asymmetry to ensure a payment from the weaker to the stronger. While certain factors aside from the coercive power of those engaged in a tributary relationship might facilitate tributary payments—loyalty (or fealty in the medieval European system of feudalism), for example, or appeals to a transcendent moral order or an ideology based upon such an order ("faith" in Europe)—these by themselves would be ineffective in producing transfers of wealth. A taxation system is considered to be resource transfers among units within a social order in which stratified relations are sufficiently clear and stable to enable collections without regular resort to coercion and in which shared cultural and social interests among units provide legitimacy for such transfers. Tax payments thus appear as essentially voluntary in the sense that benefits accuring to those who pay and those who receive are seen as mutual.

According to the distinction between taxes and tribute suggested here, a transfer of resources—income or the means of generating income—may at times be considered a tax or a tribute depending upon the relationship between those who pay and those who receive payment. It is recognized in distinguishing between tax and tribute payments that it will often be difficult to determine whether one or the other term is appropriate. Regularity in the periodicity of the payment or the rate of payment, naively considered to be attributes of taxation, may be poor indicators. Prolonged asymmetry of power between those who pay and those who receive may provide for considerable regularity whereas factors which are not directly related to power—such as drought—may produce irregularities within a taxation system. Nomenclature is possibly the most hazardous basis for deciding whether a transfer is a tax or a tribute or, more precisely, where on the continuum a particular payment ought to be located.

While the distinction between tax and tribute may have the potential for being an important feature of the relationship between the state and the economy, it is a distinction which should be refined conceptually and verified empirically. However, even as a crude marker it suggests a relevant factor with respect to the South Indian state. That is, tribute payments can hardly be associated with the managerial state which must rely upon the careful and systematic exploitation of resources. Nor does one associate the tribute system with a bureaucracy, nor a tax system with a state lacking in the apparatus for systematic collection of the surplus. Taxes imply a mechanism for assessment of demand and modification of that demand to conform in some degree with such circumstances as the capability of the payer and the requirements of the payee. It is extremely rare in medieval India to find evidence of such an apparatus in respect to what was called "the central state."

However, from Chola inscriptions it is clear that regular transfers and remissions occurred at the local level of society. The list of transfers which has been culled from inscriptions is staggering in number, indicating not a sophisticated, bureaucratic apparatus but the opposite: variegated, local systems of transfer. Hazardous inferences have been made with respect to transfers between local institutions and the Chola state. Here there is neither convincing evidence of officials (that is, rational roles and offices) involved with taxes nor particular payments to the Chola state. It is only as an extension of what is most clearly a local taxation system that assertions regarding transfers to the Chola state are made. But we really know nothing concrete about extralocal transfers.

If transfers from localities to the Chola state occurred, they were tributary in character. Any inventory of terms which refer to transfers strongly supports this proposition, for most are obviously local transfers.[29] Further, one important structural element of the Chola period supports the distinction made here between tax transfers and tributary ones. That is, there are no linkage elements connecting very well developed local networks with the Chola state.

The absence of links between local networks and the formal institutions of the state is a fact of importance in any understanding of the Chola period. If we were to accept the assertions that in the Chola period we find "the almost Byzantine royalty of Rajaraja and his successors"[30] and "a nice balance struck between centralized control and local initiative,"[31] we must be able to demonstrate the mechanisms by which "Byzantine" kingship and "centralized control" were executed. Both these terms, and similar ones which occur in the historical literature on the Cholas and other medieval South Indian states, are utterly inappropriate. Nilakanta Sastri comes much closer to a defensible proposition about the nature of the political system in a sentence which appears, remarkably, in the same paragraph as the "nice balance" statement: that Chola society "is best described as a federation of groups." For, indeed, what the evidence of the Chola period persistently and massively impresses upon us is that the society of the age was essentially oriented around local networks of relationships among well-developed corporate groups and associations.

One may well argue about what constituted the local unit of society. The primacy of the village has been denied. We have much evidence of kinship, occupational, and religious groups which were part of the village organization in the sense of cooperating segmentally within a village, but members of such groups were involved in many villages of a particular locality and their locus must be placed beyond the confines of individual village settlements. The territory called *nādu* in Tamil country and called by other terms elsewhere is the local unit of greatest consequence. The *nādu* was not an administrative unit in the sense of being a bureaucratic contrivance or convenience, as is often stated. The *nādu* predates Rajaraja I's "byzantine" order and endured beyond the time of his successors. The *nādu* was a sociological and ecological unit; it was a "social field" or "arena" comprising various ethnic groupings whose social and cultural interactions constituted a microregion. Among the crucial determinants of the size and character of the *nādu* as a microregion was its agrarian-relevant environment. These issues will be touched upon below.

Whether one agrees with the assessment of the *nādu* as the critical unit of local organization or whether other kinds of local organization are delineated, such as that implied by Noburu Karashima, in which the *brahmadēya* is seen as the integrating core institution of local society,[32] there can be no serious dissent from the emphasis upon local forms of Chola society. The burden of argument for those holding the view of a centralized governmental structure of any degree is to demonstrate how localized units of society—about which we know a good deal—were centrally affected.

Elements which might have linked localities with institutions of a central government appear to play a minor role in the society of South India from the tenth through the twelfth centuries. The most important "centers" were *brahmadēya*, which had no explicit governing functions relative to the localities in which they were, though they did have significant economic functions deriving from their pluralistic character (merchants, artisans, and cultivators resided there) and from their size. The sacred and economic functions of the *brahmadēya* may explain why it is here that one finds the largest number of inscriptions, and especially those referring to the Chola rulers and persons associated with the Cholas. Such trade centers of which we have evidence are for the most part *brahmadēya* or peasant settlements which have grown larger than most settlements without, however, losing their rural and local-centered character. *Brahmadēya* like Uttaramērūr, Eṇṇāyiram, Tiruvaḍatturai, and Tribhuvani were large, pluralistic settlements with considerable self-government (*taniyūr*), yet they are still oriented primarily to local networks rather than extralocal ones. Certain of the more ancient urban places, such as Kanchipuram and Madurai, were politically important for the Cholas and appear to have been garrison points, but there is no evidence that such places—and they were few and far between—were linkage points in a centralized governmental system. In fact, from its inscriptions it would appear that Kanchipuram remained more important as a sacred center than anything else.

If the foregoing propositions about the medieval state system, including those of South India, are correct, then the conventional understandings of the state are very largely wrong. That is, if, as argued here, the South Indian medieval states were custodial rather than managerial, tribute-receiving rather than tax-based, and the society itself was organized into relatively isolated, locally oriented networks of relations among corporate groups and associations, then much that has been written about the state is incorrect.

III

Having argued that the medieval South Indian state cannot have been a centralized, bureaucratic system of political relations as may be found in some preindustrialized societies and as claimed in the conventional historiography, how may we speak of the political order of the time? This question may be pursued in two possible ways. The first is to attempt to fit political evidence of the medieval period of South India into a framework based exclusively upon Indian textual traditions such as to create a model of political relations which is *sui generis*; the second way is comparative.

Two possible contradictory conceptions of the state may be derived from classical texts. One is a centralized state structure in which the ancient kings were conceived as the owner-managers of the territorial patrimony. This model figures prominently in *smriti* literature and appears to underlie the conventional historical views of Nilakanta Sastri and Mahalingam as well as others. Modern scholars of this persuasion have largely distorted the ancient model to conform with characteristics of the modern bureaucratic state.[33] Thus while the germinal conception of centralized monarchy comes from *nitiśāstra* texts, preeminently from the *Arthaśāstra* of Kautilya, the state has come to be presented as a curiously modern, unitary, bureaucratized system extending from the king to the lowest level of society. Depicted as efficient and ruthless, this state is an amoral vehicle for the attainment and maintenance of perfect power, *artha.*

The alternative *smriti* model of the state depicts the king—raja—within the nexus of personal relationships in which dharma as a magico-religious, or ethical, element forms the basis of kingship rather than *artha.* In a recent, provocative essay by J. C. Heesterman, the *Arthaśāstra* model is rejected:

> I think we should dismiss the deceptive appearances of a centralized setup held together by a bureaucracy reaching from the king down to the grass roots. This certainly seems to be the ideal presented in the Arthaśāstra, but its reticence of chains [of] command and reporting would suggest otherwise. Instead we find almost pathetic stress on the necessity of officials' trustworthiness, and a concomitant all-pervading spy system, which can only block administrative action and in the end reduce it to chaos. Moreover it is clear that the realization of a centralized bureaucratic setup would require objective conditions, such as a high degree of monitarization [*sic*], which would make it possible to separate the functions of government from rights in the soil.[34]

In place of the *Arthaśāstra* conception, Heesterman offers the following formulation derived from another part of the *smriti* tradition: "Kingship is constituted by a network of personal relations [as described in *smriti* texts dealing with royal ritual] . . . . The basic paradigm seems to be kinship and cunnubium spanning the whole . . . community."[35] "Community," in Heesterman's conception, is a restricted locality in which "people-cum-territory" form a political unit called *janapada* or *rashtra.*[36] The locus of state power is here seen as a "little kingdom."[37]

These two models derived from classical textual sources have at times been viewed as complementary, if not simply identical except for differences in scale. However, they appear most often as alternatives. In the *Arthaśāstra* model, an autocrat manages what might be a large territory of diverse peoples through administrative specialists augmented by a spy system and *agents provocateurs.* It is thus conceived as a very powerful unitary state. In the other model, a chief who is *primus inter pares* among other chiefs acts as a "mediator between parts of the community."[38] This would appear to be the same condition assumed by Nilakanta Sastri in his characterization of the Chola state as a "federation of groups." It is a conception of government which is very close to that called "stateless" in the current literature of political anthropology.[39]

Models of states in shastric texts change slightly over time and draw more closely together, particularly as the ruthless quality of Kautilya's conception becomes muted in later *nitiśāstra.* However, neither can be regarded as an empirical model of political relationships since they were inventions meant for didactic purposes or as a means of explicating philosophical issues (such as dharma and *artha*). Hence neither may be regarded as directly useful for the analysis of real political relationships of South India during the medieval period, however suggestive they may be for exploring ideological aspects of medieval polity. Moreover, neither of these textually derived political models permits useful comparison of Indian political arrangements with those of other societies.

The second approach to the analysis of the political order of medieval South India is to consider concepts current in modern scholarship generally. The most obvious of these is the concept of feudalism. No consideration of this concept in a non-European context can ignore the able essay by John W. Hall, "Feudalism in Japan—A Reassessment."[40] Apart from Hall's eloquent defense of comparative history, his succinct examination of usage of the concept of feudalism within European and Japanese historical contexts, and his careful concern for levels of analysis as he ponders the definition of the concept, we are indebted to him for his distinction between "feudal practices in Japan" and the origins of these practices, their development, and their decline.[41] His guarded assertion that Japanese society during part of the sixteenth century—1500 to 1550—"gave every indication of conforming in general outline with the ideal type of feudalism"[42] stands as a chastening caution to those working on Indian medieval society. For in medieval South India— and perhaps in India as a whole—there is little upon which the scholar can fasten the template of feudal practices, conditions, or behaviors; certainly there is nothing like the array of institutions and practices which one finds in Japan to justify consideration of the concept.[43]

Until very recently, historians of South India have not used the concept of feudalism in a systematic way. Terms such as *feudatory, vassalage*, and *serf* have been used, however. Thus D. C. Sircar refers to warriors of Karnāṭaka serving the Chālukya and Rāshtrakūta houses from the seventh century on as "feudatory families."[44] Nilakanta Sastri speaks of "powerful nobles" who resisted the expansion of Orissan power over Vijayanagar territory during the fifteenth century;[45] Arokiaswami refers to the *palaya-karar* of Kongu during the sixteenth century as "feudatory rulers" or "feudal chiefs," though he is constrained to admit that "we have no clear vision of how exactly these chieftains had governed the various regions entrusted to their care and control";[46] and T. V. Mahalingam sweepingly identifies locally powerful warriors as "feudatories . . . paying tribute to the royal house [Pallava] in token of their vassalage," though he also speaks of them as "tribal chieftaincies" and "hereditary chiefs."[47] In these cases, no effort is made to justify the feudal terms, so that the meanings of such terms can only be guessed to be any local ruler who recognized, in whatever fashion, the supremacy of an overlord.

Considering India as a whole, the concept of feudalism has not fared much better or differently. Two decades ago Daniel Thorner, in the Coulborn symposium volume of comparative study, *Feudalism in History*,[48] noted that at the time of his writing there was neither a monograph nor even a significant essay on feudalism in Indian history and that in two important cases where the concept had been used, major arguments could be marshaled against that usage. Thorner discussed that use of the concept by Tod in his early nineteenth-century work on Rajputana and more recent interpretations of Muslim rule in northern India. In both cases, Thorner was able to show from the work of William Crooke, A.C. Lyall, and others that the concept of feudalism in India was of doubtful validity even given the broad definition of feudalism which guided Thorner and his symposium colleagues.[49]

More recently, the feudal concept has been resurrected by R. S. Sharma in an analysis of northern India from the fourth to the thirteenth centuries. Here the full panoply of feudal terminology is used, such as *feudatories, fiefs, vassal, serfdom, subinfeudation, benefices*.[50] The theoretical framework underlying Sharma's conception is Marxist, as is clear from the following statement in defense of the use of the concept: "We see feudalism as the form of social order in which the possessing class appropriated the surplus produce of the peasants by exercising superior rights over their land and persons."[51] This conception of feudalism is very close to that used by contemporary Soviet scholars and is thus linked to a major line of historical interpretation. L. B. Alayev, while commenting somewhat critically on Sharma's emphasis upon "a definite system of institutions—economic, social, and political," states an understanding of the concept which is quite congenial to that of Sharma:

> [Soviet scholars] understand [feudalism] as a period in the history of peoples (. . . exceptions could be traced . . .), when the basis of production was the small peasant household, when the producer was not enslaved, but was also not a free hired laborer, and was compelled to give up his surplus to the lord (landlord, overlord, chieftain, and so on). . . . The social and economic status of producers and the mode of production are, according to Soviet scholars, the basis for distinguishing feudal societies out of those organized otherwise.[52]

Shortly after Sharma's lectures on Indian feudalism, but before publication of his volume referred to above, a seminar was convened at the University of Calcutta's Centre for Advanced Study of Ancient Indian History and Culture to discuss the subject. The proceedings were published under the editorship of D. C. Sircar as *Land System and Feudalism in Ancient India*.[53] Here again there was no serious effort to specify the meaning of feudalism as a general framework for ordering Indian historical evidence. Some participants in the seminar simply filled in further examples of "feudal" arrangements and conditions (B. P. Mazumdar, B. N. Yadava, H. V. Neogy); others were doubtful about the use of the concept for India (S. K. Maity and S. K. Mitra) and could go no further than to speak of a "quasi-feudal tendency";[54] and the learned editor himself, D. C. Sircar, categorically rejected the concept of feudalism for India.[55]

In the works cited above, an impressive body of evidence has been assembled suggesting some of the broad Indian similarities to very generalized models of the feudal condition. If these data relating to feudal practices and conditions are considered, and leaving aside any concern with the presumed origins of "Indian feudalism" and factors involved in its decline (if it may be presumed to have declined), then the following case can be made for the notion that the political system of medieval India—south and north—was "feudal" and that supralocal political units may have been "feudal states."

To conform with the evidence, it is necessary that "feudal" be used in its most broad (and perhaps least useful) meaning. It refers to a political order based upon the distribution of coercive authority among a large number of agencies (persons and groups) each enjoying a relatively high degree of private, local jurisdiction. This is the core of the meaning as suggested by Coulborn and Joseph Strayer.[56] The concomitant economic aspects of this kind of political order are ostensibly fulfilled in the predominantly peasant agrarian patterns of livelihood and wealth, the subordination of mercantile and industrial elements to landed ones, the low order of urbanization, and the tendency for regular income transfers among sections of the population (that is, "taxes") to be highly localized in terms of the spatial range of such transfers and the control over what was transferred. In social terms, "feudal" might seem appropriate to the local networks of social relations, the low order of spatial mobility for individuals or families, and the absence of effective centers which might link rural networks into larger patterns of organization.

Since the purpose of using the concept of feudalism assumes comparability with other feudal polities, it must be recognized that formidable difficulties are encountered. Fief, as a constituted, political subregion of a warrior's private authority, was largely absent from medieval South India. In inscriptions and other sources of this time, very few warriors can be identified as holders of some tract on service tenure under a superior warrior's authority. Here it is necessary to disagree with D. C. Sircar's unnecessary concession to the "feudal" interpretation in considering that *amara* tenure in Vijayanagar times was a form of service tenure similar to that of medieval European form.[57] Missing too from most of the presumed "feudal" relations of medieval South India were those binding ties of allegiance which characterize the lord-vassal relationship of feudal Europe and Japan. Among the rare and inconclusive references to personal loyalty of a subordinate warrior to a superior are those few records of Karnāṭaka, some undated inscriptions from Drāshārāma in Vēngī (modern Goda-vari District. Andhra),[58] and the relatively late political system developed by Vishvanātha Nayaka at Madurai in which the personal loyalty and military service due to that overlord were symbolized by his order of seventy-two bastion commanders[59] who shared a common, fictive kinship with the great *nayaka* in the institution of the *kumāravargam* ("prince's lineage").[60]

Another factor to consider in assessing the appropriateness of the feudal concept in South India is whether there existed a moral order such as to bind, or help to bind, inferior and superior warriors as one finds in the moral authority of the Roman Church organization of medieval Europe and in the samurai subculture (Bushido) of Japan. This factor, essentially a cultural one, is neglected in the general discussions of feudalism as A. L. Kroeber suggests in his introduction to the Coulborn volume.[61] It is this cultural factor which is salient in Hall's reluctance to label the Tokugawa period in Japan as feudal because, as Hall observed, "as in Europe, the 'idea of feudalism' lingered much longer [in Japan] than its substance."[62]

Hinduism ostensibly provided a politically relevant moral order if *nitiśāstra* and *dharmaśāstra* are seen as elements of Hinduism. This, of course, depends on viewing Hinduism not merely as a religion in the doctrinal and ritual sense but as a way of life with many regional variants. However, if one seeks to understand Hinduism in relationship to the political system, that is, as an aspect of ideology, then it must be recognized that it often provided for considerable instability. The power of political legitimation was vested with local Brahmans responsible to no superiors, and the religion was characterized by a basic discontinuity between relatively high-caste (Brahman and non-Brahman) participants in Vedic sect activities and the mass of Hindus involved in highly localized, non-Vedic, folk religious affiliations. This discontinuity in Hinduism considered as a morally binding force—the gulf between the high and the low—is a factor which historians have neglected. The other side of the coin of ritual exclusiveness is a discontinuous moral order.

An extension of this view of a moral order which divides the high from the low and in effect opposes Brahmans to all others[63] is the recognition of the ambiguous relationship among non-Brahman folk who claimed respectable status. For non-Brahmans of respectability and wealth who patterned their lifestyles on those of Brahmans and who were the principal supporters of Brahman culture in South India, there was the exigent requirement of maintaining close and cooperative relations with a clientele of persons of lower ritual ranks with whom they lived and shared a territory. For these patrons of wealth and secular power, special and close relations with Brahmans provided the sole means of differentiating their social positions from their clients along dimensions other than simple economic and political dominance. Participation of non-Brahman patrons in higher ritual activities was thus a way of reinforcing secular status. Hinduism, therefore, can be seen as a moral order whose very discontinuities and internal tensions afforded rank-enhancing opportunities to those of ambiguous ritual status who nevertheless possessed quite impressive secular authority. If Hinduism is to be understood as a politically relevant moral factor, that is, as an ideological element, it certainly operated far less consistently and forcibly than did the Roman Church upon the political order of medieval Europe. For the European warrior under Church interdict, no marriages and other church-mediated life cycle rites of those within his jurisdiction could be celebrated. This constituted formidable pressure upon the recalcitrant subordinate warrior which his superior might bring into play. Such pressure could hardly exist in medieval South India, where the mass of rural folk had no access to Brahmanical ritual and rustic Brahman groups could not, in any case, be controlled in the manner of parish priests of medieval Europe.

Each of the three factors discussed above goes to the matter of effective feudal hierarchical power relations involving the control of superior warriors over inferior ones. The fief, as the resource base for warrior power, was in other places held by one at the suffrance of another. In Europe, differential conditions of power and hereditary principles may at times have blunted the effectiveness of the fief as an agency of control, but it could still be converted into an effective control instrument. The same is true for personal loyalty, or fealty. A moral order which supported personal loyalty through oaths and estate honor[64] could become a control element. These are either absent or very weak in the case of medieval South Indian states. Indeed, a distinctive warrior class, or estate, cannot be said to have come into existence in most parts of medieval South India until Vijayanagar times, and then it was within a much less perfect system of hierarchical power relations as compared with that of Europe and Japan, even when due allowance has been made for the somewhat exaggerated order created by the historians of these places.

The attempt to justify the notion of a South Indian feudalism or an Indian feudalism can only prove a hazardous exercise. Medieval European and Japanese feudal systems are so fundamentally different from anything found in India that simply pointing to certain ways in which the presumed Indian feudal variant is (or variants are) different, as some scholars have done, leaves the implicit erroneous understanding that what has not been specifically excepted or qualified must exist in India as it does in some other place. Alternatively, one can follow R. S. Sharma in forcing Indian data into awkward, if not wholly inappropriate, categories. He does this in considering grants of village income to Brahmans, as individual or collective gifts (*agrahara* or *brahmadēya*), to be "feudal grants," and he argues that any income settled upon eleemosynary institutions is an indication of feudal arrangements because such alienated income diminishes the resources of "central authority." This is argued even though it cannot be demonstrated that the "center" enjoyed such resources in the first place!

IV

There is only one fully satisfying conclusion to an essay such as this: the presentation of an alternative interpretation of the historical relationship between the South Indian state and the medieval agrarian order upon which it was based. For the writer to pretend that he has no such interpretation—or at least the main outline of one—would be disingenuous and probably unbelievable in the light of the arguments posed in the discussion.

However, the validity of the critique undertaken here should not depend upon the existence of an alternative, elaborated theory and argument, and none will be offered here. To outline the alternative theory alone would require an essay twice as long as the present one, and to discuss extant historical evidence in the light of that theory would constitute a book in itself. In its present form, the critique may be justified on the basis that in any branch of ordered inquiry, it is appropriate to challenge conventional wisdom even when there may be no equally comprehensive wisdom to substitute in its place.

NOTES

1. *The Cōḷas* (Madras: University of Madras, 1935–1937). Citations here are to the revised edition of 1955.
2. *Early History of the Dekhan*: *Down to the Mahomedan Conquest* (Calcutta: Susil Gupta, 1957). Originally published in the *Bombay Gazetteer*, 1884.
3. Nilakanta Sastri, *op. cit.*, p. 446.
4. *Ibid.*, p. 447.
5. *Ibid.*, p. 461.
6. *Ibid.*
7. T. V. Mahalingam, *South Indian Polity*, rev. ed. (Madras: University of Madras, 1967), pp. 161–162.
8. A. Appadorai, *Economic Conditions in Southern India, 1000–1500 A.D.*, 2 vols. (Madras: University of Madras, 1936). The infrequency with which this important work is cited by historians of South India is a good indication of the indifference with which economic history is viewed.

9. The aberrance of medieval Karnāṭaka with respect to this political fact and other aspects is important and not adequately recognized. In this matter, however, terminological confusion—the fact that any warrior could and did take the titles of *mahāmaṇḍalēsvara* or *mahāsamanta*—makes an assessment of variation from the patterns of Tamilnad difficult.
10. *Cōḷas*, p. 461.
11. Mahalingam, *op. cit.*, p. 344.
12. *Ibid.*, p. 371.
13. *Cōḷas*, p. 513.
14. Mahalingam, *op. cit.*, p. 344.
15. *Cōḷas*, p. 514.
16. *Ibid.*, p. 508; Mahalingam, *op. cit.*, pp. 342–343.
17. *Cōḷas*, p. 515.
18. Mahalingam, *op. cit.*, p. 344.
19. A. Krishnaswami, *The Tamil Country under Vijayanagar* (Annamalai-nagar: Annamalai University, 1964), p. 81.
20. *Epigraphia Indica* XVIII, no. 34, pp. 216–233.
21. Nilakanta Sastri, *Cōḷas*, pp. 462–463, 470: "*puravu-vari-tinai-kulam* would necessarily mean the department of land revenue."
22. Nilakanta Sastri, *Cōḷas*, p. 472.
23. Mahalingam, *op. cit.*, pp. 254–255.
24. K. A. Nilakanta Sastri, "The Economy of a South Indian Temple in the Cola Period," *The Malaviya Commemoration Volume* (Allahabad, 1932), pp. 305–319.
25. *Cōḷas*, pp. 454–455; *Tamil Lexicon* VI, pp. 3839 and 3844.
26. *A.R.E.*, 1913, para. 30.
27. *Epigraphia Indica* XVIII, no. 38, pp. 330–338.
28. *Cōḷas*, p. 454.
29. This is evident from all discussions of the Chola revenue system and from the various inventories and glossaries of revenue terms; the best analysis is that of Noburu Karashima and B. Sitaraman, "Revenue Terms in Chola Inscriptions," *Journal of Asian and African Studies*, no. 5 (Tokyo, 1972), pp. 87–117.
30. Nilakanta Sastri, *Cōḷas*, p. 447.
31. *Ibid.*, p. 462.
32. In a paper presented to the Second International Conference—Seminar on Tamil Studies, Madras, January 1968: "The Power Structure of the Cola Rule."
33. See the disccussion of this issue by Louis Dumont, "Kingship in Ancient India," *Contributions to Indian Sociology* VI (1962), pp. 58 and 70–73.
34. J. C. Heesterman, "Power and Authority in Indian Civilization," Study Conference on Tradition in Indian Politics and Society, Centre of South Asian Studies, School of Oriental and African Studies, University of London, 1–3 July 1970, p. 2.
35. *Ibid.*, p. 4.
36. *Ibid.*, p. 2.
37. Dumont, *Homo Hierarchicus* (Chicago: University of Chicago Press, 1970), pp. 154ff. *Janapada* and *rashtra* as combining territory and population are compared to the French *pays* and the English country; pp. 73–74.
38. Heesterman, *op. cit.*, p. 6.

39. Among the relevant problems which have been considered by anthropologists, one involves the meaning attached to the term *state*. An important distinction has been drawn between *government* and *state*. Government is understood to exist in any society, however primitive, and comprehends the legitimate use of coercion upon its members; the state is considered to be one of the means by which this application of coercion is legitimized and executed: L. Krader, *Formulation of the State* (Englewood Cliffs: Prentice-Hall, 1968), pp. 26–28. It is thus possible to identify "stateless" societies in the manner of M. Fortes and E. E. Evans-Pritchard, *African Political Systems* (London: Oxford University Press, 1948), p. 5 and passim, where functions usually attributed to the "state" are fragmented and diffused in kinship and local community organizations. In a recent elaboration of the idea of "stateless" societies, R. Cohen and J. Middleton, in *Comparative Political Systems* (New York: Doubleday, 1967), pp. xi–xiii, distinguish some tribal organizations as relatively complex forms of acephalous ("lacking overall political organization") political systems. In this formulation, tribes may comprise relatively large populations in their territories, their economies may be based upon agriculture and stock-rearing with permanent rights in the land and herds, and their authority systems would reflect these interests.

40. *Comparative Studies in Society and History* V, no. 1 (October 1962), pp. 15–51.

41. *Ibid.*, p. 38.

42. *Ibid.*, p. 33.

43. *Ibid.*, pp. 31–32, where the principal elements are summarized as: political, where the lord-vassal relationship is understood as standing between the Weberian forms of authority called "patrimonial" and "bureaucratic"; social, where closed and ranked social strata command differential goods and services of the society; and economic, where a self-sufficient or "natural" economy places merchants outside the feudal nexus, though there is no necessary serfdom.

44. "Andhra and Karṇāṭa," *Studies in the Society and Administration of Ancient and Medieval India*, I (Calcutta: Firma K. L. Mukhopadhyay, 1967), p. 142 and passim.

45. *A History of South India* (Madras: Oxford University Press, 1958), p. 272.

46. *The Kongu Country* (Madras: University of Madras, 1956), pp. 364–365. Earlier, J. T. Gwynn, in the *Cambridge History of the British Empire*, IV (Cambridge: Cambridge University Press, 1929), p. 463, had assumed the same relationship of "poligars" ("local officials and adventurers with local influence who had seized power and asserted partial independence") to their superiors, called "feudal nobles"!

47. *South Indian Polity*, pp. 313, 320–323.

48. "Feudalism in India," in *Feudalism in History*, ed. Rushton Coulborn, reprinted edition (Hamden, Conn.: Archon Books, 1965), pp. 133–150.

49. *Ibid.*, pp. 4–5. "Feudalism is primarily a method of government, not an economic or social system. . . . It is a method of government in which the essential relationship is not between ruler and subject, nor state and citizen, but between lord and vassal."

50. *Indian Feudalism: c. 300–1200* (Calcutta, 1965).

51. *Ibid.*, p. 272.

52. "Soviet Historians on Indian Feudalism," paper presented to the Conference

on the Problems of Social and Economic History, Aligarh (U.P., India), 16–20 December 1968, pp. 2–4. See also K. A. Antonova, K. Z. Ashrafyan, and L. B. Alayev, *Istoria Indii ve Crenie Veka* (Medieval History of India) (Moscow: Institute of the Peoples of Asia, 1968).

53. Calcutta, 1966.

54. *Ibid.*, p. 114.

55. *Ibid.*, pp. 57–62 and 124–126. Sircar proposes an alternative concept, "landlordism," also not defined, then attacks the use of "feudal" as rigidly Marxist, p. 126.

56. Coulborn, *op. cit.*, pp. 4–5.

57. Sircar, *Land System and Feudalism*, p. 57.

58. These are noted by Nilakanta Sastri, *Cōḷas*, p. 270 and note 156, p. 283; T. N. Subramaniam also discusses these inscriptions in *SITI*, III, pt. II, p. 188 and places the records in the late eleventh century.

59. R. Sathyanatha Aiyar, *History of the Nayaks of Madura* (Madras, 1924), p. 58. The bastion commander legend at Madurai appears to have been used earlier by, if not introduced by, the Kākatīyas in which *nāyaka* serving these kings—seventy-seven are mentioned—were given command over part of the fortifications of Warangal; N. Venkataramanayya and M. Somasekhara Sarma, "The Kākatīyas of Warangal," *The Early History of the Deccan*, II, pt. IX, p. 656.

60. This institution is referred to in several "kaifiyats" of the Mackenzie manuscript collection which are summarized in H. H. Wilson, *Descriptive Catalogue of the Oriental Manuscripts Collected by the Late Lieutenant-Colonel Colin Mackenzie*, 3 vols. (Calcutta, 1828): "Kaifiat of Sivaganga Samsthanam" (Wilson: 431, XXX-9), in which the Ramnad Maravar ruler Tirumali Sētupati was admitted into the *kumāravargam*; "Account of Nāgaya Nāyaka, Poligar of Periyapaṭṭi in Dhārāpuram" (Wilson: 418, IV-11); "Account of Savoroy Balagovindah, Palligar (Subbarāya Valla Kondama Palle Nāyak) of Mangalam in Dharpuram District" (Wilson: 418, IV-11); "Account of Debnik Poligar of Pullakshi (Deva Nāyaka Poligar of Pollachi) in Dharapuram District" (Wilson: 418, IV-6), which speaks of the *kumāravargam* order under the Vijayanagar rulers; "Maravar Jati Kaifiat (or *caritram*)" (Wilson: 217, XXXVI), and translation by William Taylor, "Maravar Jati Vernanam," *Madras Journal of Literature and Science*, IV (July-October 1836), pp. 350–360, which relates the confirmation of *kumāra* status by Tirumali Nayaka of Madurai upon the Maravar Sētupati involving an act of commensal equality between the two. See *Tamil Lexicon*, "*kumāra-varkkam,*" p. 1005.

61. *Feudalism in History*, p. viii.

62. Hall, *op. cit.*, p. 48.

63. Dumont, "Kingship in Ancient India," p. 50.

64. Hall, *op. cit.*, p. 31, speaks of "consensus of conduct" in this matter.

Geography and the Study of South India

BRIAN J. MURTON
University of Hawaii

Geography is a wide-ranging discipline that borders on many biophysical and social sciences,[1] and before beginning our review and assessment of the nature of geographical study of South India some comment is necessary about geography as a field of study. Geography is best defined by the questions which in one form or another continually arise: "Geography is a catalogue of questions, and the questions—not the phenomena, not the facts, not the method—are geographic."[2] The distinctly geographical question is this: Why are spatial distributions organized the way they are? This question, with its wealth of implications and elaborations for both biophysical and human geography, is the foundation of the science of geography.[3] A distribution is the frequency with which something occurs in space. Today geographers focus their attention upon the internal organization of distributions, the location of the elements of the distribution with respect to each other or, put another way, the spatial structure of the distribution. Contemporary geographers devote much attention to spatial structures of all kinds and to the processes which interact casually with structures.[4] The questions which geographers ask about process and structure are what makes geography distinct from other sciences. No other discipline consistently concerns itself with distributions of phenomena in terrestrial space; no other discipline consistently concerns itself with spatial structure. The questions about spatial structure and the processes which create them distinguish geography from other sciences.

These fundamental questions apply equally well to both biophysical and human aspects of geography. In terms of this review and commentary we are basically concerned with studies which have dealt with the way in which phenomena—natural and cultural—are spatially organized, and the reasons for such organization, in South India. To accomplish this the remainder of the essay is divided into five sections: a brief sketch of early geographical study of South India; a discussion of geography as an academic discipline in the study of South India; a review of twentieth-century academic research on the geography of South India; an assessment of the research that has been carried out; and a statement on potential themes for further research.

Early Geographical Study

For most of its more than two thousand years of existence as a distinct body of thought, geography has been concerned primarily with accurately describing the locations of places. Although more recent spatial questions have now relegated inquiries about *absolute location* to an implict status, historically, "where?" questions have been preeminent. Until the basic task of accurately locating places on the surface of the earth was completed, geographers had relatively little time for more detailed questions about what existed at places and why. However, from earliest times there have also been efforts to describe places, as well as locate them. Indeed, the literature of an "informal" geography begins in the myths and sagas of every tongue. The continuing human need to locate and describe the places of the earth is the foundation upon which geography rests as a discipline. This is true in South India, as everywhere else. Geographical descriptions and locations are found in the Vedic literature, the Puranas, and in the works of Panini, Patanjali, and Kautilya. This material has been analyzed in great detail by historians concerned with the location of towns, states, and culture areas. This work will be discussed in a later section. Mentions of South India in the early North Indian materials are limited and reflect the state of knowledge existing about the south.

The earliest geographical descriptions of South India that we have knowledge of are not indigenous, but are found in the writings of the Greek and Roman geographers.[5] These works give compact and comprehensive accounts of the ports of South India and their trade with the Mediterranean world. A later account of India which can be regarded as perhaps the last Greco-Roman account dealing with South India is the record of the visit of Cosmas Indicopleustes to the Malabar coast.[6] This work attempts to disprove the theories of classical geography on the conformation of the earth and to establish notions such as a flat earth as the center of the universe, about which the sun and the planets revolved.

The first indigenous geographical descriptions of South India are found in the Sangam literature, the early centuries of the Christian era. By this time Tamils had divided the landscape of South India into five types, each presided over by a deity and named for a flower or tree characteristic of the region. In the Sangam literature the actual objective landscapes of the Tamil country became "the interior landscapes of Tamil poetry."[7] The fivefold classification reflects an appraisal of the important settings in which the men of South India lived at the time. The Sangam literature, and the later Tamil, Kannarese, Telugu, and Malayalam literature, contains many references to places, people, and activities, but little of this material can in any way be construed as specifically geographical. Certain pieces of work composed in South India were, however, more specifically geographical. For example, following the example of Kalidasa many poets of Malabar composed what are known as *Sandesa Kavya*, which describe the geography of the different kingdoms into which Malabar was divided in historic times. Most of these works date to the thirteenth century.[8]

Until the end of the eighteenth century most of the writings which are directly concerned with descriptions of places in South India (as opposed to basic source materials for use in research) were the product of Chinese travelers, Muslim geographers and travelers, and European travelers and officials. The Chinese descriptions of South India are somewhat limited in extent since only one of the noted pilgrims, Hieun Tsang, actually traveled through the area.[9] The works of the Muslim geographers and travelers are much more comprehensive and were actually carried out as pieces of geographical work. During the eighth and following centuries new zest for learning spread throughout the world of Islam. In the Muslim universities from Iran to Spain, scholars studied the geographical heritage left by the Greeks. Arab traders traveled widely and brought back new information which scholars compared with Greek ideas. A considerable number of the Muslim geographers synthesized material on South India; these include Ibn Khurdadhbeh, Abu Zaid Hasan, Ibn Al-Fakih, Ibn Rosteh, and Ishtakri.[10] The most remarkable traveler and writer was Ibn Batuta (1304–1368), whose voyages extended east as far as northern China and south along the east coast of Africa.[11] Other Muslim geographers who mention South India include Al-Beruni, Al Idrisi, Ibn Khaldun, and Abd-er-Razzak.

The first postclassical European mention of South India is in the writings of Marco Polo, who returned to the Mediterranean world via southern and western India in the late thirteenth century.[12] The greatest number of early European travelers' accounts which describe places in South India date to the sixteenth and seventeenth centuries. In the sixteenth century with the establishment of Portuguese settlements on the western and southeastern coasts the number of descriptive accounts of parts of South India greatly increased.[13] There are many other accounts by travelers and missionaries, such as de Nobli, who resided in Madurai and Salem Districts in the early seventeenth century.[14] Besides these accounts, by the late eighteenth century large bodies of official records and other materials were being generated by the European trading companies with outposts in South India. It is not the purpose of this essay to discuss this latter material, but it should be mentioned as a stage in the increase of geographical knowledge about South India. This increase in knowledge is also reflected in the growing amount of detail and accuracy of maps from the early sixteenth to early eighteenth centuries.

In the eighteenth century with the territorial struggles in South India between the Marathas, Hyderabad, Mysore, the British, and the French the need of the latter groups for detailed maps and description of places expanded. Of particular interest are detailed descriptions of routes, points of interest, and conditions in the areas in contention between the powers. After 1750 the British produced the largest volume of descriptive materials on the geography of South India. One work deserves special mention as undoubtedly the most comprehensive description of a large portion of South India: Francis Buchanan's *Journey from Madras Through the Countries of Mysore, Canara, and Malabar* (vol. I–III, 1st ed., Madras, 1807). Another body of truly geographical materials were those generated by the surveys initiated by the East India Company to establish a better knowledge of the land and people. Between 1767, when Chingleput District in Tamilnadu was surveyed, and 1843, by which time all the Company's territories had been surveyed and mapped several times, the extent of knowledge about places increased enormously. Each of the survey parties, and often individual surveyors, compiled detailed memoirs of the survey. The memoirs were compiled by men who had considerable knowledge of the areas where they worked, and they often contain insights into South Indian life found nowhere else.

This tradition of producing accounts describing areas continued in the nineteenth century and reached its culmination in the publication of the manuals and gazetteers after the middle part of the century. After 1850 the volume of travelers' accounts and personal memoirs describing places such as Ootacamund expanded greatly. These materials are the immediate forerunners of a more formal, academic approach to the description of places in South India.

I would emphasize the point that geography as informal description of places has a long history in relationship to South India. This tradition continues to the present in official publications such as the new gazetteer series and in travel books and magazine and newspaper articles. We must now, however, turn our attention to the origins and development of geography as a formal academic discipline in the study of South India.

Geography as an Academic Discipline

Geography as a formal academic discipline in South India has a longer tradition than elsewhere in India, apart from Bombay. Geography began to be taught in the schools and in the affiliated colleges of Madras University in the early twentieth century. In 1926 the Madras Geographical Association—the foreunner of the present Indian Geographical Society—was founded in Madras City.[15] The association has 152 foundation members and in its first year published a single number of the *Journal of the Madras Geographical Association*. The journal became a biannual in 1927, a triannual in 1929, and a quarterly in 1933. This journal more than anything else records the development of geography in South India. In 1940 the journal was renamed the *Indian Geographical Journal*. In 1968 a comprehensive index of papers, 1926–1967, was published.

From its inception the association did its best to promote geography. Summer schools of geography were organized for the benefit of school teachers, geography conferences were held in different towns, scholars were encouraged to undertake regional research, and branches were established at Coimbatore and Vizagapatam. Every time a conference was held in a district the papers were oriented toward aspects of the geography of that district. The proceedings of each conference were published in the journal, and thus there is material of considerable interest and value on many of the districts of old Madras Province. In 1962–1963 the second geographical periodical in South India, *The Deccan Geographer*, was established as the voice of the Hyderabad Geographical Association and the Department of Geography at Osmania University.

Madras University and its affiliated colleges was the first institution in South India to establish graduate training and research. Another graduate training program was set up at Karnatak University in Dharwar in 1952, another at Osmania University in Hyderabad in 1955, and yet another at the colleges of Mysore University in 1959. Geography is taught at the undergraduate level in the colleges of all the major universities in South India and in most of the arts colleges. I do not know exactly how many professional geographers there are in South India but the number is considerable.

A few Indian geographers teaching at universities elsewhere in India, and a few employed by the government, also are active in research on South India. Outside of South Asia, geographers specializing in South India appear to be remarkably few, although the number increases considerably if those who work on an all-India basis are included. As of 1967, the last year for which the directory of the Association of American Geographers provided a detailed breakdown of the regional interests of its membership, there were about eighty geographers in the United States who declared an interest (not necessarily a primary interest) in South Asia.[16] Relatively few colleges and universities offer courses on the geography of South Asia. In the academic year 1965–1966, of the twenty-eight colleges and universities with Class A and B membership in the American Institute of Indian Studies and/or with National Defense Education Act–supported centers for studies in South Asia or Asia as a whole, only six offered specialized geography courses on South Asia and ten others more general courses on Asia.

I have no idea of the precise number of geographers in the United States who claim to have a specific research interest in South India. Certainly it is no more than a dozen (offhand I can think of seven). When those who work within a broader South Asian framework are added, the number increases to perhaps as many as thirty. It appears that there has been a tendency in the past for American geographers to work at an all-India scale or in northern and western India. Elsewhere in the world few geographers have specialized in South India. Particularly striking is the neglect of the area in the United Kingdom. I can think of only four English geographers (undoubtedly there are more) who have worked in South India. South Asian geography as a whole is not well developed in continental Europe, although I do not claim to be familiar with the situation. At least one Danish and one East German geographer have carried out extensive field work in South India. The one bright note is found in France, where through the resources of several French universities and the Scientific and Technical Section of the French Institute at Pondicherry, considerable research has been carried out on various aspects of the geography of Tamilnadu and the general physical geography of India.

In summary, most of the research on South India by geographers has been carried out by Indians operating out of Indian universities. Since the mid-1950s a limited amount of research has been done by Western geographers and Indian geographers working in Western universities.

Research In the Twentieth Century

For nearly fifty years research has been carried out in South India by trained geographers. As in any discipline concepts and methods in geography have changed over time, and to place geographical studies on South India in context it is necessary initially to outline certain changes in approach in the discipline. As we have seen, early geographical studies of South India were primarily locative and descriptive enterprises. Once academic geographers began research in the early years of the twentieth century they followed the major conceptual emphasis distinguishable in the discipline since about 1800: regionalism, with emphasis on regionalization, or the classification of places into sets on the basis of their contents or characteristics. Geographers sought to produce areal sets of places which were as homogeneous as possible and to describe accurately the locations of the boundaries of the regions which resulted. And all geographers—physical and human, topical and regional—for a long time believed that internally homogeneous regions, based on one or a number of place characteristics, existed independently of the principles which defined them and that regions themselves were intrinsically worthy of delimitation and study.

Although variations on the regional theme dominated all types of geography until the late 1950s, many human geographers emphasized relationships between man and environment and the evolution of landscapes through time, rather than the intensive study of small areas. In a broader perspective these types of study can be viewed as early efforts to come to grips with processes generating distributions or regions.

By the late 1950s geography began to shift from a concentration on regionalism to a greater emphasis upon generalization and analysis at levels more advanced than classification. This shift has different ramifications in physical and human geography, but generally it involved a move to asking questions about spatial organization which invoke hypothesis, law, and theory.[17] This change has been labeled the "quantitative revolution,"[18] perhaps better called a "scientific revolution" since it involved the development and testing of theory, model building, and the increasing quantification of the discipline.

But perhaps more important, there has been a trend away from seeking answers to "where?" and "what is where?" questions, which are now viewed as preliminary steps toward the explanations we produce by asking "why?" (more appropriately "how?") questions. Geographers, be they physical or human in their orientations, are now interested in process questions. They are concerned with the explanation of classes of events by demonstrating that they are instances of widely applicable laws and theories. And this approach can be subsumed in the question: Why are spatial distributions organized the way they are?

To review the study of the geography of South India in its appropriate context, aspects of physical and human geography are dealt with separately here. Within these broad categories published research is evaluated with reference to international trends in the discipline.

Physical Geography

Limited research has been done in the various fields of physical geography in South India. The fields reviewed here are geomorphology, hydrology, climatology, and biogeography. Much of the basic research in geomorphology in India has been done by geologists of the Geological Survey of India, and the geographers have mainly utilized their findings. Pithawalla in 1939 was the first to develop an all-India classification of physiographic regions in India based on topography and on structural and erosional characteristics.[19] Research on physiographic regions culminated in 1962 with Chatterjee's division of India into seven major regions, three of which—the peninsula, the west coast, and the east coast—involve South India.[20] Also in 1962 Ahmad described the geomorphic regions of the peninsula.[21] More recently the results of further research into the denudation chronology of the peninsula have been presented.[22]

Descriptive studies of a geomorphological nature data back to 1930, from which time a large number of studies describing the physiological features of the districts of Madras Presidency have appeared in the *Journal of the Madras Geographical Association.*[23] Two districts in present-day Andhra Pradesh, one in Mysore, all of Kerala, and all but two districts in Madras have been described in these studies.

A limited amount of research into coastal landforms of South India has also been carried out. In 1943 Kalyanasundaram described the physical and geomorphological characteristics of the southeast coast of India.[24] Certain features of the coastline have also been outlined. Mahadevan has discussed the coastal geomorphology around Waltair,[25] and Menon the red sand hills (*teri*) of Tinnevelly and south Kerala.[26] In a more general article Krishnaswamy describes the features of different parts of the east and west coast and emphasizes the prograding nature of the Kerala coast.[27]

Most of this published research predates 1960 and in its content reflects the regionalism prevalent at the time. But since 1950 geomorphology has changed rapidly.[28] In particular there has been a trend toward more precise, quantitative field measurements of landforms and deposits, accompanied by an emphasis upon landform development processes, studied in the field and simulated in the laboratory. These trends are not yet fully apparent in published research in the South Indian geographical journals, although seminars such as that at Sagar in 1965 have been held concerning the state of geomorphological studies in India.

Little systematic research has been carried out by geographers on any aspect of hydrology in South India, and only a few papers on rivers have appeared.[29] In contrast to the small number of hydrological studies, a large amount of research has been done on aspects of climate in South India. Much of the best work has been carried out by officers of the Indian Meteorological Service or agroclimatologists working for departments of agriculture or on the faculties of agricultural colleges. The earliest published work by geographers comprised district surveys of climatic characteristics carried out in association with the district geographical conferences.[30] Rainfall in Mysore was studied by A. A. Rao in 1936[31] and that in Madras by P. R. K. Rao in 1953.[32] In the latter work it was demonstrated that the northeast monsoon rainfall of all the state and the southwest monsoon rainfall of Rayalseema (Anantapur, Bellary, and Cuddapah Districts) was highly variable and undependable. Rao pointed out that Rayalseema and the coastal districts of Tamilnadu are the areas most liable to drought during the northeast monsoon. Balasubramanian studied the rainfall of the five central districts of Madras State in 1954.[33] Using correlation techniques he shows that the pattern of rainfall in the five districts is similar. His correlation of rainfall and crop production led him to conclude that agriculture is still a gamble with the monsoon. Other recent work has assessed rainfall patterns in Kanyakumari[34] and drought in the interior parts of Tamilnadu and Andhra Pradesh.[35] Climatic zones in South India also have been studied by Legris and Viart[36] and by Bagnouls and Meher-Homji.[37] This method utilizes precipitation and temperature to establish dry and wet seasons and divides South India into ten major bioclimatic regions and seventeen secondary transitional types.

Quite appropriately, given the existence of a strong and active Meteorological Department in India, most of the recent climatological research by geographers has been in the realm of water balance and rainfall variation studies. Earlier work, which was concerned with meteorological and climatological descriptions, was quite in line with climatological research by geographers elsewhere. The research findings published since 1950 have shown awareness of trends in microclimatology in particular, although some of the methods employed have proved to be of doubtful utility for tropical conditions.

On the whole geographers have done little research on soils and vegetation, or general biogeography, in South India. It is appropriate, however, to point out that much has been done in these areas by soil scientists, botanists, and forest researchers. In the 1930s descriptions of the forests of different districts appeared in the *Journal of the Madras Geographical Association*.[38] Perhaps the most significant recent work has been the preparation of vegetation and associated soil and climatic maps by ecologists and geographers working at the French Institute at Pondicherry.[39] These maps are at a scale of 1:1,000,000 and provide a pictorial account of vegetation characteristics, environmental conditions, and land use. While this latter work deals with vegetation communities, it ignores another biogeographical focus in recent years, the application of the ecosystem concept, which can provide an analytic approach to the understanding and quantification of the relationships that exist among plants, animals, man, and the environment.

Human Geography

Human geography is a very broad field, traditionally divided into a number of topically defined subfields such as economic geography, cultural geography, urban geography, population geography, and so on. In the last fifteen years all human geography has experienced rapid change, perhaps none more important than the change in the context in which we ask our questions: we now more often than not measure space, location, and environment in relative terms.[40] To be sure, this had been done previously, but since about 1955 a large number of human geographers have made the shift to a relative space context while at the same time adopting a more theoretical approach.

The images of distance or environment that people have are the basis of relative space. Mapping places in different relative spaces appears to distort spatial relationships, but the identification and mapping of different images is a very important part of contemporary human geography. Whenever a geographer encounters a distribution determined wholly or in part by human choice—and the structures of almost all geographically relevant distributions are functions of human decisions—accurate mappings of distributions in the appropriate relative space will sometimes do more than could anything else to answer his questions.[41] Human spatial behavior is determined by the interplay of decisions made in political, economic, cultural, sociological, psychological, biophysical, and other space. People seeking to fulfill different goals in different relative contexts set in motion processes which produce spatial distributions. With the development of a theoretical approach and a concern with relative space human geographers have begun to reinterpret traditional questions of "where?" and "what is where?" Asking "where?" involves a consideration of factors other than distance: cost, time, preference, attitude, and image are now important. In summary, the move toward a relative space context is part of human geography's attempts to come to grips with process.

There has also been a change in the type of regional approach employed to classify data. Much of the early regionalization produced regions which were composed of homogeneous phenomena and which were relatively *uniform* throughout. The regions geographers require today as inputs to their analyses are more often *nodal*, or functional, delimited on the basis of spatial interaction.[42]

When we consider research on the human geography of South India we must keep these changes in mind, particularly when making assessments. Rather than deal with each of the multitude of topical approaches to human geography, we find it more satisfactory to specify major traditions and those related conceptual frameworks which give coherence to human geography. Three traditions have been identified: that dealing specifically with the historical evolution of spatial distributions and with distributions at past times; that dealing with man-environment systems; and that dealing with the study of spatial structures. In the following sections these frameworks are presented as discrete approaches to common geographical problems, but there is, of course, considerable overlap among frameworks, both in the questions asked and the methods followed.

Historical Tradition

An inherent characteristic of any place is emergence, and every place is in the process of change: diverse cultural processes have interacted with diverse environments through time, and geography although primarily concerned with spatial organization has a historical dimension. Geographers usually distinguish two approaches to the use of time. The first involves the study of a past period in terms of its spatial organization. The second use of time involves a consideration of the interplay of forces that cause a series of spatial changes through time. The approaches can be integrated, but more frequently emphasis is placed upon one or the other. Both uses of the historical dimension are valid in geography and both can be called historical geography.

As far as can be determined there are few studies of any aspects of the spatial organization of South India in past periods, although all the early research published in the *Journal of the Madras Geographical Association* can now be regarded in this context.[43] However, there has been considerable research into the evolution of certain spatial distributions. Between 1927 and 1941 a large number of papers tracing the origin and development of urban places were published in the journal, and there have also been several more recent studies.[44] Population geographers have published information on population trends. In the 1930s K. S. Raghavan presented a series of papers on district populations in the journal. Numerous other papers, mostly of all-India scope, have dealt with population growth.[45] A limited number of papers trace the development of types of agricultural activities[46] and industry.[47]

As in the case of studies of the spatial organization of past times, there are as yet few studies of "past worlds, seen through the eyes of contemporaries, perceived according to their culturally acquired preferences and prejudices, shaped in the images of their assumed needs."[48] This type of historical geographical research is closely tied to the switch to a relative space context in geography, and it is concerned with differing evaluations of resources, of hazards, and of the potentialities of different areas at different times for exploitation or conservation. Example of such research are a number of articles which discuss the geographical content of certain pieces of South Indian literature.[49]

In addition to research by historical geographers, much inquiry has also been carried out by scholars who are basically historians. Much of this is environmentally deterministic in orientation and aimed at a "historical geography which studies the effects of the surface relief and other geographic phenomena upon political and racial boundaries, and upon the whole course of material civilization."[50] K. M. Panikkar perhaps best exemplifies this approach in his *Geographical Factors in Indian History*.[51] Members of this "school of ancient geography," which is primarily concerned with locating ancient cities, territories, kingdoms, and peoples mentioned in Hindu and Buddhist texts, are more properly called geographic historians.[52] This type of research is a necessary first step for historical geographical research in that it deals with absolute location. Numerous examples of this approach can be found in the *Journal of the Madras Geographical Association*.[53]

Man-Environment Systems Tradition

We can distinguish three conceptual frameworks used by geographers to attack questions relating to man-environment systems.[54] The first and most traditional of these is the concept of *cultural landscape*, the analysis of human interaction with the physical world through the study of man's tangible footprints on its surface.[55] This concept has been little used in the study of the geography of South India. Mukherjii's work on the landscapes of Telengana Reddi villages[56] and on field patterns[57] furnishes the only examples from the eastern part of South India, and Sopher's study of Goa provides the only example from the west coast.[58] Descriptions of the landscapes of South India are contained, however, in the regional sections of O. H. K. Spate and A. T. A. Learmonth, *India and Pakistan: A General and Regional Geography* (London: Methuen, 3rd. ed. rev., 1967).

The second conceptual framework, *ecology*, focuses on processes of man-environment interactions rather than on form and content. The ecological approach to man-environment systems has a long history in geography and underlies the approaches of all three major traditions in human geography. Over the past sixty years there have been a number of interpretations of this relationship, perhaps best viewed as a series of hypotheses concerning what is going on between man and nature.[59] These hypotheses range from environmental determinism and possibilism to the current approaches of cultural ecology and the cognitive approach to environment.

Studies employing ecological approaches, with the exception of cultural ecology, have been widely carried out in South India. They generally follow the tenor of the time elsewhere in the geographical world. Those published up to the late 1930s exhibit environmental determinist tendencies.[60] Most of those published after 1940 reflect the disavowal among geographers of this approach once it was disapproved, although there were still examples of simple studies of the association between man's works and aspects of the physical environment.[61]

Many studies of population have also investigated the relationships of distribution and density and physical environmental factors.[62] Rural settlement patterns have also been examined in terms of environmental relationships. For example, in 1954 Buschmann[63] related settlement patterns and house types to site factors such as terrain and water supply. Earlier Deshpande examined geographical factors in the evolution of settlement types in northern Mysore and concluded that a supply of fresh water was the most critical variable in the location of villages.[64] Viswanath, in 1956, related settlement patterns to soils in Tanjore.[65] He found that linear villages predominated in alluvial areas and on the sandy coastal zone, whereas on black soils nucleated villages dominated. A scattered settlement pattern occurs on red soil areas. In 1938 Subrahmanyam described the four main house styles found in South India and related them to physical features and the availability of building materials.[66] Studies in agricultural geography have employed similar approaches: factors of the physical environment have been described and related to the distribution of a crop of crops.[67] More recently Noble has emphasized the idea of adjustment to changing environment in his paper on the Badagas.[68] This paper most closely approaches the cultural ecological and ecosystems perspective now commonly used by human geographers to interpret man-environment interrelationships.

The third conceptual framework, *environmental perception*, stresses man's "images" of his surroundings as a key to unraveling the nature of man-land transactions. This is the most recent framework to develop within the man-environment systems tradition in human geography. Environmental-perception studies in geography can be viewed first as a reaction to an approach that examined man principally by studying the objects around him and second as a response to the development of a behavioral approach to man in the social sciences. As yet this reaction and response has not been reflected in the published research on the geography of South India.

Spatial Structure Tradition

Studies of spatial structure can be conveniently placed in three categories: studies of *spatial diffusion*, *regional* studies, and studies of *spatial order*.[69] Studies of spatial diffusion are concerned with locational changes of men, materials, and ideas through time and can thus be heavily historical in emphasis. There have been several different approaches to diffusion in geography. The earliest, which can be traced back to late-nineteenth-century German geography and which has been significant in North America, dealt with the origin of phenomena and the identification of avenues of spread. Few such studies have appeared in the geographical literature on South India. One worthy of mention is Rangacharya's discussion of the origins of important South Indian commercial crops,[70] and there has been mention of crop origin and date of arrival in South India in articles dealing with individual crops.[71]

A more recent type of diffusion study emphasizes the spatial aspects of the communication process and the construction of models to simulate (and perhaps predict) actual or future patterns. In South India this research has been fostered by R. P. Misra, professor of geography at the University of Mysore.[72] Under his impetus Mahadev and Ramesh have used simulation techniques to predict the future pattern of hotels in Mysore City.[73] A further significant simulation study is R. Ramachandran's analysis of the diffusion of pumps in the area around Coimbatore.[74] This latter piece of research emphasizes the role of communication in the spread of an innovation. In this approach, to generalize individual communication, a mean information field is developed which specifies the probability of contact over distance. Ramachandran constructs a mean information field based upon trips to periodic markets. His simulated patterns are remarkably close to actual ones, which indicates that he may have pinpointed some of the critical variables involved in the diffusion of pumps. R. C. Mayfield has studied diffusion of hybrid corn around Bangalore and has examined the spatial pattern of marriage as a possible surrogate for the mean information field.[75] These latter examples of spatial diffusion are representative of the relative-space and quantitative trends in human geography in the past ten to fifteen years and are examples of the speed at which new concepts and techniques can diffuse.

Although the concept of *region* can be viewed as a method of spatial delimitation to classify data from all geographical perspectives, there have been innumerable studies of parts of South India as regions in their own right. The first of these studies appeared in 1926 when E. D. Birdseye prepared the first regional division and description of any part of India.[76] In this article physical structure, geology, drainage, water supply, and climate are related to vegetation and crops and through these, in an environmentally deterministic way, to human activities. Articles resulting from the district meetings of the Madras Geographical Association also provide regional descriptions of parts of old Madras Province. Collections of articles were published in the journal on the following districts: Coimbatore (1930), Malabar (1931), Madura (1932), Trichinopoly (1933), Anantapur (1935), Salem (1936), Tanjore (1937), South Kanara (1938),

Tinnevelly (1940), and South Arcot (1944). In addition, the regional settings of parts of South India have been outlined a number of times. Tamilnadu has been regionalized by Ramamurthy,[77] the regional setting of Andhra Pradesh has been discussed by Kuriyan and Prakasa Rao,[78] and the regional aspects of Mysore have been outlined by Learmonth.[79] Kerala has been described by Kuriyan, Gourou, and Dupuis.[80]

Detailed studies of small regions and portions of districts are also found in the literature. For example, Prakasa Rao's 1946 study of the lower Godavari region discusses the adaptive power of people to changing conditions.[81] Webb, in 1961, analyzed the cultural landscape of Kerala and has emphasized the physical basis for contrasts between north and south.[82] The Shevaroy Hills in Madras and the Malnad Hills in Mysore also have been described.[83] The basins of the Vellar, Kaveri, and Tambrapami were studied by Srinivasaraghavan,[84] Anantanarayanan,[85] and Muthukrishnan,[86] respectively. In 1932 Narayanaswami divided Madura District into six subregions[87] and in 1940 Iyer dealt with the regional geography of Tinnevelly.[88] More recently two excellent regional monographs in French on coastal Tamilnadu and the eastern hills have been published (J. Dupuis, *Les Ghats Orientaux et la Plaine du Coromandel*, Pondicherry, 1959; J. Dupuis, *Madras et le Nord du Coromandel*, Paris, 1960). These two studies are comprehensive accounts of land and life in the northern coastal plain of Tamilnadu.

Planners and social scientists in India have become aware in recent years of the need for regional studies to highlight spatial patterns and variations in resource endowment. As a consequence regional studies have been prepared by government departments, geographers, and statisticians. Good examples of this type of work are Prakasa Rao's regional division of Madras,[89] the regional survey of Mysore State[90] and the macroregional survey of South India.[91] These analyze spatial patterns working up from the physical base to the distribution patterns of economic and social activities. Technoeconomic surveys which examine physical resources of each state also provide regional data. The many other planning-oriented studies of regions are reviewed by Bhat and Learmonth in a 1968 article on recent contributions to the economic geography of India.[92] An important aspect of this research has been the attempt to establish better methods of identifying regions for planning purposes.

While outlining examples of the regional approach to the geography of South India, mention should be made of several atlases and the one comprehensive regional text on South Asia. Statistical atlases have been published in Madras since 1895, but as their name implies they are merely statistical compendia. Other states in South India have published similar atlases since 1950. More important, however, are the economic atlases of

Madras and Andhra Pradesh.[93] The National Atlas of India also deserves mention as an all-India item.[94] Various other specialized atlases have appeared, including Learmonth's atlas of the resources of Mysore State. Of special interest, however, are the state atlases of the 1961 Census of India. These atlases provide data at district and subdistrict levels for large numbers of variables. The one comprehensive text on South Asia, Spate's *India and Pakistan*,[95] deals basically with physical and economic geography both topically and regionally. In the latter instance the various regions and subregions of South India are described in detail. Most of the description is based upon articles that have appeared in the periodical literature.

Research that can be categorized as dealing with *spatial order*, or with patterns of order in the distribution of phenomena, has been popular among geographers studying South India. As in the case of the other research frameworks, studies of patterns of order have followed general trends in geography: up to about 1960 such studies were primarily descriptive; more recently there has been emphasis upon the use of analytic techniques and upon process. The most common type of spatial order study in South India has been that which deals with some aspect of location: descriptions of distributions, the endeavor to explain a distribution, or the study of interaction between points in a distribution. Most of these studies of location in South India have been carried out in the traditional topical fields of economic, urban, transportation, and population geography.

A large number of studies have dealt with distributions of such phenomena as industries, power, minerals, crops, cities and towns, and population. Many of these have also attempted to explain the location of the phenomena involved. Industrial location studies date back to the 1930s when Lokanathan investigated factors influencing the location of the cotton, jute, sugar, iron and steel, paper, leather, match, and heavy chemical industries on an all-India basis and later examined in more detail those of Madras.[96] In 1941 V. L. S. Prakasa Rao carried out a detailed study of location factors in shipbuilding and concluded that Vizagapatam was optimally located for this activity.[97] More recently Krishnan has discussed location factors for mineral-based industries[98] and Kuriyan has examined the spatial distribution of the textile and iron and steel industries.[99] More specialized studies of industries have also appeared in the literature since 1960. Mahadev has discussed location factors of the textile industry in Coimbatore,[100] Khan the development of Indian glass-making,[101] most of which is located in South India because of availability of suitable raw materials, and Hameed the industrial pattern of Telengana.[102] These few examples suffice to demonstrate that some research has been done on industrial location and analysis, but it should be emphasized that much more needs to be done, particularly in synthesizing and collating materials scattered throughout government reports and documents.[103]

A number of descriptive location studies have also been carried out with regard to hydroelectric power resources and development in South India.[104] A recent survey of energy sources is the *Report of the Energy Survey of India Committee*, which assesses development potential by region and actual location.[105] A number of studies have also been made of minerals in South India,[106] but little else has been done recently except by the Natural Resources Division of the Planning Commission. Crop distributions in South India have been extensively studied. Several of these studies have already been mentioned, but two are noteworthy: Vasantha Devi's study of the distribution of the individual food crops of all South India[107] and Singh's 1966 paper on changes in millet acreages in Mysore.[108]

There are many studies of town locations, hierarchies of towns, and their interrelationships. On an all-India basis Ahmad has classified Indian cities and towns,[109] and V. L. S. Prakasa Rao has attempted to do the same for Mysore State[110] and Telengana.[111] Earlier a large number of descriptive papers on towns in Madras were published in the *Journal of the Madras Geographical Association*.[112] These studies dealt with the residential, social, occupational, and land use structure of individual towns. Recently this kind of research has been elaborated by S. M. Alam at Osmania University in his analysis of Hyderabad-Secunderbad.[113] In particular, the Osmania researchers have emphasized social morphology through the use of social area analysis and factorial ecology. Other studies have dealt with the location, size, and spatial relationships of the towns of Andhra Pradesh,[114] the functional classification of urban places in Madras,[115] the service areas of market towns in northern Mysore,[116] and the location of Bangalore as capital of Mysore.[117] Population studies dealing with occupational structure on an all-India basis,[118] migration,[119] and age-sex structure[120] are also found in the literature.

Considerable descriptive research has been carried out on local and regional markets. Studies of periodic and permanent markets in the Madras Districts and in northern Mysore were carried out in the 1930s and 1940s.[121] A more analytic approach to markets is found in the work of the Danish geographer Folke, who has analyzed the central place hierarchy and spatial interaction in Nilgiri District and Coorg.[122]

Research basically concerned with interaction and flow of goods has also been carried out to a limited extent. In the 1930s Subrahmanyam outlined the communications of the Madras Districts.[123] Later studies have dealt with the deficiencies of the railroad network in Andhra,[124] road transportation in Andhra,[125] and the quality of roads in Mysore.[126] Other research has been concerned with the movement of goods. In 1966 Singh outlined the movement of coal, the most important item of freight traffic on Indian railways.[127] Dickason and Wheeler, in 1967, used a linear programming model to generate a minimum-cost system of wheat-producing and wheat-consuming regions and then, by comparing the model to actual interaction patterns, suggested that if certain two-directional movements be eliminated, wheat transportation costs could be reduced by thirty-four percent.[128] The most comprehensive study of the gross movement of goods throughout India is Berry's 1966 study of commodity flows and the spatial structure of the Indian economy.[129] This monograph consists of three essays. In the first, an atlas of Indian commodity flows is presented and repetitive themes in the maps are identified. The second essay explores and unravels the complex interrelationships between commodity flows and regional economic structure. The third essay adds an intersectoral, interregional perspective, in an input-output framework that provides forecasting ability.

Assessment of Research

There has been much research on a number of aspects of the geography of South India. Throughout my review of published research I have commented, where appropriate, upon the nature of the research. It is now my intention to summarize my remarks and assess the state of our knowledge of the geography of South India.

Let us recall the categories of research reviewed. In sum, little has appeared on the various aspects of physical geography with the exception of climatology. Within the historical tradition, with the exception of studies of "ancient geography" by "geographic historians," little geographical research has been done. Data do exist, especially after 1750, and historical geographical research emphasizing distributions, patterns, and processes could complement and supplement research in social and economic history. A marked lack of research also is evident in the cultural-landscape and environmental-perception frameworks of the man-environment systems tradition. There has been research that relates to the ecological framework, but little of this reflects cultural-ecological or ecosystems perspectives.

When we consider the tradition of spatial structure research, we find more studies. Recently several interesting studies have appeared on the spatial diffusion of innovations. A multitude of regional studies exist, the earlier ones concerned mostly with formal or uniform regions, the more recent ones with nodal or functional regions. Likewise there are a host of studies of patterns of spatial order, most of which are related to the concept of location. Studies of regions and of spatial ordering, and to a lesser extent of man-nature relationships and "ancient geography," are thus the ones that dominate the geographical literature on South India.

In summary, then, much research has been done on the geography of

South India: places have been located and described, distributions of phenomena described, regions established, interrelationships examined. Yet the research has many shortcomings: much of it follows lines outdated in Europe and North America; much of it is particularistic; much of it is inadequately related to the socioeconomic context of the study area.

With a few notable exceptions—diffusion research, social area analysis, and microclimatology—published research has followed lines which have gone out of fashion elsewhere. The recent research emphases in South India have been upon descriptive land-use location studies, urban morphology studies, urban functional studies, and regional studies. These studies stress form rather than process: they are still concerned more with absolute space than with relative space. Furthermore, as previously noted, most past research has been concerned with regions and patterns of spatial order, and there is a paucity of recent studies of man-environment systems emphasizing cultural landscape, cultural ecology, and environmental perception. Physical geography, the various fields of which have undergone radical reorientation in recent years, is particularly poorly developed, apart from climatology. The concepts of ecosystem, hydrological cycle, nutrient cycle, energy balance, and man's modification of the biosphere are strikingly absent from the literature. Even the French biogeographical literature is basically structural in nature and does not focus upon process. Climatology is perhaps the best-developed field of physical geography, but many of the best pieces of work have been done by meteorologists and agroclimatologists. Unfortunately geographers are involved in little field research in any aspect of physical geography in South India, and they certainly have not had the luxury of use of the laboratory and computer facilities so necessary to modern research in climatology, geomorphology, hydrology, and biogeography.

Another feature of geographical studies, particularly those appearing before 1950, is that many describe, often very superficially, the nature of some area usually defined for some other purpose (for example, district or village). Frequently much better descriptions are contained in the district gazetteers. A further problem is that much of the research is not of a truly original nature since it only too often uses statistics and information collected by other disciplines and agencies. Part of this problem is that South Indian geographers lack adequate funds and time for field work. Logistic difficulties therefore hinder much potential field work on interesting and significant problems. In addition, funds and facilities to analyze field and other data are not available. Since much analysis in contemporary geography involves manipulation of large bodies of data by computers, the lack of funds and facilities would seem to hamper research and also direct it into manageable avenues.

Another shortcoming of much of the research done in South India by both Indian and Western scholars has been the lack of attempts to relate individual studies to conceptual framework and theory. We have too many microstudies which lack analytic qualities, which use poor measurement techniques, and which are unsuitable for generalization—not that there is anything wrong with microscale studies if they are directed at a problem and ask questions about process as well as content. Also much of the material presented in the literature is in the form of imperfectly processed pieces of information which do little to help us understand the spatial organization of South India.

I have emphasized the analytic shortcomings of much of the research. Much analysis in modern geography employs statistical techniques and models and is directed to the search for theory, the statement of hypotheses, and the solution of problems. To employ statistical techniques presupposes a well-developed sense of problem and hypothesis. This is lacking in many of the pieces of research on South India that do use statistical techniques. A further unfortunate feature of the use of statistical techniques in South India has been the lack of effort made to adapt them to local conditions. Much of the research has involved the utilization of a method (for example, the location quotient, the Weaver crop classification method, factor analysis) which has been employed in a study, often unsuccessfully, in Europe and North America. In addition, many of the quantitative techniques make it only too easy to use census, agricultural, meteorological, and other sources of statistical data, usually collected for purposes other than geographical analysis. Studies using Indian statistical data also have been carried out in North America. Unfortunately much of this work has been done by scholars with little first-hand knowledge or sensitivity to the South Indian scene and even less feel for regional variations and complexity.

POTENTIALS

Places and phenomena in South India have been located and described in terms of absolute space, but little attention has been given to relative space and process questions: How does spatial organization in South India work? How do people and environment interact? How do people in South India cognize and perceive space and environment? How do people in South India make resource allocation decisions? These questions, and many more could be enumerated, are not only in step with contemporary geographical thinking but also have much potential for planning and development. Geographical research is not only of an academic nature: it also has a pragmatic aspect. Some geographical research has been done in South India for planning purposes, but this has usually been within a government agency and has normally involved the creation of new regional divisions or the description of existing patterns. A profitable new direction could well be toward process questions. Much of the university-based research could also be directed at policy and planning issues. This would involve a sharpening of research design, method, analysis, and presentation. But if this were done, geography's contribution to improving the quality of life in South India could be much greater than at present.

From an academic point of view it is in the areas of physical geography, and the historical and man-environment systems traditions in human geography, that more research is needed. In physical geography, research utilizing the concepts of ecosystem, energy balance, water balance, nutrient cycle, and hydrological cycle needs to be done. Any number of fascinating field problems, with pragmatic as well as academic value, could be generated for research in physical geography. Man's modification of aspects of his biosphere, both at present and over longer periods of time in South India, has received little attention: geography can contribute to a better understanding of the ecological aspects of development projects by combining physical and historical geography in a man-environment systems framework. A further fruitful area of man-environment research could be studies of resources and resource management. In this respect the cultural-ecological and environmental-perception approaches would provide appropriate conceptual frameworks, Within these contexts emphasis could be placed upon how South Indians cognize and perceive space and environment and how such conceptions and perceptions are involved in decision processes that result in patterns of spatial organization.

This focus on how decisions are made has been applied in the few studies that have been made of the spatial diffusion process. More of this type of research should be carried out. We also need more studies of patterns of spatial order, studies which ask "how?" as well as "where?" In particular, studies of industrial location, market areas, commodity flows, and transportation could benefit from such an approach. Geographers also need to study and analyze variations in institutions such as caste and joint family; the spatial components of social, economic, and political networks; and the movements of people and information on all scales and in rural and urban areas.

These few topics indicate what I feel are potential areas for fruitful academic and pragmatic research in South India. As topics they are not unique to South India, and some are currently being researched. All require that geographers be trained in the concepts, methodology, and techniques of modern geography. All require field work and access to modern data-processing facilities. In this respect cooperation between

South Indian and Western scholars could prove fruitful, both in terms of exchanges at graduate student and faculty levels and also with regard to the provision of financial assistance for field work and data processing to South Indian geographers from such sources as P.L. 480 funds. The latter use of such funds has the potential for rapidly improving our knowledge of the geography of South India. Much has been done; but much is left to do if geography is to make a continuing contribution to the study of South India.

NOTES

1. M. W. Mikesell, "The Borderlands of Geography as a Social Science," in *Interdisciplinary Relationships in the Social Sciences*, ed. M. Sherif and C. W. Sherif (Chicago: Aldine, 1969), pp. 227–248.
2. F. Lukermann, "Geography as a Formal Intellectual Discipline and the Way in Which It Contributes to Human Knowledge," *Canadian Geographer* 8 (1964), pp. 167–172.
3. R. Abler, J. S. Adams, and P. Gould, *Spatial Organization: The Geographer's View of the World* (Englewood Cliffs, N.J.: Prentice-Hall, 1971), p. 86.
4. *Ibid.*, p. 60.
5. W. H. Schoff (trans.), *The Periplus of the Erythraean Sea* (New York: Longmans, 1912); J. W. McCrindle, *Ancient India as Described by Ptolemy*, ed. S. N. Majumdar, rev. ed. (Calcutta: Chuckervertty Chatterjee, 1927).
6. Cosmas Indicopleustes, *Topographia Christiana*, trans. from the Greek and edited by J. W. McCrindle (London: Hakluyt Society, first series, vol. 98, 1897).
7. A. K. Ramanujan, *The Interior Landscape* (Bloomington: Indiana University Press, 1967), p. 108.
8. S. P. Chatterjee, *Fifty Years of Science in India: Progress of Geography* (Calcutta: Indian Science Congress Association, 1964), p. 235.
9. S. Beal (trans.), *Chinese Accounts of India*, trans. from the Chinese of Hieun Tsang (Calcutta: Susil Gupta, 1957–1958).
10. K. A. Nilakanta Sastri, *A History of South India*, 2nd ed. rev. (London: Oxford University Press, 1958), pp. 42–43.
11. See Ibn Battuta, Abu Abdallah, *The Travels of Ibn Batuta: A.D. 1325–1354*, trans. with notes and revisions from the Arabic text edited by Defremory and B. R. Sanguinetti, ed. by H. A. R. Gibb (Cambridge: Cambridge University Press, 1958).
12. See Marco Polo, *Marco Polo: The Description of the World*, 2 vols., trans. by A. C. Moule and P. Pelliot (London: Routledge, 1938).
13. For example: Vasco da Gama, *Journal of the First Voyage*, trans. by E. G. Ravenstein (London: Hakluyt Society, series 1, vol. 99, 1898); Alfonso de Albuquerque, *The Commentaries of Albuquerque*, 4 vols., ed. and trans. by W. Birch (London: Hakluyt Society, 1875–1884); Ludovico di Varthema, *Travels*, trans. by J. W. Jones (London: Hakluyt Society, series 1, vol. 32, 1863); Duarte Barbosa, *The Book of Duarte Barbosa*, 2 vols., trans. by M. L. Dames (London: Hakluyt Society, 1918–1921); Fernao Nuniz, "Chronicle," trans. by R. Sewell in *A Forgotten Empire* (London: Sonnenschein, 1900);

John H. van Linschotten, *Voyage*, 2 vols. (London- Hakluyt Society, series 1, vol. 70, 71, 1885); Pietro della Valle, *The Travels of Pietro della Valle in India*, 2 vols., ed. by E. Grey (London: Hakluyt Society, 1892); W. H. Moreland (ed.), *Relations of Golconda in the Early 17th Century* (London: Hakluyt Society, series 2, vol. 66, 1921).

14. See J. Bertrand, *La Mission du Madure*, 4 vols. (Paris, 1874–1875).

15. S. P. Chatterjee, *Fifty Years of Science in India: Progress of Geography* (Calcutta: Indian Science Congress Association, 1964), p. 32.

16. J. E. Schwartzberg, "The Position of Geography in South Asian Studies," paper presented to the Subcommittee on Development of Social Science Disciplines Relevant to National Development in South Asia, Committee on South Asia of the Association of Asian Studies, 1968, p. 1.

17. E. A. Ackerman, "Where Is a Research Frontier?" *Annals of the Association of American Geographers* 53 (1963), pp. 429–440.

18. I. Burton, "The Quantitative Revolution and Theoretical Geography," *Canadian Geographer* 7 (1963), pp. 151–168.

19. M. B. Pithawalla, "Physiographic Divisions of India," *Journal of the Madras Geographical Association* 14 (1939), pp. 423–434.

20. S. P. Chatterjee, "Physiographic Divisions of India," *Proceedings of Summer School in Geography* (Simla, 1962).

21. E. Ahmad, "Geomorphic Regions of Peninsular India," *Journal of Ranchi University* 1 (1962).

22. R. P. Singh, "Denudation Chronology of the Indian Peninsula," paper presented at the 21st International Geographical Congress, New Delhi, 1968.

23. T. N. Muthuswamy. For example: "Physical Geography of Coimbatore District," *Journal of the Madras Geographical Association* 5 (1930), pp. 85–88; P. S. Rao, "Physiography of Anantapur District," *Journal of the Madras Geographical Association* 9 (1935), pp. 214–228; P. G. Dowie, "Geology of Tinnevelly District," *Journal of the Madras Geographical Association* 15 (1940), pp. 303–329.

24. V. Kalyanasandaram, "Changes in Level in the Southern Coast of Madras," *Indian Geographical Journal* 18 (1943), pp. 30–36.

25. C. Mahadevan, "Origin of the Waltair Highlands," *Indian Geographical Journal* 24 (1949), pp. 26–51.

26. K. K. Menon, "General Features of the Teris of South Travancore," *Indian Geographical Journal* 25 (1950), pp. 1–11.

27. S. Krishnaswamy, "The Coasts of India," *Indian Geographical Journal* 29 (1954), pp. 18–22.

28. See R. V. Cooke, "Progress in Geomorphology," in *Trends in Geography*, ed. R. V. Cooke and J. H. Johnson (Oxford: Pergamon, 1969), pp. 13–26.

29. For example: C. N. R. Chettiar, "The Noyal Basin," *Journal of the Madras Geographical Association* 10 (1935), pp. 155–170; B. M. Thirunaranam, "Rivers of the Palar Basin," *Journal of the Madras Geographical Association* 13 (1938), pp. 147–160; G. K. Ghori, "The Hydrography of the Cauvery Basin, Its Geographical Significance," *Indian Geographical Journal* 30 (1955), pp. 45–64; N. Anantapadmanabhan, "Shifting of Divides and River Capture," *Bombay Geographical Magazine* 8–9 (1961).

30. For example: M. S. Subrahmanyam, "Meteorology of Coimbatore District," *Journal of the Madras Geographical Association* 5 (1930), pp. 89–94; B. G. Narayan, "Meteorology of Malabar," *Journal of the Madras Geographical*

Association 6 (1931), pp. 103–110; C. K. Ananthashbrahamanyam, "Meteorology of Anantapur District," *Journal of the Madras Geographical Association* 9 (1935), pp. 229–231; K. Ramamurthy, "Climate of South Kanara," *Journal of the Madras Geographical Association* 13 (1938), pp. 263–268.

31. A. A. Rao, "Statistical Study of Rainfall of Mysore State," *Memoirs of the Indian Meteorological Department* 7 (1936).
32. P. R. K. Rao, "Rainfall of Madras State," *Memoirs of the Indian Meteorological Service* 30 (1953).
33. C. Balasubramanian, "Rainfall in the Central Zone of Madras State," *Indian Geographical Journal* 29 (1954), pp. 23–34.
34. C. Balasubramanian and M. S. Dorairaj, "Rainfall Pattern in Nagercoil," *Indian Geographical Journal* 33 (1958), pp. 79–82.
35. V. P. Subrahmanyam and C. V. S. Sastria, "Drought Climatology of the Dry Sub-humid Zones of South India," paper presented at the 21st International Geographical Congress, New Delhi, 1968.
36. P. Legris and M. Viart, "Study of Xerothemic Index in India, Burma, Pakistan, and Ceylon," *Travaux de la Section Scientifique de l'Institut Français de Pondichery*, tome 1, fasc. 4, Pondichery, 1959.
37. F. Bagnouls and V. M. Meher-Homji, "Types Bioclimatiques du Sud-Est Asiatique," *Travaux de la Section Scientifique de l'Institut Français de Pondichery*, tome 1, fasc. 4, Pondichery, 1959.
38. For example: W. C. Hart, "Forests of Madura District," *Journal of the Madras Geographical Association* 7, 3, 1932; A. H. Khan, "Forests of Anantapur District," *Journal of the Madras Geographical Association* 9, 4, 1935; E. V. P. Pillai, "Forests of South Kanara District," *Journal of the Madras Geographical Association* 13, 3, 1938.
39. For example: see "International Map of the Vegetation and of Environmental Conditions at 1/1,000,000: Cape Comorin Sheet," *Indian Council of Agricultural Research Vegetation Map Series*, no. 1 (New Delhi: Swan Press, 1962).
40. Abler, Adams, and Gould, p. 72.
41. *Ibid.*, p. 76.
42. *Ibid.*, p. 85.
43. A. B. Mukherjii's "Succession of Cultural Landscapes in Telengana Reddi Villages," *Indian Geographical Journal* 39 (1964), pp. 42–58, which seeks to explain the present landscape in terms of a succession of past landscapes, most closely approximates this approach.
44. For example: C. S. Srinivasachari, "Growth of the City of Madras," *Journal of the Madras Geographical Association* 2 (1927); C. M. R. Chettiar, "Growth of Modern Coimbatore," *Journal of the Madras Geographical Association* 14 (1939), pp. 101–116; B. P. Rao, "Evolution of Visakhapatnam," *National Geographical Journal of India* 6 (1960); R. L. Singh, "Evolution of Bangalore City," *National Geographical Journal of India* 7 (1961).
45. For example: B. C. Mamoria, "Growth of Population in India," *Geographical Review of India* 19 (1957).
46. For example: G. K. Ghori, "Coffee in Mysore," *Indian Geographical Journal* 27 (1952), pp. 198–239; S. Folke, "Evolution of Plantation, Migrations, and Population Growth in Nilgeris and Coorg (South India)," *Geografisk Tiddskrift* 65 (1966).
47. For example: C. V. V. Iyengar, "The Mill Industry in Coimbatore," *Journal*

of the Madras Geographical Association 5 (1930), pp. 114–119; K. R. Dixit, "Growth and Distribution of Indian Paper Industry," *National Geographical Journal of India* 9 (1963), pp. 218–235.

48. H. Prince, "Real, Imagined and Abstract Worlds of the Past," *Progress in Geography* 3 (1971), p. 4.
49. For example: C. Sivaramamurthy, "Venkatadhwari's Account of India," *Journal of the Madras Geographical Association* 9 (1934), pp. 1–23; K. Kuriyan, "Geographical Basis of Legendary Origin of Kerala," *Journal of the Madras Geographical Association* 16 (1941), pp. 340–354.
50. K. A. N. Sastri, "Presidential Address: Relation of Geography to History," *Journal of the Madras Geographical Association* 8 (1933).
51. K. M. Panikkar, *Geographical Factors in Indian History*, 2nd ed. rev. (Bombay: Bharatiya Vidya Bhavan, 1959).
52. For example: B. C. Law, *India as Described in Early Texts of Buddhism and Jainism* (London: Luzac, 1941); B. C. Law, *Historical Geography of Ancient India* (Paris: Souété Asiatique de Paris, 1954); Sir A. Cunningham (ed. S. N. Majumdar), *The Ancient Geography of India*, 2nd ed. (Calcutta: Chuckervertty Chatterjee, 1924); N. L. Dey, *The Geographical Dictionary of Ancient and Medieval India*, 2nd ed. (London: Luzac, 1927).
53. For example: P. T. S. Iyengar, "Geographical Control of Early Kongu History," *Journal of the Madras Geographical Association* 5 (1930), pp. 54–58; C. M. R. Chettiar, "Geographical Limits of Pandyan Kingdom," *Journal of the Madras Geographical Association* 7 (1932), pp. 287–294; K. S. Vaidyanatham, "Geography of Ancient Puli-Nadu," *Indian Geographical Journal* 25 (1950), pp. 16–20.
54. The frameworks used here follow P. W. English and R. C. Mayfield (ed.), *Man, Space, and Environment: Concepts in Contemporary Human Geography* (New York: Oxford University Press, 1972), but they have been in common use for the past ten years.
55. *Ibid.*, p. ii.
56. A. D. Mukerjii, "Succession of Cultural Landscapes in Telengana Reddi Villages," *Indian Geographical Journal* 39 (1964), pp. 42–58.
57. A. D. Mukerjii, "Field Patterns in a Telengana Village," *Indian Geographical Journal* 37 (1962), pp. 153–163.
58. D. E. Sopher, "Cultural Landscapes of Portuguese India," *Yearbook, Association of Pacific Coast Geographers* 22 (1960), pp. 34–39.
59. H. and M. Sprout's *The Ecological Perspective on Human Affairs* (Princeton: Princeton University Press, 1965) provides an excellent survey of the literature on man-milieu relationships.
60. For example: A. Appadorai, "Rural Life on the West Coast—A Study in Environment," *Journal of the Madras Geographical Association* 3 (1928), pp. 15–37; C. A. K. Rao, "Influences of Physical Features on the Human Geography of Trichi District," *Journal of the Madras Geographical Association* 8 (1933), pp. 144–150; K. S. Gopalan, "Human Geography of the Tanjore District," *Journal of the Madras Geographical Association* 12 (1937), pp. 160–166.
61. N. Subrahmanyam, "Seasonal Control of Rural Life and Activities in Conjeeveram," *Indian Geographical Journal* 17 (1942), pp. 100–109; B. M. Thirunaranam, "Influences of Geology on Human Geography Near Rajahmundry," *Bombay Geographical Magazine* 2 (1954).

62. G. Kuriyan, "Population and Its Distribution," *Journal of the Madras Geographical Association* 11 (1936), pp. 42–53; K. S. Ahmad, "Environment and the Distribution of Population in India," *Indian Geographical Journal* 16 (1941), pp. 117–134; N. Anantapadmanabhan, "Density of Rural Population and Terrain Types in Madras State," *Bombay Geographical Magazine* 5 (1957).
63. K. H. Buschmann, "Settlements and Habitations in India," *Geographical Review of India* 16 (1954).
64. C. D. Deshpande, "Settlement Types of Bombay Karnatak," *Indian Geographical Journal* 17 (1942), pp. 115–131.
65. M. S. Viswanath, "Soils and Settlement Patterns of the Tanjore District," *National Geographical Journal of India* 2 (1956).
66. K. M. Subrahmanyam, "Four Main House Types in South India," *Journal of the Madras Geographical Association* 8 (1938), pp. 168–175.
67. For example: G. Kuriyan, "Rice in India," *Indian Geographical Journal* 20 (1945), pp. 28–36, 76–84, 110–126; R. Ramachandran, "Crop Regions of India," *Indian Geographical Journal* 38 (1963), pp. 58–64; M. N. Vasantha Devi, "Some Aspects of the Agricultural Geography of Southern India," *Indian Geographical Journal* 39 (1964), pp. 1–14, 59–122.
68. W. A. Noble, "The Badagas, Entrepreneurs of Southern India," paper presented at the 21st International Geographical Congress, New Delhi, 1968.
69. English and Mayfield, pp. vi–vii.
70. V. Rangacharya, "Studies in the History of Some Common Commodities," *Journal of the Madras Geographical Association* 4 (1930), pp. 113–121.
71. For example: K. N. Pashupathi, "Cinchona Cultivation in India," *Journal of the Madras Geographical Association* 14 (1939), pp. 410–415; S. Velayudham, "Ground-nut in Madras," *Indian Geographical Journal* 21 (1946), pp. 113–125.
72. R. P. Misra, *Diffusion of Innovations* (Mysore: Prasaranga, University of Mysore, 1968).
73. P. D. Mahadev and A. Ramesh, "Spatial Distribution of Hotel Industry in Mysore City: An Application of a Probability Model," *National Geographical Journal of India* 13 (1967), pp. 208–213.
74. R. Ramachandran, *Spatial Diffusion of Innovation in Rural India: A Case Study of the Spread of Irrigation Pumps in the Coimbatore Plateau* (Ph.D. dissertation, Clark University, 1968).
75. R. C. Mayfield, "The Spatial Structure of Selected Interpersonal Contact: A Regional Comparison of Marriage Distances in India," *Technical Report*, no. 6, Spatial Diffusion Study, Department of Geography, Northwestern University, 1967.
76. E. D. Birdseye, "Some Aspects of the Geography of Madras," *Journal of the Madras Geographical Association* 1 (1926), pp. 45–58.
77. K. Ramamurthy, "Some Aspects of the Regional Geography of Tamilnadu," *Indian Geographical Journal* 23 (1948), pp. 24–35; 24 (1949), pp. 33–35; 25 (1950), p. 34.
78. G. Kuriyan and V. L. S. Prakasa Rao, "Andhra State: Its Regional Setting" (Waltair: Andhra Chamber of Commerce, Silver Jubilee Volume, 1953).
79. A. T. A. Learmonth and A. M. Learmonth, "Landscapes of New Mysore," *Indian Geographer* 2 (1957).
80. G. Kuriyan, "Some Aspects of the Regional Geography of Kerala," *Indian*

Geographical Journal 17 (1941), pp. 1–41; P. Gourou, "Quelques observations de géographie tropicale dans l'Inde," *Revue de l'Université de Bruxelles* (1950–1951); J. Dupuis, "Kerala," *Cahiers d'Outre-Mer* (Bordeaux), 2 (1958), pp. 213–231.

81. V. L. S. Prakasa Rao, "The Lower Godavari Region," *Calcutta Geographical Review* 8 (1946).

82. M. J. Webb, "The Coast Plains of Kerala," *Indian Geographical Journal* 36 (1961), pp. 1–27.

83. V. Natarajan, "The Shevaroys Region," *Journal of the Madras Geographical Association* 11 (1936), pp. 162–173; G. K. Ghori, "The Human Ecology of the Malnad," *Journal of Mysore University* 18 (1958).

84. K. Srinivasaraghavan, "A Geographical Study of the Vellar Basin," *Journal of the Madras Geographical Association* 11 (1936), pp. 213–234.

85. T. S. Anantanarayanan, "The Cauvery Region of the Trichy District," *Journal of the Madras Geographical Association* 8 (1933), pp. 191–194.

86. S. M. Das, "The Tambraparni Basin," *Journal of the Madras Geographical Association* 13 (1938), pp. 161–167.

87. G. Narayanaswami, "Subregions of Madura District," *Journal of the Madras Geographical Association* 7 (1932), pp. 191–195.

88. T. S. S. Iyer, "Regional Geography of Tinnevelly District," *Journal of the Madras Geographical Association* 15 (1940), pp. 86–104.

89. V. L. S. Prakasa Rao, "Regional Grouping of the Districts of Madras State," *Indian Geographical Journal* 28 (1953), pp. 33–43.

90. A. T. A. Learmonth and L. S. Bhat (eds.), *Mysore State—Vol. 1–An Atlas of Resources* (Calcutta, 1960); A. T. A. Learmonth (with others), *Mysore State—Vol. II—An Atlas of Resources, A Regional Synthesis* (Calcutta, 1962).

91. *South India: A Macro-regional Survey* (New Delhi: Indian Statistical Institute, Regional Survey Unit, 1962).

92. L. S. Bhat and A. T. A. Learmonth, "Recent Contributions to the Economic Geography of India: Some Current Preoccupations," *Economic Geography* 44 (1968), pp. 189–209.

93. *Economic Atlas of Madras State* (New Delhi: National Council of Applied Economic Research, 1962); V. V. Ramanatham and V. L. S. Prakasa Rao, *Economic Atlas of Andhra Desh* (Vizagapatam, 1949).

94. *National Atlas of India* (Hindi edition, Calcutta, 1957; English edition, Calcutta, 1959).

95. O. H. K. Spate, *India and Pakistan: A General and Regional Geography*, 2nd ed. (London: Methuen, 1954; revised with A. T. A. Learmonth, 1967).

96. P. S. Lokanathan, "Localisation of Industry in India," *Journal of the Madras Geographical Association* 7 (1932), pp. 16–35; P. S. Lokanathan, "The Industries of Madras," *Journal of the Madras Geographical Association* 14 (1939), pp. 155–163.

97. V. L. S. Prakasa Rao, "The Geographer and the Localisation of Industries," *Indian Geographical Journal* 17 (1941), pp. 216–331.

98. M. S. Krishnan, "Geographical Control in Relation to Mineral Industries," *Bulletin of the National Geographical Society of India* 16 (1952).

99. G. Kuriyan, "Spatial Distribution of Industry in India," *Indian Geographical Journal* 31 (1962), pp. 1–7.

100. P. D. Mahadev, "Textile Industry of Coimbatore District," *Deccan Geographer* 4 (1966), pp. 74–77.

101. M. N. Khan, "Development of Glass Industry in India," *Deccan Geographer* 4 (1966), pp. 1–9.
102. S. A. Hameed, "Industrial Pattern of Telingana—A Geographical Analysis," *Indian Geographical Journal* 37 (1962), pp. 45–56.
103. One such paper that has done this is L. S. Bhat and R. B. Mathur's "Cement Industry—A Case Study in National and Regional Perspectives—1967," *Bombay Geographical Magazine* (1967).
104. For example: G. Kuriyan, *Hydro-Electric Power in India* (Madras: Indian Geographical Society, Monograph no. 1, 1945); K. Rangappa, "A Study of the Hydro-Electric Development in Mysore," *Indian Geographical Journal* 31 (1956), pp. 59–68.
105. Government of India: *Report of the Energy Survey of India* (New Delhi, 1965).
106. For example: P. G. Dowie, "A Geographical Study of Manganese with Special Reference to India," *Journal of the Madras Geographical Association* 11 (1936), pp. 235–256.
107. M. N. Vasantha Devi, "Some Aspects of the Agricultural Geography of South India," *Indian Geographical Journal* 39 (1964), pp. 1–41, 59–122.
108. G. S. Singh, "Relative Change in Area under Jowar and Ragi in Mysore State," *National Geographical Journal of India* 12 (1966), pp. 51–57.
109. Q. Ahmad, *Indian Cities—Characteristics and Correlates* (Chicago: Department of Geography, University of Chicago, Research Paper no. 102, 1965).
110. V. L. S. Prakasa Rao, *Towns of Mysore State* (Calcutta: Asia Publishing House and Indian Statistical Institute, 1964).
111. V. L. S. Prakasa Rao, *Urban Telengana* (New Delhi: report prepared for the Research Programme Committee, Planning Commission, 1964).
112. For example: R. Dann, "A Note on the Urban Geography of Coimbatore," *Journal of the Madras Geographical Association* 5 (1930), pp. 132–133; V. Tyagarajan, "Tuticorin, A Town Study," *Indian Geographical Journal* 14 (1941), p. 179.
113. S. M. Alam, *Hyderabad-Secunderbad Cities: A Study in Urban Geography* (Bombay, 1965).
114. V. V. Ramanadham and Y. Venkateswarlu, "Economic Aspects of Town Formations in Andhra Pradesh," *Indian Geographical Journal* 32 (1957), pp. 63–85.
115. N. Anantapadmanabhan, "Functional Classification of Urban Centers in Madras State," *Proceedings of Summer School in Geography* (Simla, 1962).
116. G. S. Kulkami, "Service Area of a Market Center in the Transitional Belt of Mysore State: Yamkanmardi, a Sample Study," *Bombay Geographical Magazine* 10 (1962), pp. 86–95.
117. G. K. Ghori, "Choice of Capital for New Mysore State—A Plea for Revision," *Deccan Geographer* 11 (1964), pp. 175–177.
118. G. S. Gosal, "Occupational Structure of India's Rural Population," *National Geographical Journal of India* 4 (1958).
119. P. S. Lokanathan, "Migration of Labor with Special Reference to South India," *Journal of the Madras Geographical Association* 6 (1931), pp. 1–57.
120. For example: J. C. Sen, "The Sex Composition of the Population of India," *Deccan Geographer* 2 (1963), pp. 43–62.
121. For example: V. Krishnan, "Fairs and Trade Centers of Madras and Ramnad Districts," *Journal of the Madras Geographical Association* 7 (1932), pp.

237–249; C. D. Despande, "Market Villages and Periodic Fairs of Bombay Karnatak," *Indian Geographical Journal* 16 (1941), pp. 327–339.

122. S. Folke, "Central Place Systems and Spatial Interaction in Nilgiri and Coorg Districts, South India," paper presented at the 21st International Geographical Congress, New Delhi, 1968.

123. For example: N. Subrahmanyam, "Communication Lines of Trichinopoly District," *Journal of the Madras Geographical Association* 8, 3 (1933).

124. H. Rangachar, "Development of Railways in Andhra Desa" (Waltair: Andhra Chamber of Commerce, Silver Jubilee Volume, 1953).

125. S. Venkatarangam, "Road Transport in Andhra" (Waltair: Andhra Chamber of Commerce, Silver Jubilee Volume, 1953).

126. S. M. Adrashannawar, "Geographic Analysis of the Quality of Roads in Mysore State, India," paper presented at the 21st International Geographical Congress, New Delhi, 1968.

127. J. Singh, "A Perspective on the Patterns and Problems of Coal Transport in India," *National Geographical Journal of India* 12 (1966), pp. 96–113.

128. D. G. Dickason and J. O. Wheeler, "An Application of Linear Programming: The Case of Indian Wheat Transportation," *National Geographical Journal of India* 13 (1967), pp. 126–140.

129. B. J. L. Berry, *Essays on Commodity Flows and the Spatial Structure of the Indian Economy* (Chicago: Department of Geography, University of Chicago, Research Paper no. 111, 1966).

Anthropological and Sociological Research in Kerala: Past, Present, and Future Directions

JOAN P. MENCHER
Lehman College of CUNY and
Columbia University
K. RAMAN UNNI
School of Planning and Architecture, New Delhi

In this essay we have attempted to explore in some detail a fairly wide range of studies of Kerala sociology, cultural anthropology, and related fields.[1] We have tried to deal with published studies and with research currently underway, and also to indicate some areas we believe to be important for future study. We do not claim to be exhaustive, though we have tried to cover most of the basic fields of sociology, taken in a broad sense. Prompted by the nature of the material, we have divided our presentation into a number of subjects which coincide, more or less, with these fields.

TRADITIONAL BACKGROUND

Kerala is a long, narrow territory bounded on the west by the Arabian Sea and on the east by the Western Ghats. The central, coastal area forms the main region of traditional settlement. Visually the central region presents a picture of a continually undulating countryside with long, narrow paddy fields surrounded by hills. Rural settlements in Kerala were not villages as in most of India, but rather residential clusters focused around large, rice Nayar houses, with their fortress-like appearance, and wealthy Nambudiri households (*illam*). Each Nayar house had its own area of influence, often coinciding with its area of economic domination. Thus traditionally there was no nucleated village as may be found in other parts of India. Politically the focus of any given area was the local Nayar "manor."

It has been pointed out by many writers that subcaste proliferation reached its most extreme elaboration in Kerala. There is, however, considerable variation. Both historically and today, for example, it is striking that within one community, the Tiyyars or Izhavas, who make up close to twenty-four percent of the total population of the state, there are few subcastes. The main Tiyyar divisions were regional: those belonging to the north are called Tiyyar; those in the central areas, Izhavas or Chovan; those in the south, Tandan. Traditionally these divisions of the larger community did not intermarry. Apart from territorial divisions, the only subdivision was that of the Tiyyar barbers and priests, both very small groups. The greatest amount of subcaste elaboration was in the matrilineal Nayar, Ambilavasi, and Samandhan groups, but it is doubtful whether these were castes in the traditional sense of the term.[2] Only five or six of the Nayar subcastes were of appreciable size.

Two factors stood out as important in creating a social milieu conducive to subcaste proliferation, especially in the case of the small groups which Dumont calls "status groups" rather than castes. These factors were the presence of a matrilineal (and usually matrilocal) family system which stressed hypergamous unions and the relative spatial isolation of the individual unpartitioned Nayar households (*taravād*). The *taravād* in its ducal isolation was freer to engage in the various maneuvers we describe below.

If one wants to understand the caste system as it existed in traditional Kerala, it is essential to look at it in terms of the political and economic structure of the region as well. Politically, up to the eighteenth century there were a large number of small kingdoms. It is possible (though still to be documented) that there was some degree of integration during the early Chera period, but it is clear that even if the regional political system was integrated, it fell apart easily because there was little pressing need, and few facilities, to hold it together. There were no roads linking regions to one another, and no waterworks to be coordinated. Each area could function quite well by itself. Within each kingdom there was a rigid, hierarchical structure with (at least from the tenth century on) a clear militaristic base.[3] Descriptions of the position of the "slave castes" as late as the eighteenth and early nineteenth centuries leave no doubt as to the complete authority wielded by the Nayar aristocracy and the wealthy Nambudiri Brahmans.

During the fourteenth and fifteenth centuries, the Zamorin of Calicut, with the help of the coastal Muslims who controlled the trade, gradually expanded his state by taking over some of the inland kingdoms and part of the area controlled by the Maharaja of Cochin. However, this expanson was stopped when the Portuguese began to give help to the latter. In Kerala prior to the eighteenth century, when an army like that of the

Zamorin defeated someone else and took over control, this conquest did not involve a mass movement of people or even individuals moving in to administer the acquired territory. Thus even at that time the subcastes represented in one area did not move to another.[4]

In medieval Kerala there were small groups of Christians, each seemingly deriving from different castes, though nothing like the proliferation found later. The early Christians were all high-ranking and, like the Nayar landlords, owned untouchable "slaves" who worked their land. Since the Muslims were confined mostly to the coast, they did not have access to low-caste villagers and thus had little chance to convert many people to Islam.

The traditional Kerala Nayar male was expected to be always in good physical condition so that he could go out as a soldier if called upon. For this reason gymnasiums (*kalari*) were maintained by each large Nayar *taravād*, not only for training men of the *taravād* but also their followers, the poorer (though not the poorest) Nayar retainers of each local chieftain (*nāḍuvaḻi*). It is important to understand this fact in dealing with the economics of modern Kerala. Because Nayars were relatively free of managing cultivation, during the nineteenth and twentieth centuries most had a clearly articulated middle-class identification since they were able to withdraw from the land whenever other employment made it possible. This did not preclude their role as absentee landlords who spent their holidays and retirement in their native village.

As in the rest of India, a clear picture of the caste system in Kerala is difficult to obtain without an understanding of the traditional economy, which was very exploitative of those at the bottom but which provided those at the top with tremendous economic, political, and social power. The rigidity of the caste system in Kerala was enforced with the sword, not through any ideas of "knowing one's place" or "being secure." The Pulayan "slave" who did not obey caste rules was liable to be killed.

Economically Kerala was traditionally better off than other parts of India. Even if the rains were bad, they never failed totally. Besides, there were always valuable goods, such as pepper, which could be traded for rice. It is reported that there were ships bearing rice in Calicut harbor at the time Vasco da Gama arrived there.

This is not to imply that all Nayars were wealthy in the period preceding European contact, but they did not generally have to cultivate their own fields. It is clear that in this rich environment, prior to the nineteenth eentury, the same amount of land could provide food for several layers of a complex feudal structure. In many ways, the structure of medieval Kerala resembled that of feudal Europe with its various forms of infeudation and subfeudation.

There continues to be a large Nayar population in rural Kerala, but among rural Nayars a sizable percentage hold nonagricultural jobs. Many Nayars are located in the cities and towns of Kerala, as well as in urban centers in other parts of India. Although poor Nayars in north Malabar and some parts of the former Cochin and Travancore do manual work in the fields, this situation relates to phenomena of the eighteenth to twentieth centuries and not to earlier conditions. The lack of a tradition of agricultural work is often given as an explanation of why Nayars are not as competent at it as others. Apart from the Nayars, the only other South Indian group with such a high percentage of civil service and professional employment is the east coast Brahmans, a group of subcastes whose members on the whole refuse to dirty their hands in the soil. Nayars differ from other South Indian land-owning communities such as the non-Brahman Vellalas in Tamilnadu in this respect. Though the Vellalas clearly have a middle-class identification which goes quite deep, they also work the land and take pride in being agriculturists. This has also been reported for the Okkaligas and Lingyats, the Mysorean equivalents of the Vellalas. These non-Kerala groups could be considered a peasantry in the sense that they constituted a subclass of people who owned and cultivated land at least partly with their own labor and considered themselves agriculturists. Nayars never fit this category.

The hierarchy of land rights was typically multilayered. Nayars traditionally held land on lesser (that is, indirect) forms of tenure from other Nayars or from Nambudiri Brahmans. The land was generally worked by Izhava or Tiyyar sharecroppers, or by "slave caste" laborers, under the supervision of a senior member of the Nayar family. Thus the Izhavas did not constitute a peasantry either. Except in the extreme north, few held land on direct forms of tenure, and on the whole their position in the rigid caste system of traditional Kerala was very low. One of the chief traditional occupations of Izhavas was the cultivation of palm trees, a more substantial business in Kerala than in any part of Madras. In the Middle Ages,[3] some of them were also used as soldiers by the local chieftains and rulers of Malabar, especially north Malabar. Today the majority of Izhavas are engaged in agriculture. The more well-to-do, on the whole, have taken to business, especially on the coast. Proportionately only a few may be found in the professions, though the numbers are increasing at present. The majority are quite poor, and many have become agricultural laborers in recent years.

The traditional system was not seriously disturbed by the arrival of the Portuguese and the Dutch in the fifteenth and sixteenth centuries. What really led to significant changes was a series of events which occurred in the eighteenth century, starting with the invasions of Malabar by Haider Ali and his son Tipu Sultan. They built roads, converted many people to Islam (including large numbers of low-caste laborers, as well as a few high-caste people), introduced a new system of land taxation, and changed the entire communication network of the area. During this period, Marthenda Varma was in the process of breaking the power of the local warlords and unifying Travancore. Somewhat later, the same thing was done by the Maharajah of Cochin under the guidance of Travancore.

The defeat of the Mysoreans and the betrayal of the Zamorin by the British led to British rule in Malabar. This completed the series of events which led to a really significant change in Kerala social structure.[6] A large bureaucratic machine was introduced in each of the areas (British Malabar, Cochin, and Travancore). During the nineteenth century, within each of these three areas which had formerly been ruled by powerful local chieftains, various administrative divisions were carved. They were divided into districts, taluks, and smaller units on a model copied from elsewhere in territories under British control. In addition, railways and roads were bult and it became fairly easy to move about. Families moved from one region to another, castes which had never existed in a region moved in, and altogether there was great change in the makeup of rural areas. This process continued into the mid-twentieth century.

These events led to many changes in traditional Kerala caste relations during the nineteenth and twentieth centuries. To begin with, under Tipu many low-caste people were converted to Islam. As a result of Portuguese influence and various later missionary groups, many low-caste people were converted to Christian sects in Cochin-Travancore. The result of this conversion was a decrease in the absolute percentage of people belonging to the lowest castes. While conversion did not automatically mean an end to economic discrimination, it did ease the situation and at least potentially provide the possibility for some individuals to come up. Among the Tiyyars, a movement against their being treated as "semi-untouchables" was led by Narayana Guruswami (1856–1928). Other Tiyyars had previously improved their situation as a result of their willingness to associate with the British.

Among the Nayars two things happened. On the one hand, the increased mobility, and especially the gradual breakup of the large *taravāds*, led to a far larger number of Nayar subcastes being represented in many areas. On the other hand, there has been a movement toward breaking down Nayar subcaste distinctions and an attempt (often said to be primarily political) to unite all Nayars. This has been one of the aims of the Nair Service Society in Travancore. This breakdown of Nayar subcaste distinctions has occurred more in Travancore than elsewhere, though it was striking to Mencher in 1959 that even in a conservative part of south

Malabar, many of the younger Nayars did not know to what subcast they belonged, and that when it came to marriage, many traditional patterns had changed. Thus arranged marriages were occurring between females of high subcastes and males of lower subcastes without any comment in the community, as long as the families were of equal social status, that is, equal economic position and education.

Today many of the inequities of the caste system are still operative in Kerala. There certainly is a correlation between caste and economic position, though it is not absolute. Caste has entered another arena, namely that of modern politics. We disagree with Leach[7] that castes cease to function as castes when they enter the political arena. There was always a correlation between caste and politics. In Kerala, high-ranking Nayar subcastes were primarily rulers (local chiefs) and Nambudiri Brahmans had considerable political power.[8] Occasionally a low-ranking Nayar or a rich Tiyyar gained control over a small kingdom. Gough notes the following: "Each of these aristocratic lineages tended to set itself up as a separate subcaste, acknowledging ritual superior but no peers. In the course of time following the vicissitudes of political fortunes, such lineages could rise or fall in the ritual hierarchy."[9] While ritual status among Nayars of different subcastes was generally agreed upon, there was some change as they gained in wealth and social status.[10] What has changed is the nature of politics itself. Politics in feudal times was different from politics today, and the caste system has proved itself so strong that it has so far managed to adapt to other changes in the society. We return to this point later in our discussion of social class.

The social history of Kerala needs a more objective sociological interpretation. The institutions and processes which maintained the traditional stratification intact have been inadequately studied, though some indications of forces at work are discussed by Unni[11] and Gough.[12] Apart from Gough, most studies reveal a kind of reverence for the colonial power, and thus they have failed to explore the ways in which colonial diplomacy manipulated and made use of the mechanics of traditional social control to govern with minimal political and administrative effort. The ways in which the British helped to bolster traditional authority and administration by their policy of indirect rule need to be explored fully in their sociological perspective.

We have only a limited number of studies of the historical socioeconomic situation. One is a doctoral dissertation by an economist, Thomas Shea; others include a few pieces by anthropologists.[13] Varghese, an economist, has worked out in some detail an analysis of some of the differential forces at work in Travancore, Cochin, and British Malabar from about 1800 to the formation of Kerala State in 1956. However, these studies leave much data remaining to be analyzed. In some of the old Nambudiri, Nayar, and Syrian Christian houses, there still exist palm leaf (*ola*) land records which would yield a veritable mine of information if they were studied by economically oriented historians or anthropologists. In many instances, such records relate to the time before Tipu (who died in A.D. 1799). A study of these palm leaf manuscripts could provide a tremendous amount of insight into economic relations during that period.

Studies of Caste

When it comes to an understanding of the caste system as it has been played out in Kerala over the last century, we have various sources at our disposal. To begin with, there are accounts presented in the early part of the century: L. K. Anantha Krishna Iyer's *Cochin Tribes and Castes*, the *Travancore State Manual*, and E. Thurston's *Castes and Tribes of Southern India*.[14] But such works are not sufficiently localized nor detailed to answer many of the questions asked today by anthropologists and sociologists. The literature by anthropologists is limited. Most of the research deals with Nayars,[15] and studies of other castes are few. A. Aiyappan has written two books in which he deals with Izhavas,[16] though his later book also deals with intercaste relations in one village. He has also written about the Nayadis, a small untouchable community,[17] and Mencher has dealt with the Nambudiri Brahmans.[18]

Since 1950, several papers on Kerala tribes have appeared, each dealing with selected aspects of the people studied.[19] As Aiyappan[20] points out, ethnographically the least-known region of Kerala is Wynad. He has nearly completed a report on the Kurichiyars of Wynad. There are also sixteen other tribes in Wynad; all of them are becoming modernized in various ways.

One of the tendencies noted in studies to date has been that of focusing on the higher castes in the area and then looking at the system from the top down. This is not accidental. The sociologist working in Kerala is likely to become involved with the higher castes, and once one works from that point of view, it is hard to shift focus. Yet on the basis of Mencher's work among untouchable groups in Tamilnadu, it is clear that the world can look very different indeed from the vantage point of the man at the bottom.[21] In Kerala today, after losses due to conversion to Islam or Christianity, scheduled castes (untouchables) form 8.49 percent of the total population of the state and close to 12 percent of the population in the main rice-growing areas. Some of these castes are small in number; a few are exceedingly large. The majority of the large scheduled castes continue to be engaged in agricultural labor. Of the others, some are quite small in number and may have originally been tribal groups living in the hilly areas. Today all these groups are changing. Among the agricultural laborer castes, a new political awareness has led many to give up some of their traditional practices. This trend can only increase over the next few decades. At this juncture, it is essential to learn more about these groups and document their distribution, economic relations, and interrelations with other castes, as well as their own unique traditions.

The scheduled castes (the large ones are the Pulayans or Cherumans and the Paraiyans) have hardly been studied by modern anthropologists, though several excellent reports appear in the early "castes and tribes" volumes. A full description of their role in the socioeconomic structure of traditional Kerala has never been attempted, but numerous writers have attested to the fact that they were considered to be little more than slaves:

> In Malabar, Cochin, and Travancore, slavery seems to have prevailed from a remote period. . . . These agrestic serfs continued to exist in a state of hereditary bondage exposed to the caprice or at times to the brutality of the owner, and were disposable according to his will and pleasure. . . . On account of the law of castes, these slaves have all been engaged solely in field work, and not in domestic service, because they could not enter the houses of their masters. . . . As to the class of soil slaves the lowest were the Pulayans. . . . They were so wretchedly provided with the necessities of life that the most loathsome things were a treat to them. They were bought and sold like cattle and were often badly treated. . . . The children of slaves did not belong to the father's master, but were the property of the mother's owner. . . . The succession was by the female line, in accordance with the custom of the Nayars, the principal slave holders of the country. . . . One of the usual clauses in the deed of transfer of slaves was "you may sell him or kill him." . . . By the influence of the Madras Government, the Raja's Proclamation in 1853 set free the future offspring of Government slaves. . . . Although thus legally emancipated, the slave population could not for a long time take advantage of the opportunities afforded to them for their improvement, owing to caste tyranny which kept them to starvation limits.[22]

Of the ones who were converted to Christianity, many did manage to improve their condition considerably. On the other hand, despite their conversion, they are not allowed to sit with other Christians in the same churches. Klausen,[23] comparing the fishermen who were converted to Christianity with others, shows very clearly how the Christian fishermen, because of their affiliation with a wider social milieu and because of the influence of the Catholic Church, have been able to take far more advantage of the boons of development than those who stayed within the Hindu fold.

Alexander[24] has studied the Pulayans of the southern part of Kerala. He deals with groups from three areas, including the city of Trivandrum, and with the problem of their social mobility. However, this study is only an introduction to the kind of work which is needed among these low-caste communities. Most of his conclusions deal with the applicability of reference group theory to closed societies.

In connection with a recent study by the authors of this paper, an economics student from Kerala University in Trivandrum, P. Sivanandan, himself a member of one of the scheduled castes, did a small study of the condition of the low castes in three villages. This report is currently being prepared for publication.

In Kerala today, many of the other small caste groups are either changing their occupations or being absorbed in some other way into the modern economy. Carpenters may continue to work with wood, but some have moved to nearby towns where they can make more money, and the sons of many are now taking occupations where they can have a more secure livelihood. It would be useful to have more detailed studies of such artisan groups, their traditional practices, kinship system, and economic relations with others while they can still be identified.

THE CHRISTIANS

Except for what is available from work of the early writers,[25] we have very few analytic studies of Kerala Christians. There is perhaps no study that can compare favorably with Aiyappan's examination of Izhavas cited above.

George Kurian[26] has published a study dealing with the changes in the family structure of Syrian Christians, both urban and rural. Residents of Bombay City constitute his urban focus, and they were selected, he notes, because of the "absence of typical modern urban areas in Kerala State." Rural Syrian Christian groups in Kerala are mostly planters and businessmen with a "fairly high standard of living." He further notes that these groups "were studied as future indicators of a society where much planned economic development is taking place to raise the standard of living." Kurian concludes that these Christians "have shown significant changes in their attitudes towards marriage and family." It is probably desirable to wait for intensive studies of these groups rather than to accept his conclusions about Christians and other castes mentioned in the study.

Pothan[27] and Thomas[28] have also given us accounts of Kerala Christians, but we still feel that too little is known about the Christians with their internal differentiation, their distribution, and their wide range of occupations. Recently a study of Christians in the Changanachery area was undertaken by a Ph.D. student from Cambridge University, Christopher Fuller; it should add to our knowledge of this group. Among other things, we know little about why, and by what financial means, Christians expanded into the former Malabar and Cochin regions after reorganization of states in 1956. This would surely constitute a rich field for future investigation.

The Muslims

A recent advance in anthropological studies of Kerala is the extension of social anthropological investigation into the Laccadive Islands off the Kerala coast. Leela Dube[29] has contributed a study of matriliny and Islam based on data from Kalpeni Island, and she describes "a matrilineal system characterized by duolocal residence involving the absence of conjugal family either as an independent residential unit or as one embedded in a larger kinship grouping." Dube's book also announces a forthcoming volume by A. R. Kutty which will present fuller ethnographic data on the island society and will deal in depth with marriage and kinship. One striking fact that emerges from Dube's study is the persistence of all the significant structural features of the matrilineal social system in spite of Islam, the only religion of the island. She suggests that the expressions of religion appear to reaffirm the solidarity and unity of matrilineal groups and to buttress the relationships and values of existing social structure. Her book offers a promising source for comparative study with the matrilineal Muslims of north Kerala. Our knowledge here is limited to Gough's work.[30] Dube[31] also has shown how some Laccadive Muslims, despite centuries of Islam, still cling to their memory of the Hindu caste they were converted from and still continue to marry within the same endogamous unit.

Social Class

While much of the sociological literature on Kerala has focused on the study of various caste groups, we find lacuna in materials dealing with problems of social class formation and development. In studies of Indian society both by foreigners and by Indians, there has been a general tendency to be fascinated by the rich materials for the structural study of caste and to ignore the importance of class factors. A partial explanation of this tendency is offered by Barber:

> By stressing the absolute differences between Indian stratification and that of the West, by describing a condition of radical inequality and complete lack of mobility in India, Westerners could, in the light of their own values, be asserting a moral superiority to the Indians which helped to justify their imperialistic policy in India. . . . The moral self-satisfaction of outsiders to India may have combined with native upper-class ideologies in perpetuating a distorted conception of the caste system.[32]

In studies of social stratification in Kerala, very little attention has been given to the way in which the diverse social classes were integrated into the traditional village structure. Wealth, property, and power dimensions have been described in terms of caste, overlordship of the land, tenancy, and labor relations to some extent;[33] they still remain to be explored in coherent class terms for the past and today.

A study by Varghese,[34] an economist, provides us with a rough picture of some class differences among the three main regions in Kerala in historical perspective, but there still is a need for many studies in depth on problems of delimiting socioeconomic classes. A current research project of Unni and Mencher includes eight village areas (one census ward in each of eight villages, as established by the 1971 census, or 250 to 400 houses per village) located in the northern part of Trichur District and in parts of Palghat District. This study should give us a picture in some depth of the class structure in this central Kerala region. A study of approximately eighteen villages over the length and breadth of Kerala, conducted by Professor Eapen in the Indian School of Social Science and sponsored by the Indian Council of Social Sciences, is expected to provide a picture of the range of variation in class structure in different parts of the state.

Today in Kerala, class elements which were dormant in the traditional structures appear to be increasingly active in shaping movements which are rapidly destroying what remains of the traditional bases of stratification. It is thus extremely important to identify these foundations of the emerging class system and emerging class movements. A full understanding of this would help to clarify the nature of the social unrest which may be noted in all rural and urban parts of Kerala. It would be of much use if we could understand the crucial factors leading to mass movements in some areas and impeding them in others. Clearly literacy is one such factor,[35] but it is not the only one. Much more research remains to be done on problems of this kind, both on the micro and on the macro levels.

Another area where further investigation is needed is on the relationship between social class and economic development. Some dimensions of this relationship have been examined by Mencher,[36] but more need to be explored. We need to know which communities are being favored by progress and why. It is exceedingly important in the Kerala context to ask why there has been the creation of a kind of backwater of less favored places or communities and what effect this is to have on the society, both today and in the long run. Another concern of such an analysis would be the way in which the very nature of development programs in the area has been leading to cleavages between the middle class and the landless laborers.

Socioeconomic Studies

It is clear that studies of the socioeconomic structure and processes have a great deal to contribute to our theoretical knowledge of social factors in development, to our broader knowledge of Kerala both as a unique area and as a part of South Asian culture, and to our understanding of practical problems facing contemporary Indian society. In this respect, although some preliminary studies have been made and some work is currently underway, much still remains to be done.

One area that is of particular significance is the relationship between traditional social structure and economic development. In studies of economic anthropology, there is a pressing need to emphasize resources for change and development, as well as for the preservation of traditional structures. Earlier studies by anthropologists and sociologists appear to have extolled, at least implicitly, the integrative features of the social structure and culture of caste groups. In today's context, the impediments that these traditional structures pose must also be identified. It is essential to identify those sociocultural variables that can be used to promote change, as well as those economic and social forces that might be used to promote stability while other disruptive (but necessary) changes are taking place. Sociologists have asked: What are the social and cultural structures of economic development and to what extent can we limit the injuries of economic change? These questions have great relevance for Kerala, where unemployment (including a large educated unemployed group) poses serious challenges.

We want to explore, in the Kerala context, the relationship between what has been called the "opportunity structure" of a peasant society and the position of an individual in the social structure. Does the farmer's position in society significantly influence his perception of economic opportunities? It appears from the qualitative data of the Mencher and Unni study that it does in Kerala. A poor, small landowner in a central Kerala village normally will see very little scope for using new agricultural inputs under present distribution and credit arrangements. The poor man cannot afford artificial fertilizer, nor can he afford to make trips to government offices to obtain seeds or pesticides when he needs them. The rich landowner can afford to do so. In one village of our project, the government has set up a new program (called the Ela Program) which does make it easier for small farmers to make use of new seeds and other inputs that were previously unavailable.

It is important to understand the underlying structural reasons why certain avenues to development may be open to some groups and different avenues to others. Is it possible simply to place the blame on "cultural values" (which has been the excuse used by anthropologists)? Or must we look deeper at the underlying socioeconomic base? Why do some Kerala Muslims in northern and central Kerala, or Christians in central and southern Kerala, take to business more readily than do members of other groups? What has prevented Hindu Araya fishermen from taking advantage of the facilities affored to Catholic and Araya fishermen alike under the Indo-Norwegian project? Klaussen[37] clearly indicates that it is not simply a question of values, but that two structural factors were equally, if not more, important: the credit facilities available to the Catholic fishermen through church connections and the restrictions placed on the Arayas by virtue of the caste hierarchy in their village. But this study is only a beginning. It is clear that groups which carry considerable political weight, can mobilize credit facilities, and are part of larger social networks have a decided advantage in the modernizing process. We need to know more about how this advantage operates.

In the matter of obtaining a job, different castes tend to follow different paths. A superficial explanation, and one which Malayalis are fond of offering, bases this choice on the value system. But is that really the case? To what extent does one act because of values or because of contacts? Much of Malayali economic life is based on contacts. If one's contacts are in civil service, one seeks opportunity there; if they are in business, then it is easier to go there. The employment structure is not an open one, and a man's choice is clearly limited to the horizons of his contacts. Credit also follows contact lines, and for new ventures credit is very important. Certainly values influence the way in which capital is utilized, but these values in turn are related to the need to maintain one's position in the structure because of other pressures, often economic pressures.

In central Kerala, there tends to be a close correlation between certain occupations (such as tailoring, small industries, or trading in specified commodities) and membership in particular caste clusters or religious groups. Structural analysis of the forces which lead to the "monopolization" of different expanding occuaptional fields by different groups would reveal much about the process of socioeconomic development.

In view of the ever-increasing need for employment in Kerala, it would also be useful to explore the effect of new industries on local regions. One question which immediately comes to mind in this connection is the need to determine to what extent new industries absorb locally unemployed as opposed to bringing in people from elsewhere in the state or elsewhere in India. Our recent research has clearly shown that to date the development process has been quite uneven, creating a large number of backwaters of less favored subregions while other regions seem to be developing rapidly.

We need much more study of the labor-use cycle during the crop year.

Mencher[38] has done a little of this. We want to know both the traditional and the modern cyclical fluctuations in the demand for family and hired labor under different conditions. Clearly there is a difference between a Kerala locality with its multicrop pattern and a Tamil rice area, but even in Kerala there is considerable regional variation. Does ecology alone explain why there is less variation in socioeconomic status in certain Travancore areas where tapioca, a perennial, is the major corp, as compared to the major rice-producing areas? Can labor get a better deal in areas where they are wanted all the time? To what extent can one expect differential response to modernization under different crop conditions? Such questions demand detailed sociological inquiry.

It is also important to know more about year-to-year fluctuations in labor use. How does it go down in a poor year, up in a good year? How do these fluctuations affect different segments of the population? What was the condition previously—that is, prior to 1750, in the nineteenth century, and prior to independence? The data for early periods are harder to ascertain, but not impossible. It is also important to learn more about the nature and functioning of rural labor markets, as well as structurally feasible ways to improve work conditions and job opportunities in rural and semirural areas.

Anthropologists and sociologists are particularly concerned with the role of social structure in channeling—at times helping, at times impeding—economic development. Some preliminary papers have been published which deal with this role,[39] and we expect several others to emerge from our project during the next two years. However, much remains to be done in this field. There has been work on the relationship between land tenure relations and development, though much of it remains impressionistic. In the changing Kerala context, it would be interesting to compare areas where the 1970 Land Reform Act has really made a significant change with areas where it has had less of an impact. It has been predicted by a number of observers that in the future, the main arena for conflict in rural areas will be between landless laborers and landowners. We need to explore the effects of a variety of social parameters on this conflict. Reports on two villages currently being studied reveal that a strike by the landless laborers in their Nayar-dominated village was successful because the Nayars would not work in their own fields, whereas in the Christian-dominated village the landlords broke the union's strength by getting together to bring in the harvest themselves. We need to know to what extent this sort of thing has occurred and to learn the underlying forces at work. A simplistic explanation in terms of cultural values is probably inadequate.

Another important area for investigation in economic sociology is that of labor union activity, both in industry and among agricultural workers.

Kerala has been one of the areas where agricultural labor unions have been most active, especially in villages. It would certainly be of importance to our understanding of Indian social structure to know more about the reasons for this. Two papers by Mencher currently in preparation deal with this matter, but much empirical work remains to be done.

Ecological and Demographic Studies

Ecologically, Kerala (and south Kanara) are quite unique in the Indian subcontinent. Kuriyan[40] has shown that there exists in Kerala a high correlation between agricultural practices (such as methods of ploughing and irrigation) and linguistic and cultural distributions. C. A. Menon[41] has further shown how ecological factors have exerted a striking influence on the distribution and pattern of settlement. In Kerala, as noted above, a rural settlement was not the nucleated village as in most of India. In the early period, it was the manor house of the main local landlord that formed the nucleus for each "neighborhood." Indeed, according to one Malayali historian, within the historical period the smallest political unit was a household,[42] meaning of course a large landlord's household. Within the jurisdiction of each such household were the homes of their landless laborers, their Nayar vassals, and their other servitors. All land belonged to some landlord, and there was no village common land as elsewhere. A brief description of Kerala ecology appears elsewhere,[43] but it is mentioned here because it sets the background for a study of modern Kerala.

One thing that emerges from ecological studies in Kerala is a range of variation which is enormous. Thus, as Nair[44] points out, even within one district cropping patterns tend to vary greatly from subregion to subregion, and these have profound implications for social life. We do not know enough about which of these variations are significant and which are of minimal importance, nor for which functions a given structural and ecological variation might be meaningful.

We want to learn more about the extent and the ways in which ecological factors influence social structure. For example, we find in north Malabar many places where swidden (slash and burn) cultivation is practiced, either exclusively or alongside permanent rice cultivation. There appears to be some indication that caste barriers are lower where swidden cultivation dominates, but this matter needs further investigation. We know very little about the role of rice and coconuts, as opposed to other crops, in influencing social structure. We know, for example, that there are more large landowners in the interior districts Palghat and Trichur (the "rice bowl" of Kerala) than in the rest of the state. We also know that in these areas today caste barriers remain strong. Is this a fortuitous connection?

When we examine studies done by anthropologists in Kerala (as well as elsewhere in India), we need to go beyond the traditional province of anthropologists. We want to know whether the villages reported on by anthropologists are typical of their areas or typical of a certain type of village. We all know how villages are chosen for study: a house is available, there is a large and interesting distribution of castes, people seem friendly, or the investigator comes from nearby. This is well and good for getting intensive materials, but it is now time for the person working intensively to determine how the place he works in fits into a larger regional and state nexus. This larger perspective is even more necessary in Kerala, where the degree of variation is profound.

We are certain that within the variation, patterns will emerge; but these may differ considerably from any patterns suggested in present studies. Thus there is a great need for combining traditional anthropological field work with as much knowledge of demography as possible, coupled where possible with collaborative surveys by trained survey sociologists.

Obviously we cannot get demographic materials for early periods (except perhaps by inference from old documents). However, it may be useful to study the censuses of the late nineteenth century, which will enlighten us about the distribution of population local area by local area (*desam* by *desam*). Though these censuses are probably quite inaccurate and incomplete, we can at least hope to get a better picture than what we have now. From old records, we might get some idea of the range of variation in land tenure systems of the past and even in the early twentieth century. This knowledge is extremeley important in building a picture of present-day Kerala society.

Political Anthropology

While political scientists have published a number of studies of Kerala, little has been done on the sociological study of political behavior. Gough[45] is perhaps the only anthropologist to have dealt with this exceedingly important aspect of Malayali life. Various other writers have dealt with traditional political structures,[46] but little work has been done on the Kerala of the mid-twentieth century.

Gough has dealt with some of the ways in which village politics function. She has tried to show the mechanisms by which political allegiance is sought and the pertinent sociological factors. She has also examined how village panchayats function. Mencher[47] provides some contrasting material for the east coast.

A new Panchayat Act is to be passed shortly which will give considerable power to local bodies. The bill will provide for current district-level powers to be vested with the panchayat. Panchayats have recently been enlarged to include what were previously two or three panchayats. In some areas a panchayat may cover a fairly large area, as much as fifteen to twenty miles square. Each new panchayat, which consists of about ten old local neighborhoods (*desam*), provides an important unit for the study of local political processes.

There has been an increase in the process of politicization through the working of panchayats during the past ten years. Gough[48] shows how and why villagers of different castes and classes, in both farming and suburban areas, support the Congress or the Communist Parties. She also shows how interparty conflict is pursued through local institutions and what factors hold conflict in check. Another article[49] shows the relationship between the panchayat, the smallest unit for local administration, and the Community Development Program. This study suggests some of the constraints these programs impose on panchayats, in some cases limiting the effectiveness of panchayat leaders. But clearly more research remains to be done in a variety of settlements on problems of local politics.

There has been a perceptible drift of loyalties from the traditional territorial unit of *desam* to the cluster of *desam* which form the panchayat. To understand why and how this is occurring, we need considerable study of the relationship between political processes and other aspects of rural social structure. Among these relationships are kinship, such structural components as age, authority within the family, relations between former tenants and their ex-landlords and those between different social classes. Work on most of these problems still remains to be done.

Urban Studies

Sociological study of urban areas has so far been a neglected field, even though urbanization in Kerala has features which are unique compared to the trends obtaining in other states of India. At present, census reports and a few socioeconomic surveys give us quantitative information about towns, but descriptive accounts of a qualitative nature are few and lack precision and depth. Social anthropological studies of towns will make a substantial contribution in this direction.

In 1961 Kerala had ninety-two towns, in which 27 percent of the total population of the state lived. In contrast to the rest of India, most of the urban population of Kerala lived in smaller towns. Class III towns (having 20,000 to 50,000 population) and class IV towns (having 10,000 to 20,000 population) have 53.2 percent of the total urban population of the state. Reflecting the pattern of scattered rural settlements, the urban areas in Kerala have a spot density which does not exceed 36,400 persons per square mile in any city. The corresponding figure for cities of comparable size in India as a whole is 260,000 persons per square mile. At the same time, in terms of urbanized area Kerala is more urbanized than India in general, the figures being 2.88 percent for Kerala and 1.20 percent for India.[50] Another noteworthy feature of the urban situation in Kerala is that 57 percent of the total number of towns, and three out of the four class I towns (those with one million or more inhabitants), have "service" as their main function. Manufacturing towns belong mostly to the class III and IV category. Also, 60 percent of the total urban population of the state resides in service towns and 35 percent in manufacturing towns. Some ecological factors are also noteworthy in this context. Of the ninety-two towns, fifty-two are located on low lands and are developing fast.

Zacharia,[51] studying the trend of urbanization in Kerala on the basis of data from census figures, notes that migration to towns in Kerala was not very substantial during the two decades 1941–1961; quite a few urban centers actually lost population through migration. Although preliminary data show increasing urbanization between 1961 and 1971, Unni[52] points to several features which minimize the gap between the urban and rural scenes of Kerala in comparison with other parts of India. For example, as Unni points out, only 46.96 percent of the rural population is engaged in the primary sector of the economy. This fact makes the rural social matrix conducive to the emergence of characteristics of urbanism.

Against the background outlined here, the study of Kerala towns offers much promise to the social anthropologist. A recent study of Trichur town by Ittaman of the University of Saugar is to be published by the Census Department, Government of India.

Kinship

Kinship systems in Kerala stand out in marked contrast to the rest of South India. Even early travelers to the region saw fit to comment on some of the Kerala systems, especially on those versions of Nayar and Nambudiri practice visible to the casual visitor in a port town. What intrigued these travelers most was the matrilineal system found among the Nayars. From Barbosa on, we have writings dealing with Nayar kinship.[53]

Despite all the work that has been done, we still do not have a clear idea of the range of variation of the various practices described by these authors. Unni[54] and Abraham[55] provide us with some details about variations in Nayar polyandry; Unni's study also highlights the situation in the context of intercaste relations, showing in detail how nonfraternal polyandry functioned in an area where the pattern of visiting husbands was common. We have no way to document how long polyandry has been in existence in Kerala, nor whether it always took different forms in different parts of the coast. Unni[56] shows how in south Malabar the visiting custom was an integral part of the way in which matrilineal households functioned. He also showed some of the changes going on at present.

A great deal of debate has focused on the famous *tāli-kettu-kalyānam* ceremony among the Nayars. Considerable regional variation occurs in this custom, as well as variation according to subcaste and family prestige. In some instances the *tāli* (marriage necklace) was tied by a member of a linked or *enangar* lineage, in others by a member of a higher subcaste of Nayars or one of the matrilineal Ambilavasi or Kshatriya castes or (in the case of North Kerala) by a Nambudiri Brahman. In many instances the ceremony would be performed once every ten years or so, at which time all the girls down to the baby in the cradle would be married in this fashion as an economy measure. When a rich family held a *tāli*-tying ceremony, all the poor girls of Nayar families also had their *tāli* tied in the same courtyard.

Although the functions of this ceremony have been discussed in detail by numerous writers,[57] we lack the historical data which would enable us to come to a definitive conclusion. There is some evidence to suggest that the *tāli*-tying ceremony may date from the tenth century. If it did occur about this time, then our somewhat static picture of Kerala society clearly needs revision. If we look at that society prior to 1750 not as a static system but as a society undergoing transitions of various kinds, considerable light might be shed on our understanding of things observed today. For example, with the present-day breakup of all the large Nayar *taravād* and the gradual economic impoverishment of others, certain types of marriage patterns are emerging as dominant and most desirable. Some of these existed previously, but the degree of importance given to them has if anything increased. We refer here to three types of marriage pattern: mother's-brother's-daughter, father's-sister's-son, and the much desired brother-sister exchange pattern. Among Izhavas, this was quite common earlier. We suspect that it was an old Nayar pattern, rooted in the need to maintain close family ties in geographically isolated communities.

Marriage patterns differ among subsections of Nayars.[58] However, we do not know to what extent social class in general influenced marriage patterns. For Nambudiri Brahmans, Mencher[59] has shown how their need to maintain themselves as a wealthy aristocracy was a dominant factor in their prohibition of marriage for younger sons. E. K. Pillai[60] has shown that the Nambudiris rose to their dominant position in the Kerala socio-economic scene between the tenth and the fourteenth centuries. If this was so, then it is clear that kinship patterns of other groups may also relate to economic considerations.

At the other end of the caste spectrum, Iyer[61] notes that, in some areas at least, the Pulayan and Paraiyan castes were matrilineal because they belonged to Nayar landlords: "The children of slaves did not belong to the father's master, but were the property of the mother's owner. . . . The succession was by the female line, in accordance with the custom of the Nayars, the principal slave holders." Iyer also found considerable variation in the marriage customs among Pulayans, and Mencher (unpublished notes) found that the Pulayans in an area dominated by Nambudiri Brahmans were patrilineal.

In a recent paper Rao[62] examines how, during recent years, reform movements have affected family organization, and in turn caste unity, over wide areas. He examines changes in Nambudiris, Nayars, and Tiyyars, and he points to drastic changes in such matters as the observance of customary ceremonies, lineage exogamy, subcaste endogamy, and birth and death pollutions. Notwithstanding such changes, Rao reports a strong affinity toward one's caste as well as toward one's joint family. His work indicates that future studies might fruitfully explore the ways in which these changes, as well as the newly created horizontal unity, have influenced the structure of kinship and caste at the microlocal level. Gough is currently working on the correlation between political party membership and marriage patterns; Mencher and Unni are studying the relationship between education and social class membership on the one hand and marriage patterns on the other.

Clearly we need to know more about the economic factors underlying marriage patterns and kinship structure. Since we can observe radical changes going on in the economy of Kerala today, we are provided with an excellent laboratory to study these complex interrelations.

Other Areas for Study

Very little work has been done in the field of sociology of religion on the west coast. Unni[63] has dealt with the "social mobility of deities," that is, the ways in which deities came to acquire a halo of sanskritized status. A few other references to similar phenomena are found in early books.[64] Mencher[65] has dealt with the opposite process, namely, the way in which high castes come to accept non-Brahmanical worship as important in their lives. Clearly we need far more study of both phenomena. We want to know more about how Sanskritic and Dravidian cultures influenced one another.

Another important area of study is that of low-caste religious belief. A considerable literature exists dealing with high-caste belief, the values of the shastras, the concepts of karma and dharma, and the like. But how important are these in low-caste belief? Do the Cherumans in Kerala (when no high-caste person is around) really espouse these ideas? It is clear that low-caste people have used black magic as one method of exercising some control (economic and social) under extremely difficult circumstances. Thus if a Nayar family feared that an untouchable Paraiyan might do some harm to the females of the Nayar family, the Nayar might be especially careful how he treated the Paraiyan when he begged for food or medicine for a sick child. Iyer[66] describes in great detail how this cult operated. But what is not analyzed is the role it must have served as a counterbalancing force in traditional Kerala society. The fact that it is virtually gone today may be related as much to improvements in the Paraiyan's position, and to the opening of new avenues for protest (as through political action), as to fear of punishment by government officials.

The way in which religious movements have tried to foster horizontal unity of castes is also quite important. We have yet to find, however, a detailed sociological study of the movement of Guru Nayaranaswami (the Tiyyar saint). Similarly, the growing interest in the Sabrimala festival, and Aiyappan worship even by high-caste people, clearly need study.

In Kerala today, with the opening of temples to all castes, one finds a resurgence of interest in religion and a great premium placed on certain non-Sanskritic forms of worship. This phenomenon needs to be studied in more detail. Today many more families are celebrating marriages at the temples, especially Guruvayur and one or two others. Local festivals appear to be becoming more important, not less. It is clear that, with current changes, some temples are becoming poorer as they lose their sources of wealth whereas others have become much richer. We need a sociological description of the forces which favor certain temples and disfavor others. Too often, accounts of village festivals emphasize the pageantry of a festival without any further interpretation.[67]

Another area for research here would include an exploration of how religious institutions are bringing secular institutions of all kinds into their folds. For the various churches in the southern part of the state this is not a new phenomenon, but it has certainly increased since independence. Today Hindu temples are also involved in such secular activities as the running of colleges and welfare centers. This trend clearly needs further study.

Literary and Film Resources

Literary works and the cinema provide important areas for sociological research that remain to be explored. Malayalam fiction started around the end of the nineteenth century.[68] A few examples of the range of works available are:

1. Folk songs and proverbs of Kerala were briefly analyzed from a sociological perspective by M. S. A. Rao in 1955. He has shown how rich a source they are for anthropologists.
2. O. Chandu Menon's *Indulekha* (English translation available) and

Sarada are early novels dealing with the complexities of Nambudiri-Nayar relationships around the turn of the present century.

3. C. V. Ramam Pillai's work, *Premamritam* (Nectar of Love) reveals aspects of matrilineal Nayar joint families of south Travancore around the turn of the century.

4. Bhavatratan Nambudiripad's *Appante Makal* (Paternal Uncle's Daughter) sheds light on Nambudiri-Nayar relationships in Walluvanad taluk in the 1930s.

5. Pottekkatt's novel *Visha Kanyaka* (Poison Maiden) deals with the land hunger of Christians in the hilly tracts of Malabar in the 1940s, and his *Moodupadam* (The Veil) deals with Hindu-Muslim conflict.

6. Surendran's novel *Jwala* (Flame) deals with political struggle in Trivandrum in the years 1920 to 1940.

7. Basheer's *Balyakala Sakhi* (The Female Playmate of Childhood) deals with the customs of Muslims in central Travancore during the 1940s, and his novel *Ntuppappakkoranentarnnu* (My Grandfather Had an Elephant) presents a picture of aspects of internal differentiation among Muslims as well as aspects of social change in rural areas during the 1940s and early 1950s.

8. Vivekanandan's *Kalli Challamma* (The Thief of a Woman) is a social novel dealing with peasants and workers in rural Kerala between 1935 and 1945.

9. Parapurath's *Adya Kiranangal* (First Rays) is a social novel of programs of social change in a central Kerala village in the late 1950s.

10. Pisharoti's novel *Ayiram Kunnukal* (Thousand Hills) discusses the impact of social change and urbanization in the rural interior of Malabar in the 1950s.

11. Kesav Dev's *Ayalkar* is a social novel highlighting caste tensions between Nayars and Izhavas in Kuttanad between 1923 and 1943.

12. Takazhi's *Chemmeen* (Prawns) (translation into English available) is an excellent examination of the life of fishermen in Travancore in the 1950s. His *Randu Edangazhi* (Two Measures of Rice) is another novel which reveals the relationship between landlords and untouchable landless laborers during the same period. Another novel of Takazhi, *Tottiyude Makan* (Son of a Refuse Collector), provides a clear look at the poverty and misery of this caste in central Travancore, and still another novel of his, *Ouseppinte Makkal* (Children of Joseph), shows the preconversion status of Christians in Travancore in relation to other groups.

13. P. C. Kuttikrishnan (also known as Uroob) has written an excellent novel, *Ummachu*, which provides us with insights into the conflicts and adjustments worked out between Muslims and Hindus of Ponnani taluk (south Malabar) in the 1950s.

14. Malayattur Ramakrishnan's *Verukal* (Roots) deals with the lack of

ancestral roots of immigrant Tamil Brahmans (Iyers) in Kerala, the locale being the Cochin-Travancore border areas in the 1950s and early 1960s.

15. Malayattur Ramakrishnan's *Ponni* (translation into English by P. Susheela forthcoming) provides some understanding of the nature of intertribal conflicts between the two scheduled tribes of Mudugar and Irular in the Attappadi hill ranges.

16. Vijayan's novel *Khasakkinte Irihasan* (The Saga of Khasak) is concerned with the immigrant trading Muslims of Palghat (Ravuttar) and their relations with other local communities.

17. Vasudevan Nair's *Nalukettu* (literally the traditional house of a matrilineal joint family) portrays Nayar joint family life in the 1940s, and his *Asuravittu* (The Devil Seed) offers insights into Nayar-Muslim relations in Ponnani taluk of south Malabar.

18. S. Menon Marath's novel *The Wounds of Spring* (in English) deals with the problems of a Nayar *taravād* during the 1930s and the effects of the Moplah rebellion and intercaste marriage in central Kerala.

Kerala films often focus on stories of sociological import, and it would be of interest to see a content analysis of some of these. Numerous stories deal with landlord-tenant relations, problems of family partition, and intercaste relations. The cinema reflects real-life situations to an impressive extent. Themes of social life known widely among all except the very few low castes occupy the cinema screen. The emphasis on the life of luxury and sophistication, so often found in Hindi films, is markedly absent here. Generally, Malayalam novels and short stories which have achieved popularity and critical acclaim are the film producer's mainstay.

The conflicts between tradition and modernity among Nayars, Nambudiris, and Muslims of the former south Malabar area have been popular themes. Films which highlight social injustice (except at intercaste levels) have also met with a good deal of appreciation. Muttattu Varkey's *Gangasamgamam* is an example of this, dealing with the exploitation of Catholic Christians by their priests. Knowledgeable intellectuals tell us that exploitation at intercaste levels is kept out of the cinema world for fear of rousing communal tensions.

Class struggle between laborers and employers has occupied an important place. The landless agricultural worker, or the factory worker in the context of unionization, are familiar themes. In the last five years there have appeared about two dozen films revealing the leftist ideology, all dealing with class struggle in one form or other. Participation in political life has, in the last five years, entered the cinema as an area rich with thematic possibilities. Much care is taken in this matter to steer clear of arousing unhealthy political party conflicts.

Nearly all films have a primarily rural background. This poses the question of whether this is because in Kerala there is really no urban social matrix distinct from the rural, except in Erankulam and Cochin. Also we find that the social life of the lower castes is a neglected field, apparently because script writers come from the higher castes and communities and have had no opportunity to observe their social life.

NOTES

1. This essay was written while the authors were working together on a joint Columbia University–Delhi School of Planning and Architecture research project, sponsored by the National Science Foundation of the United States. The authors are grateful to Professors F. C. Southworth and O. M. Anujan for their help and suggestions.
2. J. P. Mencher, "Kerala and Madras: A Comparative Study of Ecology and Social Structure," *Ethnology* 5 (1966), pp. 135–171.
3. Elamkulam Kunjan Pillai, *Studies in Kerala History* (Trivandrum: National Book Stall, 1970), p. 237.
4. S. Shahani, "A Comparative Study of the Traditional Political Organization of Kerala and Punjab" (Doctoral thesis, School of Oriental and African Studies, University of London, 1965).
5. E. Thurston, *Castes and Tribes of Southern India*, 2 (Madras: Government Press, 1909), p. 393.
6. David M. Schneider and Kathleen Gough (eds.), *Matrilineal Kinship* (Berkeley: University of California Press, 1961).
7. E. R. Leach (ed.), *Aspects of Caste in South India, Ceylon and North-west Pakistan* (Cambridge: Cambridge University Press, 1960).
8. J. P. Mencher, "Namboodiri Brahmins: An Analysis of a Traditional Elite in Kerala," *Journal of Asian and African Studies* 1 (1966), pp. 7–20.
9. E. Kathleen Gough, "The Nayar Tarawad," *Journal of the M.S. University of Baroda* 1 (1952), pp. 1–13.
10 K. R. Unni, "Caste in Southern Malabar" (Doctoral thesis, M.S. University of Baroda, 1959), chap. 5.
11. *Ibid.*
12. Schneider and Gough, *op. cit.*
13. Unni, *op. cit.*
14. L. K. Anantha Krishna Iyer, *The Cochin Tribes and Castes*, 2 vols. (Madras, 1901–1912); Travancore, India, *The Travencore State Manual*, 3 vols. (Trivandrum, 1906); Thurston, *op. cit.*, in 5 vols.
15. The following works of K. R. Unni: "Visiting Husbands in Malabar," *Journal of the M.S. University of Baroda* 5 (1956), pp. 37–56; "Polyandry in Malabar," *Sociological Bulletin* 7 (March and September 1958); "Caste in Southern Malabar." The work of E. K. Gough: "The Nayar Tarawad"; "Changing Kinship Usages in the Setting of Political and Economic Change among the Nayars of Malabar," *Journal of the Royal Anthropological Institute* 82 (1952), pp. 71–88; "Female Initiation Rites on the Malabar Coast," *Journal of the Royal Anthropological Institite* 85 (1955), pp. 45–80; "The Nayars and the Definition of Marriage," *Journal of the Royal Anthropological Institute* 89 (1959), pp. 23–34; and chapters on the Nayars in Schneider and Gough, *op. cit.* The work of J. P. Mencher: "Changing Familial Roles Among South

Malabar Nayars," *Southwest Journal of Anthropology* 18 (1962), pp. 230–245; "Growing Up in South Malabar," *Human Organization* 22 (1963), pp. 54–65; "Possession, Dance and Religion in North Malabar, Kerala, India," forthcoming in the *Collected Papers of the VIIth Congress of Anthropological and Ethnological Sciences* (Moscow, 1964). Also: J. J. Puthenkalam, "Marriage and Family in Kerala" (Doctoral thesis, University of Bombay, 1963) and C. M. Abraham, "Nayars of Kerala" (Doctoral thesis, University of Lucknow, 1962).

16. A. Aiyappan, *Iravas and Cultural Change* (Madras, 1943) and *Social Revolution in a Kerala Village* (New York: Asia Publishing House, 1965).

17. A. Aiyappan, *Social and Physical Anthropology of the Nayadis of Malabar* (Madras, 1937).

18. J. P. Mencher, "The Namboodiri Brahmins of Kerala," *Natural History* 75 (1966), pp. 14–21; "Namboodiri Brahmins"; J. P. Mencher and Helen Goldberg, "Kinship and Marriage Regulations Among the Namboodiri Brahmins of Kerala," *Man* 2 (1968), pp. 87–106.

19. Among these are: M. K. Nag, "Family Structure of the Kanikkar and the Urali of Travencore," *Man in India* 5 (1956), p. 219; and P. T. Thomas, "Adjustments to Changing Environment (on Muthuvans of Travencore)," in *Anthropology on the March*, ed. Bala Ratnam (Madras, 1963).

20. A. Aiyappan, "Urgent Anthropology for Southern India," paper presented to the Conference on Urgent Research in Social Anthropology, Indian Institute of Advanced Study, Simla, 1968.

21. See J. P. Mencher, "Group and Self-Identification: The View from the Bottom," for a volume edited by Dennis Walton on the question of "identity" in South Asian societies (in press); also J. P. Mencher, "Socio-Economic Constraints to Development: The Case of South India," *Annals of the New York Academy of Science* (in press).

22. L. K. Anantha Krishna Iyer, *Anthropology of Syrian Christians* (Cochin, 1926), pp. 208–214.

23. Arne Martin Klausen, *Kerala Fishermen and the Indo-Norwegian Pilot Project* (Oslo: Scandinavian University Books, 1968).

24. K. C. Alexander, *Social Mobility in Kerala* (Poona: Deccan College Postgraduate and Research Institute, 1968).

25. L. K. A. K. Iyer, *op. cit.*; and Thurston, *op. cit.*

26. George Kuriyan, *The Indian Family in Transition—A Case Study of Kerala Christians* (The Hague: Mouton, 1961).

27. S. G. Pothan, *The Syrian Christians of Kerala* (Bombay: Asia Publishing House, 1963).

28. P. Thomas, "The Early Christians of Kerala," *March of India* (1958).

29. Leela Dube, "Matrimony in Islam," *Religion and Society in the Laccadives* (Delhi, 1969).

30. Schneider and Gough, *op. cit.*

31. Leela Dube, "Social Stratification in the Laccadives," *Caste and Social Stratification among the Muslims*, ed. Imtiaz Ahmad (Delhi, 1972).

32. B. Barber, "Social Mobility in Hindu India," *Social Mobility in the Caste System in India*, ed. James Silverberg, Supplement III of *Comparative Studies in Society and History* (1968), pp. 18–36.

33. See E. K. Gough, "Communist Rural Councillors in Kerala," *Journal of Asian and African Studies* (1969); and Thomas W. Shea, "Barriers to Economic

Development in Traditional Societies: Malabar, A Case Study," *Journal of Economic History* 9 (1959), pp. 504–522.
34. T. C. Varghese, *Agrarian Change and Rural Consequences: Land Tenures in Kerala* (Bombay: Allied Publishers, 1970).
35. Donald S. Zagoria, "The Ecology of Peasant Communism in India," *American Political Science Review* 65 (1971), pp. 144–160.
36. J. P. Mencher, "Change Agents and Villages: An Analysis of their Relationships and the Role of Class Values," *Indian Economic and Political Weekly* 5 (July 1970); J. P. Mencher and F. C. Southworth, "The Tera Ceremony of Kerala," *Illustrated Weekly* (20 February 1972), pp. 40–43.
37. Klausen, *op. cit.*
38. Mencher, "Change Agents."
39. *Ibid.*; and Mencher and Southworth, *op. cit.*
40. George Kuriyan, "Population and Its Distribution in Kerala," *Journal of the Madras Geographical Association* 13 and 14 (1938–1939); and George Kuriyan, "Some Aspects of the Regional Geography of Kerala," *Indian Geographical Journal* 17 (1942), pp. 1–41.
41. C. A. Menon, *Kali Worship in Kerala* (Madras: University of Madras, 1953).
42. K. A. Menon, *Ancient Kerala: Studies in Its History and Culture* (Trichur, 1961).
43. Mencher, "Namboodiri Brahmins of Kerala."
44. K. N. S. Nair, "Constraints That are Limiting Agricultural Production and Causing Uneven Distribution of Gains—A Case, Palghat District, Kerala State" (Doctoral thesis, Indian Agricultural Research Institute of New Delhi, 1972).
45. E. K. Gough, "Politics in Kerala," *Peace News* (Canada), (January 1965) and "Village Politics in Kerala," *Economic and Political Weekly* (20 and 27 February 1965).
46. For example: Shahani, *op. cit.*
47. "Politics, Religion and Caste in Madras Villages: An Analysis of Their Inter-Relations and Implications for Development," paper presented to the American Anthropological Association, 1968, under revision for publication.
48. Gough, "Village Politics."
49. Gough, "Communist Rural Councillors."
50. J. H. Ansari, "A Study of Settlement Patterns in Kerala in Urban and Rural Planning Thought," *Quarterly Journal of the School of Planning and Architecture, Delhi* 12 (1969).
51. K. C. Zacharia, "Migration and Population Growth in Kerala," *Population Growth in Kerala and Its Implications* (Trivandrum, 1966).
52. K. R. Unni, "Toward Comprehending Kerala in Rural and Urban Planning Thought," *Quarterly Journal of the School of Planning and Architecture, Delhi* 12 (1969).
53. Mansel Longworth Dames (ed.), *The Book of Duarte Barbosa*, 2 (London, 1921); Fred Fawcett, *The Nayars of Malabar*, vol. 3, no. 3 of *Bulletin of the Madras Government Museum* (1915); Iyer, Gough, Unni, and Mencher as cited above.
54. "Polyandry in Malabar."
55. C. M. Abraham, "Custom of Polyandry as Practiced in Travencore," *Eastern Anthropologist* 12 (1958–1959).
56. "Visiting Husbands in Malabar."

57. Nur Yalman, "On the Purity of Women in the Castes of Ceylon and Malabar," *Journal of the Royal Anthropological Institute* 93 (1963), pp. 25–58; and Gough, Fawcett, Iyer, and Mencher as cited above.
58. Schneider and Gough, *op. cit.*
59. Mencher, "Namboodiri Brahmins of Kerala."
60. Pillai, *op, cit.*
61. Iyer, *Syrian Christians*, p. 213.
62. M. S. Rao, "Caste and Joint Family in Kerala," *Essays on Sociology of Economic Development and Social Change* (Bombay: Popular Prakasam Press, forthcoming).
63. Unni, "Caste in Southern Maliabar."
64. For example: Fawcett, *op. cit.*; and K. M. Panikkar, "Some Aspects of Nayar Life," *Journal of the Royal Anthropological Institute* 48 (1918), pp. 254–293.
65. Mencher, "Possession, Dance and Religion."
66. Iyer, *Cochin Tribes and Castes* 1, pp. 76–81.
67. See, for example, *Census of India*, 1961, "Fairs and Festivals."
68. An excellent survey appears in K. M. George, *A Survey of Malayalam Literature* (Madras: Asia Publishing House, 1968).

BIBLIOGRAPHY (IN MALAYALAM)

Basheer. *Balyakala Sakhi.* 1946.

———. *Ntuppappakkoranentarnnu.* 1951.

Bhattathiripad, K. A. B. *Samudayamitiam.* Published by Parayil Raman Namboothiri. Printed by Trichur Mangalodyam Press. 1910.

Bahttathiripad, M. R. *Changes Befallen to Namboothiris Within Quarter Century.*

Cherumukkil Pachcha.

Dev, P. Kesav. *Ayalkar.* 1963.

Granthavari of 1723. Perumanam temple in Malayalam.

Kuttikrishnan, P. C. (alias Uroob). *Ummachu.* 1955.

Menon, Karatta Achuta. *Ammayi Panchatantram.* Trichur: Managalodyam Press, 1912.

Menon, O. Chandu. *Indulekha.* (Republished in English trans. by Mathrubhumi Press, Calicut, 1963)

———. *Sarada.* 1903.

Nair, K. N. Damodaran. *Marriage of Nayars.* In Malayala Rasyam Annual Issue. 1949–1950.

Nair, M. T. Vasudevan. *Nalukettu.* 1956.

———. *Asuravittu.* 1958.

Nair, S. K. "Kerala Castes and Customs," *Mathrubhumi Weekly*, 28 October 1956.

Nair, T. Balakrishnan. "Chirakkal Gymnastics." Read on the All-India Radio.

Namboothiri, Parayil Raman. *Namboothirimar.* Trichur: Mangalodayam, 1903.

Namboothiripad, E. M. S. *Atmakadha.* pt. I. Trivandrum: Deshabhimani Book House, 1969.

Namboothiripad, Kanippayoor Sankaran. *Namboothiri and Marumakkathayam.* Kunnankulam: Panjangam Press, 1961.

Nambudiripad, Bhavatratan. *Appante Makal.* 1933.

Parapurath. *Adya Kiranangal.* 1961.

Pakazhiyam Chandangu. Kunnankulam: Panjangam Press, 1928.

Pillai, C. V. Raman. *Premamritam.* About 1916.

Pillai, Elamkulam Kunjan. *The Dark Periods of Kerala History*. 2nd ed. Sahitya Pravarthaka Co-operative Society, 1957.
———. *Kerala Charitratille Chilla Prasnangal* (English translation available). Kottayam: National Book Stall, 1956.
———. *Kerala in 5th and 6th Centuries*. 1961.
Pillai, P. N. Kunjan. *Early Kerala*. Trivandrum, V.V. Book Depot.
Pillai, Takazhi S. *Chemmeen*. 1955.
———. *Randu Edangazhi*. 1952.
———. *Tottiyude Makan*. 1948.
———. *Ouseppinte Makkal*. 1959.
Prisharody, Attoor Krishna. *Kerala Charithram*. Trivandrum: S.R. Book Depot, 1930.
Pisharody, K. Rama. *Neelakantan's Cochin Royal Ancestry*. Ernakulam: Santhana Dharmam Pub. Works.
Pisharoti, N. N. *Ayiram Kunnukal*. 1963.
Pottekad, S. K. *Visha Kanyaka*. 1948.
———. *Moodupadam*. 1949.
Raja, K. Kunchunni. "Janmis of Ancient Kerala," *Mathrubhumi Weekly*.
Ramakrishnan, Malayattur. *Verukal*. 1964.
———. *Ponni* (English translation forthcoming). 1967.
Sastry, K. *Kerala Charithram*. Trivandrum: Government Press, 1939.
Surendran, K. *Jwala*. 1965.
Vijayan, O. V. *Khasakkinte Irihasam*. 1969.
Vivekanandan, G. *Kalli Chellamma*. 1956.

Approaches to Changes in Caste Ideology in South India

STEPHEN A. BARNETT
Princeton University

Why do anthropologists go to India? We know that castes will diversify occupations, that industries will develop, that roles will become functionally more specific. We know in general that modernization is enhanced through education, communications, ideology—especially that related to nationalism and charismatic leadership. So again, why go to India? Does modernization theory suffer from what has been called elsewhere "the dead hand of competence"? To paraphrase Bob Dylan, is something happening out there and modernization theorists don't know what it is?

The following is one person's reading of data and theoretical conjectures. I emphasize this because no pretense is made to bibliographic completeness. Rather than simply describe research to date, I shall attempt to criticize various approaches and to offer alternative models for conceptualizing change.

This is a large order, and in an essay of this size I am forced to say too little and therefore too much. My hope is that the attempt to criticize and reorder will be stimulating to the specialist and can provide some organization to guide the nonspecialist through minute ethnographic debate. The discussion will concentrate on caste *ideology* and caste change, on the changing meanings of the symbols of caste culture, because typical studies of caste change focus on behavior, not culture. An anthropological analysis worth its salt, however, should attempt to integrate ideological and behavioral levels.

It is a thankless task to summarize the very diverse views of the authors mentioned below, and no doubt some will object to being placed in unexpected company. Still, I think it worthwhile to look at these writings with one basic question in mind: Is the caste system fundamentally breaking down or is it successfully adapting to new conditions? While writers on recent change in caste offer any number of justificatory conjectures, they tend to preside over the demise of caste or hail its phoenix-like qualities. Some see caste declining in favor of class; some note a sharp break between rural and urban caste forms; others describe a more general split between tradition and modernity; still others emphasize the flexibility of caste overriding any dichotomous distinction.

This essay starts with a different premise. Rather than working through these alternatives, taking each at face value, it will develop a theory of caste structure and only then ask: What in the urban situation enhances or challenges this structure? This approach can lead to unexpected results. Certain urban settings favor caste; certain extensions in kinship networks, previously thought to be a clear case of caste adaptation, will be seen as undercutting the very bases of caste ideology. Such an approach seeks to order the incredible complexity of contemporary South Indian society where new factories border on ancient paddy-producing villages, where hereditary leadership rights conflict with electoral politics, where communists and orthodox Brahmans live next to each other, where some landless agricultural laborers organize unions and go on strike while others still call their employer "master," where violence periodically erupts as leaders talk of Gandhian nonviolence. Too many theories of South Indian change simplify this complexity, creating a fantasy world of harmonious incremental development.

In this essay, I wish first to discuss the most general problems of dealing with change, problems that reappear in all discussions. Second, I shall discuss levels of change from descriptive to structural as a way of coping with these problems. Third, I shall illustrate the usefulness of such a level shift by an example of kinship change in one South Indian caste. Fourth, I shall suggest a way to integrate these levels in a general statement of South Indian change. And finally, as a result of this discussion I shall propose avenues of future research. The general orientation of the essay can be summarized here as a guide to the reader:

1. David Schneider[1] has suggested that the culture of American kinship turns on the concepts of natural identity (or inherited biogenetic substance transmitted from parents to children) and code for conduct (or guides to correct behavior). Sexual intercourse is the core symbol that links relations through natural identity and conduct and through conduct alone (in-laws). Extending this line of thought to South India, we might say that purity as a quality of the blood contains *both* substance and code,

and therefore, unlike the American case, one must marry a relation, a person of equivalent substance and code.

2. Substance and code are thought of in terms of blood and the physical body in the South Indian theory of conception and procreation. Blood is the locus of purity, and blood purity is transmitted from both parents (semen is concentrated blood, breast milk is also concentrated blood, the fetus may also absorb uterine blood) to children. If a person does not conform to caste codes for conduct, blood purity is affected and can result in outcasting. The substance and code aspects of blood purity are basic to understanding caste culture. This notion of blood purity gives meaning to marriage rules, intercaste transactions, and local caste rank orders.

3. Recent changes in caste culture can be seen as a limitation of the criteria of blood purity to substance or ancestry only. Many previously restricted codes for conduct can thus cross caste or subcaste boundaries. This separation of substance and code (since purity is a matter of substance, not of how one lives) is the critical shift in caste culture.

4. This change in the conceptualization of blood purity paves the way for new components of personal and social identity given India's emergent state capitalism. Ideas of race, ethnicity, cultural nationalism, and class become thinkable only given a separation of substance and code. South Indian castes now resemble ethnic groups; untouchables are excluded from ethnicization and are coming to be thought of as a separate race; Tamil cultural nationalism posits a common code for all castes; and class formation leads to codes crosscutting castes.

This approach seeks to delimit an ideological field, to specify the range of possibilities through which a person must move and make choices at a particular historical moment. I suggest it can make sense of the data we now have on contemporary South Indian caste.

Problems in the Study of Change

Recognition of Change

Superficially we might expect that modernizing change is easily perceived, and even casual writers write as if the observation of change posed no problems. But a notion of what is changing presupposes some knowledge of what was. Benchmarks are usually established by fiat, by supposing a traditional *status quo ante*. Recently the question of mobility in traditional caste has been raised[2] and although, as a modern reflex, the picture of mobility is more optimistic than its documentation, Still it is difficult to estimate the significance of present-day attempts at caste mobility. Even drastic changes initiated by the non-Brahman movement may have parallels in medieval South Indian Hinduism and before.

System-Maintaining versus System-Challenging Change

Even when we can be confident of change (industrialization, parliamentary democracy, westernization, and so forth), the significance of these developments is far from obvious. Does the particular instance of change fundamentally change the system or does the system adapt to it? Theorists have developed a complex vocabulary to handle this issue—rejection, mixture, and combination according to Dumont,[3] compartmentalization and vicarious ritualization according to Singer,[4] and interpenetration according to L. and S. Rudolph.[5] But, the same datum can be seen as system-maintaining by one author and as system-challenging by another. In one sense, we can oppose the theoretical orientation of Max Weber,[6] who saw Hinduism as an impediment to economic development, to that of Milton Singer,[7] who suggests that Hinduism may even be conducive to Indian modernization. If one considers the caste *system* to be of such a nature that any modernizing change challenges it at the root, then of course the problem is easily solved. Thus we have the views of Weber and also Edmund Leach,[8] according to which competition among castes destroys the caste system because caste relations are essentially perceived in terms of cooperation. Yet this is too facile: one has the sense of a system being set up expressly to be knocked down.

With hindsight we can excuse Weber; after all he was working secondhand with intractable texts and British government reports. Singer has carefully evaluated Weber's work and concludes that what for Weber is system-transforming is, given another concept of the caste system, system-maintaining. Social transformation is a far more complex process. For Singer, Hindu asceticism can be adapted to meet the needs of a poor but developing nation; the joint family can persist and even administer aspects of modernization; and the industrialist can effectively compartmentalize his office and home life. L. and S. Rudolph suggest that this "interpenetration" of forms moves us to the heart of process of South Indian change by pointing to the adaptiveness of caste; caste associations and parliamentary democracy foster the democratic reincarnation of caste.

These formulations certainly advance our understanding of process and direct our attention to fruitful research, but perhaps they do not so easily dispose of the question of the relative nonadaptiveness of caste as a system. Rather, Weber and Leach in contrast with Singer and the Rudolphs seem to be describing different levels of analysis, levels which are confounded at our peril. Within a rigid conception of the caste system, any modernizing change would almost have to terminate that system; given an adaptive caste system, change can be accommodated within it. Take Singer's suggestion that an individual can eat meat or eat with lower castes at the office but keep an orthodox kitchen at home. Some industrialists may actually compartmentalize in this way; however, given one understanding of orthopraxy, a meat-eating industrialist could never eat in his own house to maintain requisite household purity. Something is adapting, but something else is fundamentally changing.

If we demarcate levels of analysis, in essence defining system, structure, and process more closely, the problems of system-maintaining or system-challenging change become clearer. At this point, I can only reiterate that what for one writer is system-maintaining is for another system-challenging. The difficulty lies with the notion of what is caste as a system. I shall return to this point and try to clarify it, but here I can suggest that any reasonable discussion of change must, implicitly or explicitly, include some indication of what the caste system is all about.

Isolation of Changing Subsystems

This is another way of opening up the part-whole problem. One way of getting a grip on change is to limit a study (or publication) to change in some unit within a larger whole of some sort: economic, kin, religious, caste, village, or town. An implicit assumption here is that these units are viable divisions of any cultural whole. Thus, for example, it is reasonable to examine changes in traditional family organization across many cultures. However, there are subtle traps here. While Singer's discussion of the joint family given industrialization is illuminating and unexpected, he does not feel constrained immediately to place family change or persistence within a particular South Indian kinship system, a system which I would argue is undergoing profound change. But why stop at kinship? If parameters of kinship change have to do with alliance units of equivalent purity, then we must talk about pure and impure in a modernizing context. And this brings in religion. Can we then separate the family from Hinduism? This raises a difficult and arguable point. It seems to me that we must start with the categories of South Indians themselves, with their construction of the world. If we follow their construction, however, then subsystems may not be immediately comparable cross-culturally nor should we expect this.

This summary of puzzling questions recapitulates the basic problem. Is caste basically altering or is it only changing in its minor aspects? Can we say more than that the old is continuing in the new or that the modern is substituted for the traditional? If both are occurring, can we specify in what areas and with what consequences?

Levels of Change

In order to proceed, consideration must be given to levels at which changes are considered. Apart from the descriptive level—detailed accounts of specific developments in South India for the past two hundred years—there is the *processual level* pertaining to persistence and transformation. This is the level of much work on South Indian change. There are, for example, studies concentrating on the significance of caste seen as a variable in economic modernization[9] or elaborating the concept of vicarious ritualization whereby daily rituals may be given over to other household members. Processual analysis confounds Weber and Marx, for the accountrements of caste persist reasonably intact in most areas. Even where process is seen as a caste-to-class shift, the processual analysis per se merely identifies the flux and notes contradictions. Again we return to caste associations as an example, for these organizations are at once caste-based and at the same time operative in an electoral political context.

By itself the processual level is incomplete and can in fact be deceptive, substituting a shallow empirical confidence for theoretical acumen. Rather these processes must be seen in terms of their significance for structural alternations; a structure "is present or absent, it does not change."[10] I take *Structural level* to mean that a structure organizes and gives meaning to its components or elements, but that apart from movement and change among the elements, these principles of organization ("structure") must remain constant. If these principles change, we can speak of the replacement of one structure by another. Process then includes two possibilities—the movement of elements in a structure in line with unchanging principles of organization, or the replacement of one set of principles by another. If we move to the structural level, we no longer give primacy to elements as basic analytic units but to relations between these elements. It may be the case that while certain elements or symbols persist, there has been a substitution of one structure for another, so that given a new set of relations of elements, these persisting elements or symbols take on opposite meanings or significations.

By embedding process in structure (and vice versa), we can begin to deal with our original conundrums. Benchmarks are understood in terms of the presence or absence of a particular structure. System maintenance or change can be seen as a processual transformation within one structure or the replacement of one structure by another.[11]

Relating the Levels by Illustration

To make these levels concrete, I shall use recent change in the marriage alliance patterns of one caste. Tonṭaimanṭala Konṭaikkaṭṭi Vēḷāḷar Mutaliyārs (hereafter KV) are one of six vegetarian South Indian Vēḷāḷar castes. Vegetarian Vēḷāḷars have been historically linked with both Brahmans and local rulers,[12] and today KVs are dominant landowners in parts of Chingleput, south Arcot, Tanjavur, and Tirunelveli. Apart from caste myths of dispersions from Chingleput, up to fifty years ago there was little if any contact between KVs of different districts and the only overarching institution was the caste religious retreat and residence of the caste guru (and the location of caste records) at the Sri Gnanaprakasa Swamigal Maṭam, in Kancheepuram.

Within some districts, KVs were further divided into unequivocally ranked bilateral kindreds (*vakaiyara*). These kindreds were transactionally ranked (prohibitions on interdining and water exchange) with clear, nondisputed boundaries until about 1930. Cultural distinctions between KV units of varying size and geographical range are complex and involve, most importantly here, degrees of purity. KVs express purity distinction this way: purity is a matter of the blood (*irattam*) and we are all one blood since our ancestors are the same (given the KV origin myth). At the same time we are not all of equivalent purity since purity is also a matter of the way a person lives: a person may be outcaste for certain violations of KV purity requirements (sexual intercourse with a woman of lower caste, meat-eating). Sexual intercourse with a lower-caste woman involves purity considerations since she will literally suck an excessive amount of semen (concentrated blood for KVs) from her partner, so jeopardizing his purity. Meat-eating directly affects the blood. In this vein, higher kindred KVs will say that lower KVs live looser, less pure lives. One KV put the unity and subdivisions of KVs this way: "We are all like gold, some of us may be pure gold, some 18 karat, but we are all gold."

The growth of Madras City as an industrial, educational, and governmental center attracted KVs of various districts there, and eventually a caste association was formed. At the same time, the non-Brahman movement emerged as a significant force in South Indian development, and KVs were early attracted to the Justice Party.[13] Given the unique position of KVs and all vegetarian Vēḷāḷar castes, which ranked distinctly between Brahmans and other upper non-Brahmans, the non-Brahman movement was an arena for a peculiar upward mobility movement. If Brahmans were removed from the top of the hierarchy, vegetarian Vēḷāḷars were all too willing (and able, given their extreme orthodoxy and orthopraxy) to replace them. While the concept of Brahman has all-India range, however, each vegetarian Vēḷāḷar caste was known only in its local region of dominance and therefore more "visibility" was needed to set Vēḷāḷars up as an effective alternative to Brahmans at the highest rank.

The KV caste association considered two steps to increase vegetarian Vēḷāḷar visibility and unity: interdistrict marriage among KVs and then intermarriage among all vegetarian Vēḷāḷars (the latter was never carried out). KV reformers passed a resolution endorsing interdistrict marriage, and the debate leading to passage is most significant. First note the strength of the opposition. Orthodox KVs objected that there was no way to know whether the purity of a woman from a district four hundred miles away was equivalent to that of a woman of their own kindred. The purity of women is crucial for KVs since their traditional theory of conception includes transmission of purity/blood from father (semen) and mother (breast milk, also a product of the blood). In fact, some orthodox kindred members broke off all contact with those KVs who initiated interdistrict marriage alliances.

KV reformers, however, successfully argued that, after all, this was the Kali Yuga and there was no way of really knowing the purity of another KV. Who could have access to another's private or sexual life? Therefore all that mattered was that a person was a KV, that he had descended from KV ancestors as delineated in the origin myth. Put another way, KV identity was "substantialized."[14] Following David Schneider's suggestive line of thought, "natural" identity, rather than castewide codes for conduct oriented toward the whole, became decisive.[15] Substantialization involves a shift away from the whole and toward the person, or groups conceived on the model of the person. It situates primary identity within that person or group rather than the whole itself. The whole is a secondary system, built up from these primary persons. Rank based on interdining (and other) transactions, an aspect of code for conduct clearly related to purity and one which defines the operational whole, can no longer hold where codes for conduct can cross caste lines.

I want to draw your attention to two consequences of this substantialization, this emergence of caste as a "collective individual."[16] First non-vegetarian castes in the non-Brahman movement immediately challenged vegetarian Vēḷāḷar pretences to preeminence. Articles appeared in non-Brahman journals pointing out that the "orthodoxy" of vegetarian Vēḷāḷars was Brahmanical and therefore misguided at best and pernicious at worst. Here we see the radical results of substantialization and the shift away from a structural universe encompassed by Brahmanical concepts. Vegetarian Vēḷāḷars could no longer appeal on the basis of a universally accepted hierarchy and relative purity (through transactional rank); rather if membership is based not so much on a caste code for conduct as on natural identity, then the struggle for control and power among castes is one between separate, independent units, each with an inviolable substance (pluralism).

The second consequence has to do with a recent KV wedding. An orthodox KV in Madras City did not invite a KV leader who had publicly eaten with lower castes, on the ground that the KV leader could not then eat in an orthodox house. Invoking interdining sanctions is of course the traditional way of drawing distinctions of relative purity. But in this case, the response of other KVs was unusual. They communicated to the orthodox man that while they might attend the wedding, they certainly would not eat at his house since he was snubbing an important KV who represented the caste to the outside world. Here interdining retained significance as a crucial symbol of rank, but with precisely *inverted* meaning: interdining restrictions were used to validate an individual code for conduct rather than enforce and sanction a castewide code for conduct. Traditionally one should eat only with persons of equivalent purity (substance and code); here KVs were refusing to eat with such a man. The orthodox KV was being told that caste purity was not related to conduct, that the KV leader was as pure as anyone in the caste despite his eating with lower castes. This is not an idiosyncratic event, but has had profound impact on KVs as a whole. The "other" ("nonorthodox") KVs, also important caste and political leaders, were publicly extending the implications of the resolution on interdistrict marriage, for if code is separated from caste membership in one arena it might as well be separate in all arenas.

As a final twist, note the response of the orthodox KV who, faced with these threats of food boycott, capitulated and invited the KV leader. In a caste context, orthodoxy is dictated by the caste as a unit, so if the caste decides to sanction individual deviance, paradoxically the orthodox man must go along since he has no cultural base for holding out as an individual.

What does this summary amount to in terms of the demarcation of levels of change? The descriptive backdrop is crucial to any analysis of the position of KVs and other vegetarian Vēḷāḷars with respect to Brahman and upper non-Brahman relationships, Madras City urbanization, and the development of the non-Brahman movement. The processual flow is quite complex. First I chronicled a change in the KV unit of endogamy from local, ranked, bilateral kindreds[17] to, at the largest remove, all those calling themselves KVs. At the same time, the KV concept of purity and blood retained significance but with altered meanings, since the relevant distinction is no longer transactionally validated rank in one locality but attributional rank in the non-Brahman movement and throughout the state. Other symbols (such as interdining) also continue but with different significations.

Are these processes system-maintaining or system-changing? Caste obviously continues in South India; it is still deemed important to be a

KV, so we can say that these processes indicate caste adaptiveness. But if we move to the structural level, this seeming adaptiveness must be evaluated as either a transformation within caste as a system or as the cutting wedge destroying it. Or we must distinguish the persistence of named groups called "castes" from the persistence of the caste system. If we accept as a first approximation that the caste system involves a stress on a relational universe of structure (interdependence) rather than independence (meaning and substance inhering in each unit) and therefore an emphasis on transactional rather than attributional rank, then these processes have vital implications for caste as a system. Caste is substantialized in terms of the attribute of natural identity while that aspect of purity/blood relating to transactions and castewide codes for conduct is devalued (except of course for codes directly related to natural identity transmission—that is, marriage). Once this is accomplished, castes can compete as equivalent "ethnic groups," each claiming a unique natural identity and substance, and we see nonvegetarian castes challenging vegetarian Vēḷāḷars.

Edmund Leach has stated that competition among "like groups of *different caste*" defies caste principles. Such competition has to do with the ideology of the competing units rather than with attempts at mobility per se. Where that ideology is holistic, mobility implies, through transactional rearrangements, a reordering of all elements of the whole. Only where castes are substantialized does caste competition approach a Western view of competition. Once caste is defined by natural identity, the importance of caste members conforming to a castewide code for conduct diminishes—what one man does need no longer affect his caste fellows (in certain arenas)—and so the scope of individual choice is widened and may even be sanctioned as we have seen by the traditional method of invoking interdining prohibitions. And these fundamental shifts occur not through the obliteration or negation of the symbols of caste but precisely through complex processes of symbolic shifts and operations leading from one structure to another. It is this structure level that enables us to see the particular KV shift in units of endogamy not simply in transformational terms, which need not necessarily affect the whole, but as having more basic implications.

I have followed Dumont[18] in seeing the two relevant structures (castes and substantialized castes) in hierarchical versus egalitarian terms and wish to add one point. It is striking that while attempts have been made to equate castism and racism, only Harold Gould[19] has stressed similarities between castes and ethnic groups. Substantialized castes (based on ancestral blood and territory) show important ideological similarities to Western ethnic groups (based also on blood and territory). In each culture, ethnicity is downgraded, either as something to be eradicated from an egalitarian, individualistic universe or as something not to be admitted in a hierarchical, holistic universe. For this reason, if for no other, the ethnicization of caste seems a constructive way of opening the flux of change to analysis.[20]

As castes are substantialized, as blood purity becomes primarily a matter of natural identity, the ideological floodgates open. Caste blocs resemble ethnic groups; codes for conduct cross caste lines, allowing the possibility of a unitary code (Dravidian cultural nationalism) or diverse codes (voluntary associations and, most importantly, class alliances). This profound ideological shift goes along with the emergence of state capitalism in contemporary India and suggests a holistic understanding of Indian life. Such an analysis remains to be done, but a hint of some directions is possible. In Madras City, urban untouchables are *excluded* from ethnicization; thus while consistent transactions among urban castes are breaking down, they are carefully maintained vis-à-vis untouchables. And correspondingly, the concept of a separate "untouchable race" is emerging among upper-caste city dwellers. So the caste-to-substantialized-caste vector ideologically allows cultural nationalism, racism, ethnicity, and class consciousness—in short, the essential elements of modern ideological conflicts.

This understanding of caste ethnicization (the shift from caste as a religious system to castes as substantialized, competing units) suggests a solution to a puzzling aspect of recent changes mentioned by many authors. Given modernization, commensality seems relaxed, although marriage alliance patterns are still bounded by caste. Even when formerly distinct subcastes now marry, overall caste boundaries are still assiduously kept up. Rules of commensality have to do with castewide codes for conduct whereas marriage has to do with the transmission of "natural identity." Therefore we might expect that where castes become substantialized, certain castewide codes for conduct are devalued but the heritability of natural identity assumes new significance.

Other Date Relative to the Levels of Change

Having briefly illustrated the significance of description, process, and structure in understanding change, let me elaborate these levels in terms of other South Indian data. At the descriptive level, data on land and labor are critical. The significance of population increases and the creation of ownership along with land revenue levies by the British are discussed by Dharma Kumar.[21] While she avoids final statements, work of this order invites future research and detailed comments. Also crucial were such developments as the growth of a mercantile economy, changing relationships between moneylenders and peasant farmers, and the extension of cash crops tied to trade within the British imperialist sphere. These changes can be followed in postindependence times. We note differential receptivity to economic development given caste and local relations.[22] The penetration of capital to villages continues as payments tend to be in money rather than in kind, and there are important legal and social shifts in land held as *panku* ("original" rights over the land) or *maniyam* (land given to village service castes). Finally the development of new cultivation techniques is relevant. The construction of electric pumps, the replacement with artificial fertilizers for animal manure and "green" manure, and the introduction of new seed types presaging a "green revolution" at least in some areas[23] can be seen in South Indian villages.

The growth of Madras City has implications for change throughout South India. First as a governmental and later as an educational and industrial center, Madras has been a magnet attracting reformers throughout the south. Especially important are the development of a legal network, the creation of electoral procedures (first with a property qualification, then universal suffrage) and political parties and movements, and finally the dissemination of British ideas of education including awareness of empiricist and classical liberal philosophical ideas, the "scientific" worldview, and English literature.

At the same time, caste and traditional institutions persist in neighborhood organizations of Madras as well as Bangalore.[24] These institutions concern themselves with the arts[25] and religious activities and, as caste associations, press for a share of the new occupations, university seats, and bureaucratic positions. And rural-urban networks ramify, maintaining a sense of contact with the land and bringing villagers in touch with new lifestyles.

Industry has developed in Madras City, especially after independence, leading to the construction of industrial estates, a huge oil refinery, and the emergence of industrialists as an economic and social category. Industrial growth has stimulated entrepreneurial activities[26] and shopkeeping[27] as well. But we must guard against an optimistic picture of incremental economic development. The conditions of urban untouchables and lower castes in general seems grim. There are few opportunities for schooling, much unemployment, and an increase of tin and mud hut urban slums.[28]

While developments in agriculture, urbanization, and industrialization are all-India in scope, another widespread phenomenon in modern India—anti-Brahmanism—reached an apex in South India.[29] The development of the Justice Party, DK, and DMK culminates with the present DMK rule in Tamilnadu State.[30] Also backward castes became politicized and formed caste or caste-cluster parties (Tamilnad Toilers, Forward Block, and Commonweal). The influence of non-Brahman leaders in literature, plays (especially *Vellaikkaran* by C. N. Annadorai), and the cinema (especially *Parasakti* by Mu Karunanidhi) significantly shaped caste and social reform attitudes.

Analysts of one or another aspect of this total picture have elaborated explicit processes to handle the complexity. K. Gough speaks of changing subsistence base relations and changing relations with a wider society.[31] It seems rather that each "interpenetrates" the other, although that bald assertion does not solve the problem of just how. However, most authors describe processes that are most relevant to one or the other of these divisions and I shall follow them here.

Within villages and small multivillage foci, there is a shift from long-term agricultural and service jajmani relations to relations of contract involving only the parties to the agreement.[32] This process has ramifications beyond the economic; in fact, one might say that only with contractual relations penetrating agricultural villages does an economic system appear as an autonomous element in local thinking. The previous arrangement located economic relations within the ideology of caste. The implications are strikingly and controversially drawn by T. Scarlett Epstein when she argues that, given traditional agricultural and service relations, redistribution was more equitable in lean years and only in good years did a clear consumption difference emerge between castes.[33] Now we find contractual relations in many villages leading to layoffs and general underemployment for landless agricultural workers in lean years rather than an attempt to ration paddy equitably. Or new kinds of economic calculations (personal maximization in a monetized system) supersede the idea of labor being directed toward a local whole.

New contractual relations (not including those traditional relations of traders and artisan castes), an increase in extravillage economic transactions, and greater absentee landownership imply different social relations, most obviously between dominant peasant landowners and landless agricultural workers. Gough offers a dramatic example of a Kallan of a different village bloodying a Brahman's head with a staff and the Brahman's inability to retaliate lest the Paḷḷan Adi-Dravidas of his own village join the other side.[34] I have elsewhere[35] presented evidence that Adi-Dravidas are playing off KVs against other upper non-Brahmans to their own (small) advantage and, in villages with occupational diversification and rural industry, these low-case workers are beginning to take an independent political stand.

But the question remains: To what extent are these conflicts limited to politics and economics and to what extent do they challenge the caste hierarchy directly in its ideological forms in terms of transactions and the domain of purity/impurity? Transactionally, Adi-Dravidas have attempted equivalence. Epstein reports that in the Mysore village of Wangala, untouchables tried to hold a drama in which an untouchable actor sits on a throne in the presence of an upper-caste audience (that is, inverting traditional sitting arrangements).[36] Upper-caste men boycotted the performance and eventually untouchables capitulated and paid a fine. And in the neighboring village of Dalena, she writes that untouchables no longer performed ritual functions for other castes owing to a general breakdown in hereditary relations between peasants and untouchables.[37]

Gough, writing of a Kerala village, says that since 1964, untouchables "have ceased to perform any of their religious festivals."[38] And in 1967, they claimed equal rights in the village goddess temple, taking the case to local government officials. However, Nāyars padlocked the temple and the untouchables did not storm it, so the issue was a standoff. Edward Harper states that untouchable Holerus in a Mysore village have

> given up beef consumption, refused to move dead cattle for Haviks [Brahmans], have refused to supply wood for Havik funeral pyres, and are now attempting to refuse to clean Havik cattle sheds. . . . In sum, Holerus appear to be trying to make a radical change by substituting the criteria of achievement, a principle associated with an open class system, for that of heredity, a principle associated with a Hindu caste system. They are joining with other like-minded low rank groups to accomplish this end, groups with whom they previously competed for social position. Although my evidence on this is insufficient I suggest that their desires for upward mobility are oriented towards an idealized and generalized Indian middle class culture.[39]

Of these significant changes. Dumont writes:" In the caste system profession is linked to status only by its religious aspects. . . . At most it is likely that Jajmani has become restricted to properly religious and personal services and has let escape some professions which it covered previously."[40] The preceding statements suggest that something drastic is changing, at least in some villages, where even personal and religious service may "escape." There are examples of untouchables no longer removing dead cattle, of washermen no longer washing menstrual clothes, of barbers no longer cutting hair or nails or doing services during death rites. In many of these changes, upper castes must do at least some of these tasks themselves or hire anyone available. Often this implies a purity breakdown since available help is of much lower rank than traditional service help (in one KV case, the shift is from a middle-rank caste to a tribal group). Consider the use of non-Brahman priests by some upper-caste members convinced by Dravidian ideology. Many urban KVs and some rural KVs have KV leaders, not Brahmans, officiate at weddings and other rituals. To the extent that each caste itself does all or most tasks, religious, personal, or other, the very basis of caste hierarchy (that is, interdependence) is challenged. Dumont then poses a basic question: Given modernization, can we simply see a process where caste shunts aside unnecessary aspects to emerge "purified" or are aspects basic to caste itself modified? The data on occupational diversification and religious challenge are fundamental seen in this light.

There is another aspect of religious change in some South Indian villages—the ending of annual or cyclical (typically every twelve years) village goddess festivals.[41] Given transactional challenges and claims of equivalence by lower castes, locally dominant castes (who must initiate the village goddess festival) may call the whole thing off rather than risk losing a confrontation. But other (verbal) reports indicate that these festivals are flourishing in Tirunelveli and elsewhere. This seems a crucial aspect of change to follow up since it raises a number of questions already mentioned. What are the relational aspects of local hierarchies that encourage or discourage village goddess festivals? Does abandoning village goddess festivals have larger implications for village organization in terms of other religious activities such as the use of Brahmans as priests? Do village goddess festivals continue in new forms that confront hierarchical ideologies?[42]

It is no accident that Gough and Harper stress a processual shift from caste to class since this theme is picked up by other authors, especially those writing of recent change in Tanjavur.[43] These writers indicate a divergence of caste hierarchy and class stratification in certain South Indian contexts. Given occupational diversification, the same person may be a "landowner and a manual worker, a tenant and an agricultural laborer."[44] For Béteille, the caste hierarchy is moving toward westernization and secularization, and the class system is widening scope due to the marketability of land and a cash economy. Harper suggests that untouchable Holerus are trying to change the principles of rank from ascription (heredity) to achievement, a caste-to-class movement.

These are provocative statements, but caution is needed. The model of the caste system used by these authors is wanting; they are too ready to accept an a priori sociological scheme relegating caste to one end of the social stratification continuum as "frozen" class. Béteille sees caste through Weberian lenses in terms of distinctive lifestyles ("status groups") but does not come to grips with caste culture or hierarchy as a whole. Counterposing Dumont and Béteille is helpful here. Dumont develops a structural view of caste ideology stressing the encompassing nature of purity/impurity and the encompassed domain of power (politics and economics). So, for Dumont, the system-maintaining versus system-challenging question is this: To what extent is this encompassing-encompassed relation being inverted? Class considerations may still be encompassed by the ideology of caste. Caste-to-class analysis for the most part avoids this problem by not concentrating on the symbolic operations necessary to move from caste hierarchy to class stratification. In fact, one might argue that relative divergencies between caste hierarchy and the distribution of power and relations to the land have periodically developed throughout South Indian history. If the caste-class vector is to be convincing, we need more evidence of the symbolic operations at the heart of the process. A caste-to-class shift ignores the concomitant rise of ethnicity, racism, and cultural nationalism in South India. Indianists are thus recapitulating the errors of earlier students of American society who, because of their own "liberal" ideology, did not seriously analyze American ethnicity or black cultural nationalism. The model of caste substantialization offers a way of seeing an entire ideological field, including the continuation of caste, ethnic-like caste blocs, racism toward untouchables, cultural nationalism, and class ties. The analytic problem then becomes this: How do persons or groups pick and choose among these alternatives, and how, having made a choice, do they relate to other persons and groups? In such a framework, class is still critically important, and ethnicity, racism, and cultural nationalism are ways of blunting class consciousness. Thus the complex realities of South Indian ideological struggles are not artificially simplified.

Another way to consider occupational diversification and caste change is to focus on networks. I mentioned a change in KV marriage alliance networks that raises the issue of structural change, but networks of all kinds are changing in South India with differing implications. Again we are guided by a consideration of the structural implications of network change, since the caste system can accommodate differing levels of segmentation and changes in these levels within its ideology. So the structural form of segmentation is critical. A. M. Klausen, writing of a fishing village in Kerala, notes a typical network change;

> Thus if a low-caste person wants to improve his socioeconomic position, he very often does so by breaking off his connection with his native home village and his caste kindred. He may get a job in a city-milieu, and very often get a new occupation not represented in the traditional caste system. If he succeeds in this he will enter a milieu where representatives of many castes live side by side in a new employment situation and where caste attachment therefore will be subordinate.[45]

Unfortunately there are scant comprehensive data on networks since little research has been oriented toward this end. I have completed extensive friendship sociograms of KVs varying in age, education, occupation, and residence. There are clear shifts among the young and educated away from same or adjacent caste friends. Close friends may now include members of service castes, a very few Adi-Dravidas, and even tribals. The magnitude of this is indicated by the remarkable fact that around 1950 when urban KV members of the non-Brahman movement gathered to discuss political affairs on one KV's porch, the only other persons allowed on that porch were Brahmans! These KVs felt they could intimately associate with no other caste despite allegiance to the Dravidian ideology. Also on-the-job networks have not been studied. My own data from one fire station in the Madras port indicate that the single KV fireman there maintains a studied aloofness from his compatriots, always waiting for them to initiate contact.[46]

Network change, especially across caste, may involve greater scope for individual choice. A. Aiyappan describes this process in a Malabar village:

> I have suggested . . . that the little community of Mayur is getting atomized, that the pressure of want makes individuals think more about themselves and less about others and give up several traditional rites and ceremonial gifts. Also at the same time I have shown examples of the way in which the villagers are trying to take advantage of the opportunities for co-operation and education. A new sense of equality is slowly growing, and the younger generation is building a slender bridge across the separatism of caste.[47]

Epstein elaborates for a Mysore village:

> Greater individualism has entered Dalena's social system since the diversification of its economy. The multifarious economic changes that have taken place in Dalena since irrigation reached the area are responsible for the changes in the political and social system. The diversification of Dalena's economy widened the economic horizon of Dalena villagers and consequently also their political horizon. They now have so many different economic links with the regional economy that their political attitude and social relations have changed. . . . As the range of [economic] relations increases, the degree of dependence upon neighbors and contemporaries diminishes. Thus as Dalena men increase the range of their economic relations, the dependence between farmers and their agricultural laborers decreased and consequently the hereditary economic relations between Peasants, Masters, and Untouchable clients disappeared.[48]

One symbolic operation of substantialization needed for an emergent individualism was discussed in the KV example given above. And it should be clear that caste substantialization paves the way for increased individualism, allowing greater personal choice in codes for conduct. Of course, as Karl Marx long ago pointed out, this ideological individualism (this sense of independence) becomes prevalent just as the interrelations of society reach a higher stage of development.

A consideration of networks leads us to a discussion of caste change in the wider society. The pioneering research techniques and theories of Milton Singer will serve as a basis for noting these processes. Singer has studied urban sects, the great tradition in Madras City, and South Indian industrialists—throughout emphasizing the adaptiveness of caste and Hinduism. For Singer, adaptiveness is enhanced by the processes of "compartmentalization" and "vicarious ritualization." Both reduce conflicts between traditional and modern arenas. Compartmentalization achieves this by separating the conduct and norms of work and residence; vicarious ritualization achieves it by delegating responsibility for ritual observances to domestic priests and other family members. Thus the Indian tradition can adapt to change, and the following observation by Joan Mencher seems a reasonable possibility: "The individuals who are most eager to take advantage of certain aspects of modernization are often the most vociferous and insisting on the maintenance of 'purity' of caste and family."[49]

These processes confront all the major issues. Singer and Mencher imply that Hinduism and caste, given change, can continue. However, one implication of compartmentalization as noted above is that it changes the nature of orthopraxy since a vegetarian who eats meat at the office should not then eat in his own house. It should be observed that nine of Singer's nineteen "compartmentalized" industrialists are Brahmans. To what extent is this a Brahman or an industrialist response to change? In any event, Singer raises the central issue of what need change in caste and what not. The processes he describes have much in common with Dumont's separation of religious status and power and will certainly stimulate future analysis.

Incidentally, KV urban compartmentalization takes a different form. Rather than dichotomize home and place of work, KVs separate their neighborhood from the rest of the city. What happens in these neighborhoods (on the street, in the temples, during temple processions) is as important as home life. The reason for this Brahman-KV difference in compartmentalization is clear following the earlier argument. Brahmans are secure as Brahmans since "Brahman" has meaning to all, but KVs are not widely known as a caste ranked between Brahmans and other upper non-Brahmans. Therefore KVs must be primarily concerned with maintaining rank in urban localities given changes of residence and the constant influx of people who must learn who KVs are. Thus the neighborhood becomes the focal arena of urban KV transactional rank. These divergent forms of compartmentalization point to a basic methodological premise: analysis must start with caste structure, with the relational position of castes. Following this, it makes no sense to generalize one form of compartmentalization for all castes or even to assume that all castes will compartmentalize in some fashion.

Compartmentalization occurs both in space and as a cognitive process. Spatially, we can talk of home versus office, neighborhood versus rest of city. Cognitively, compartmentalization is more elusive since neither compartment is the same as it was before compartmentalization (for example, changes in ideas of household purity to accommodate office meat-eaters). In fact, I see attempts at compartmentalization, attempts to avoid conflict by separating arenas of conflict, as ultimately futile. Compartmentalization only postpones, or changes the nature of, basically opposed views. Thus compartmentalization is important not so much as an avoidance technique but as a marker of fundamental tensions.

Singer's discussion of the continuation of the joint family in modern industry follows his concern for adaptive strategies. There are parallels between joint family management and business management that favor joint family continuity since the joint family can incorporate both the old and the new elements of Indian life. On the other hand, Epstein[50] indicates that rural joint families may break down through partitioning as a result of conversion to a cash economy. As was suggested by the KV example, however, joint family units may persist while other aspects of kinship are undergoing fundamental change. Singer is careful to point to joint family changes as well as continuity, but one overlooked aspect of the joint family is a shift in stress from a unit of transactionally pure equivalents (culturally seen in purity terms) to one based upon the achievement of family members with respect to such things as university posts, other prestigious jobs, and housing. In other words, the significance of joint family persistence is an open topic.[51]

Singer's concern with the adaptiveness of Hindu society led him to an important study of bhajanas (multicaste, devotional singing and worship groups) in Madras City.[52] For him, the Rādha-Krishna bhajanas reduced tensions among castes (especially Brahmans and non-Brahmans) and among linguistic groups. This reduction[53] is all the more significant in the light of the Dravidian movement and non-Brahmanism. In fact, one might see bhajanas as a subset of all modern bhakti forms, keeping in mind that the bhakti stresses individual salvation and is thus well suited to the substantialization of caste and the increasing individual choice of caste members. Urban bhajanas (including the increasingly popular Ayyappan bhajanas among Madras City workers) are but one instance of changes in worship. Gough suggests the following broad range for Nāyars:

> Some Nāyars who still hold their traditional beliefs in ancestral spirits and deities deliberately "purged" their rites of non-Sanskritic elements in order to gain respectability. Others have changed both rites and beliefs to a modified form of the Brahmanical religion even while they are busy repudiating the religious authority of the Brahman. Yet others, whose

numbers are probably increasing, are repudiating both Brahmanical and non-Sanskritic religions in their orthodox forms. Instead, they work out for themselves a more or less agnostic world view with humanitarian ideals, in which ceremonies, if they figure at all, figure only as acts of piety towards respected persons.[54]

Conversion to Christianity is also occurring among low castes for the most part, but also among some upper castes, and Klausen discusses Catholicism and modernization at length.

One other process must be delineated since M. N. Srinivas described sanskritization and westernization as important Indian adaptive mechanisms. Two additional possibilities are significant for South India: tamilization and the Vaishya model.[55] Vēḷāḷars trying to validate status under the British argued that they were "Vaishyas," not "Sudras" as Brahmans claimed nor Kshatriyas as some North Indian dominant peasant castes claim. Tamilization (Tamil cultural nationalism) is more complex and has radical implications for caste as a system. It includes speech patterns,[56] the nonuse of Brahman priests, and the general acceptance of the Dravidian-North Indian dichotomy as coloring all else. Tamilization cuts across caste, and "tamilized persons" may be a distinct grouping within a single caste.

The processes outlined above focus on the same things from slightly different vantage points. The shift from jajmani to contract overlaps with a caste-to-class process and both can be studied in terms of network changes. We have noted changes in relations between peasants and landless agriculture workers, in the services performed by the barber and washerman, and in religious services (including the use of Brahman priests). The effects of these changes can be seen in altered or moribund village goddess festivals. There seems to be a tendency for each caste to do a wider range of services for itself, and the Gandhian notion of self-help may be a latent function of modernization.

Caste-to-class analysts point to increasing role contradiction (for example, a single man as landowner and factory worker) and role specificity in an emerging capitalist economy leading to class conflicts (and the breakdown of jajmani loyalties); they have also noted the effects of unemployment, education, and industrialization in fostering these conflicts.

Role specificity and role contradiction alter traditional networks. One result is a stress on fusion (network extension) rather than fission (reduction).[57] KV kindred erosion is a good illustration of the former. The KV picture is actually more complex. Rural KVs keep a semblance of kindred commitments; tradition-minded urban KVs look both ways—to their rural kindred and to alliances with tamilized KV leaders who form an interdistrict marriage alliance at the apex of the caste. But networks can also cross caste lines as KV sociograms and other evidence show. Socio-economic class, occupation, and education all now affect the scope of a person's relations. Network extension, involving intimate contact across caste, goes along with the process of greater individual choice or of generalizing formerly highly specific values. With an emphasis on substance and a deemphasis on transactional rank, a person's code for conduct need not affect the rank of his caste fellows. The development of bhakti movements, especially urban bhajana groups, is a kind of network extension designed in part to bridge the modern boundaries of Brahman–non-Brahman and linguistic groups and also to foster individual salvation.

If we move to a cultural analysis, what is implied in such processes as compartmentalization, vicarious ritualization, and tamilization is a reconstruction of the perceptual, emotional, and cognitive universe. The change in the meaning of "blood" by KV caste association meetings in the late 1920s is an example of general symbolic process. Here there is the utilization of traditional symbols in new ways or contexts such as to make possible caste substantialization in the minds of men.[58] At the caste level, this involves the ethnicization of castes, now competing as equivalents (for example, the nonvegetarian challenge to vegetarian Vēḷāḷars). There are other possibilities for substantialization, such as the imposition of *one* substance for all castes. Dumont provides an apt example:

> This is how the conservative circles of this very traditionalist region [Madras State] responded to the movement and measures aimed to grant the Untouchables the right to enter the Brahmanic temples: there was at first resistance against the Gandhist movement, but the reform was more or less generally imposed, and laws ("Temple Entry Acts") were passed in various states (in Madras in 1947). Then a sort of puritan reaction by the vegetarians established itself in Madras, which flourished after Independence; prohibition on sacrificing animals in the immediate vicinity of the great temples, as the meat eating castes were wont to do; prohibition by certain municipalities (Dindigul) on butchering, even by Muslims; finally in September 1950 the vote by the Madras Assembly (the state was not yet divided between Tamils and Telegu-speaking people) prohibiting by law animal sacrifices in general (and so even in the private worship of a locality, a caste of kinship groups). As the majority of the population was given to such sacrifices, one cannot see either how such a law can really be applied, or how it could have been adopted if democracy had functioned normally. But the reason for all these measures is clear; from the moment the Untouchables enter the temple, the purity of the high castes and their very idea of worship and god is jeopardized: so the only solution is the forcible reform of the Untouchables, so that they would cease to be abettors of impurity. The aim is even exceeded, and there is a tendency to impose vegetarianism on everybody. This is a con-

> siderable event: the traditional hierarchical tolerance gives way to a modern mentality, and this is a totalitarian mentality: hierarchical structure is replaced by a single, rigid substance. The fact is extremely significant: egalitarianism, leaving the limited zone in which it is well tolerated, causes a profound modification and brings the threat of religious totalitarianism.[59]

Here vegetarianism becomes an attribute for all castes. As such, it is a change in the opposite direction of the changes noted for the symbol "blood," for it extends one form across caste lines to embrace all castes. Thus, by using the symbols of South Indian culture, we can move away from castes in either of two directions: toward the individual and pluralism or toward totalitarianism. "Totalitarian" is a strong term and refers specifically to the attempted imposition of vegetarianism. The emergence of Tamil cultural nationalism is basically different, without any necessary totalitarian implications. In either case, one or a number of substances may emerge. This discussion of blood and vegetarianism, like the KV interdining case given above, indicates how symbolic persistence from the point of view of particular elements becomes structural replacement once these symbols take on altered meanings in new relations. The argument is that particular symbols derive meaning from and change their meaning according to structures of which they are elements.[60] Blood purity for KVs is derived from both substance and code; in the late 1920s, KVs emphasized substance rather than code. We are really talking here of a shift in ideology (or symbolic structure) from caste hierarchy to a kind of ethnicity. Blood is a critical symbol in such a shift.

We now have a provisional way to broach the original question of caste demise or caste adaptiveness. Processes which enhance caste substantialization challenge the traditional idea of caste.

To the extent that castes perform polluting, religious, and personal tasks formerly delegated to others; to the extent that transactions do not have castewide implications but are more a matter of personal (or class, or ethnic) choice which does not jeopardize caste standing; and to the extent that the ideology of purity/impurity is being redefined and limited, caste as a system is no longer viable and we must therefore look to non-caste structures. This development occurs despite (more precisely, because of) the persistence of concrete symbols of Indian culture owing to changed meanings of these symbols. Basic change in the forms in which the world is given to man occurs in part through antecedent forms already laden with emotive, perceptual, and cognitive significance.

But this merely deepens, extends, and opens basic problems. The operative phrase "to the extent that" is purposefully vague since we know so little about the scope and depth of South Indian change. What I have conjectured should not be taken to imply that all South India is pell-mell undergoing the most basic changes. Rather, *if* these changes become pervasive we must recognize the replacement of one structure by another and account for it. A more realistic picture, and one far more difficult to say anything about, is that distinct elements stand in different relations as a result of recent change. Thus we must control for rural and urban;[61] for region, village, and state, for educated and uneducated, for those practicing traditional occupations and those involved in new occupations; for the rural agnostic and the city "fundamentalist"; and so on. The question then becomes thus: How does a South Indian orient himself in these "multiple worlds?"[62] How does a universe so divided, layered, interconnected, and disconnected make sense to him? Compartmentalization deals with only two spheres, but even there some continuity must pervade both. We have seen how a change in the meaning of blood allowed a basic kinship change and incipient ethnicization; how interdining restrictions were used to validate an individual code for conduct; how vegetarianism was extended to become a totalitarian substance. But these changes only suggest the need for an extended analysis.

Indication for Future Research

If the preceding breakdown and reintegration of levels of change has utility, then certain directions for future research are indicated beyond the usual "we need more of everything." This analysis suggests a concentration on transformations within a structure and on the replacement of one structure by another. Processes must be delineated in terms of their implication for system maintenance or system change.

First we need bolder structural theories defining benchmarks. Students of India are fortunate in having the high-level groundwork laid by Dumont and Marriott, both demarcating caste and noncaste structures. But while holism/individualism, purity/impurity, Brahmanical model/kingly model/merchant model, transactional rank/attributional rank are basic, their content still needs to be filled in for South India. Burton Stein and I[63] indicate historical and contemporary Brahman-peasant alliances, but the significance of these alliances (for example, the import of vegetarianism among many Vēḷāḷar castes) for the separation of Brahmanical and kingly functions needs more research. Also the right/left[64] separation seems to relate to Brahmanical and kingly model, right castes stressing purity and left castes dominance. Right/left and vegetarian Vēḷāḷar considerations are interconnected, for it appears that vegetarian Vēḷāḷars were above a right/left split and so the split demarcates dominant castes not overly concerned with orthopraxy. The relations of merchant and trader castes to agricultural hierarchies remains problematical. Merchant Seṭṭiyārs are an obvious, untapped focus of study. Since the contractual emphasis of the merchant model is most relevant to state capitalism, perhaps supplying a traditional frame for recent changes, this gap is all the more regrettable.

These research suggestions all entail a much closer look at local rank, at the parameters of transaction, and at the ramifications of purity considerations in concrete normative expressions. In short, if we look for consistency at the level of relations rather than elements, then these relations (not elements per se) must serve as benchmarks and any serious discussion of relations involves a structural model of caste at a given point in time. These benchmarks involve elaboration of regional differences in local structures. Examination of the distinctions among the structural positions of Kavuntars in Coimbatore, Vēḷāḷars in Chingleput, Brahman landowners in Tanjavur, and Maravars, Tēvars, and Akamuṭiyars (also Kaḷḷars) in Ramnad will go a long way toward explaining the different paths of change of these castes and different Adi-Dravida and service caste strategies in these regions.[65] Critical transformations across space (region and subregional hierarchies) must first be outlined before we can gauge the significance of processes through time.

An additional aspect of benchmark construction is relevant: the organization of traditional towns. The significance of recent urbanization is all too often seen against a rural image of caste hierarchy, yet the existence of traditional temple and administrative centers is documented throughout South Indian history and it is still possible to do fruitful research on places like Kancheepuram and Madurai. Such studies might tell us the extent to which it was (and might still be) possible to organize large numbers within a traditional caste system, a critical question.

Benchmarks apart, studies of change need innovative research designs to comprehend process and the replacement of one structure by another. If the understanding of process is located at the level of relations rather than elements, then shifts in intracaste and intercaste relations and in the ideology of rank are an obvious study. Let me recapitulate. Joan Mencher suggests that an excessive concern with orthodoxy by some south Indians may go along with an active interest in modernization, and my data suggest that in one cluster of villages caste orthodoxy forces "withdrawal" from modernizing change. Are we to see these positions as blatant contradictions? Before doing so, I would suggest an exploration of the forms and significance of orthodoxy for the units under analysis. Orthodoxy should not be taken as a variable *in itself* (unless it emerges as a substance; for example, vegetarianism), but rather it may have different significance in different local hierarchies (where there are a number of dominant castes, for example, or where left/right distinctions still have relevance or where Brahmans are also landowners).

Take another example. K. Gough and I suggest that village goddess festivals are not being performed in certain villages involved in strain-producing change. Yet there is evidence that in some parts of South India (also undergoing change), village goddess festivals are enjoying a resurgence of popularity. Again I would venture that the generalization "village strain and change cause village goddess festivals to be abandoned" commits a fallacy of misplaced concreteness. To understand the abandonment of village goddess festivals in KV villages, we must *start* with the relational position of KVs between Brahmans and other upper non-Brahmans, and this structural position need not hold for other dominant peasant castes.

Processual research then starts with the structure of caste and notes changes in the transactional bases of rank and in the symbols of hierarchy. The utility of network analysis methods is obvious here. The shift from local kindreds to interdistrict alliances is a change in the network of marriageable KVs (previously defined in interdining transactions) and in the ideology determining network boundaries (from an emphasis on transactional purity considerations to a stress on secular attributes and substance).

Once relations are central to analysis, the persistence of symbolic elements with altered significations in different structures allows us to move to the core of change, for we perceive how the man in caste can accommodate modernization while not simply abandoning his cultural universe.

These methodological and programmatic suggestions must apply to concrete research, and there are critical areas of South Indian change central to these concerns. First regional spread is essential so that relational differences in local hierarchies can be developed. Everywhere, however, the changing options of Brahmans[66] and Adi-Dravidas provide clues to structural change since to the extent that the top and bottom ranks most reflect purity considerations, we are directly confronting the encompassing/encompassed distinction.

New sects, some challenging caste rank, are developing in South India. The Muslim-Hindu syncretism of Sai Baba, the intercaste commensality of Rādha-Krishna bhajanas, and the working-class, possession-oriented, Ayyappan bhajanas—all are obvious research choices. In addition to Bishop Diehl's work,[67] there are as yet unpublished studies of Christianity in Tirunelveli that should throw light on Christian ideology in caste hierarchy. The arts are another area of change. The use of the cinema and plays for non-Brahman propaganda is well known, but close analysis of the content of presentation of non-Brahman concepts remains to be done. Less known are debates between orthodox artists and artists closely linked to South Indian cultural nationalism on musical and dance forms.

City life is largely unanalyzed. The relation of new professions to caste life, caste in urban neighborhoods, the nature of urban rank, and rural-urban relations have only been broached.

Finally the effects of British imperialism are underplayed. The influence of British rule on taxation, on bringing peasants into wider supranational markets and law courts, on the creation of local governments, and on the development of state capitalism—all need further study.[68] Most significantly, we know little about the South Indian colonial mentality fostered by the dispersion of British education and values and by forcible subjugation.

Conclusion

The complexity of South Indian life should be apparent. While there is a general shift away from jajmani to contract, a cash economy, industry, and state capitalism, not all South Indians are equally affected. Castewide transactions are diminishing in scope, but they are kept up in some villages by all castes and by all urban castes toward untouchables. Regional ethnic-like caste blocs, voluntary associations, political parties, and class links all contribute to a person's sense of identity. The non-Brahman movement, now a cultural nationalist movement, has affected all Tamilians through mass media.

In this welter of possibilities, we must first organize and describe the range and divergence of ideological stances and see how particular persons and groups work through this range. The total range is an "ideological field," the universe in which people think but which they do not think about. To describe that field for South India, I emphasized a shift in the meaning of blood—from blood purity as both heritable substance and code for conduct to blood purity as essentially a matter of the transmission of ancestral blood. This shift frees codes (except marriage rules) from caste constraints. This shift in the symbol, blood, is seen as basic to the development of ethnicity, racism, cultural nationalism, and class alliances.

Once blood purity is not a matter of a wide range of intercaste codes for conduct, we note the movement from holism to individualism, from transactional rank to attributional rank, as persons act on a greater freedom of choice in codes for conduct. Personal freedom of choice means that castes can no longer be ranked on the basis of asymmetric transactions binding upon all caste members. As castes begin to organize around regional ethnic-like caste blocs, the interdependence of castes in a local whole is superseded by the relative independence of caste blocs: caste members can now take on occupations traditionally assigned to other castes. This holds even in villages where, given labor shortages or high labor casts, upper-caste members are beginning to do formerly proscribed work.

An understanding of changing caste culture in terms of a South Indian ideological field allows us to situate the data accumulated on recent South Indian change. Various options are given meaning by reference to the overall South Indian ideological field. In the same caste, we find people clinging to a transactional universe, caste leaders regularly violating these caste codes for conduct, and other members forsaking the caste for DMK or Communist Party affiliation. It is no wonder that caste gatherings are settings for harsh words and, occasionally, physical fighting. I see future analysis of caste change delineating far more carefully the nature of such disputes: how people talk to and past each other.

This essay has concentrated on changes in South Indian caste ideology; other areas of change were considered only as they bear on this topic. Valuable data from other parts of India were ignored and certain aspects of South Indian change (such as caste and politics) were treated perfunctorily. The core problem was the development of techniques and theories allowing us to distinguish system maintenance from system challenge, for only then can the significance of various processes of South Indian change be assessed. Since named groups called castes and aspects of caste culture persist, does this imply that the caste system is facilely adapting to modernizing change (and in fact shaping it)? Or can symbols persist given structural replacement?

Both solutions are viable alternatives, and we are directed to emphasize symbolic operations linking distinct levels of analysis as seen in the KV kindred and Temple Entry Act examples. Through this emphasis, we get a sense of the cultural universe of the man in caste and the operations on that culture which allow him to remain in caste and may ultimately replace caste as a system.

In part, these formulations emerge in the writings of theorists concerned with caste change in South India, but they are couched in pseudodialectic forms. L. and S. Rudolph write of "interpenetration," and Milton Singer speaks of simultaneous persistence and change in the joint family. I have tried to make the issues more explicit by separating process and structure and by suggesting that the movement from one to the other entails a relational understanding of caste symbols.

This essay also attempts to make more explicit an important theoretical difference emerging in studies of Indian change. This difference is between an emphasis on adaptation in caste and an emphasis on dichotomizing tradition and modernity. Harold Gould has forcefully stated the issues in a recent paper,[69] following the lead of Richard Fox.[70] Fox criticized the idea that caste associations are to be seen as an adaptation of caste to modernization, preserving caste more or less intact. While Gould's analysis and mine differ somewhat, I tried to indicate here that distinguishing process and structure (at both the behavioral and cultural levels) may blunt the adaptation versus replacement controversy. To that end, I have adduced specific examples of symbolic persistence and structural replacement. Persons at different points (that is, with distinct situational logics) in the "multiple worlds" of South India retain different aspects of tradition (adaptation), but these aspects also recombine in new structures (tradition versus modernity).

The general approach of this essay can be summarized: change brings into focus the multiple world views of contemporary South Indians. These worlds may be seen in contradiction, as when transactional rank is opposed to attributional rank, fission opposed to fusion, substantialization opposed to hierarchy. Contradictions generate tensions in particular arenas (for example, orthodox KVs insist on transactional rank in determining connubium, KV reformers urge attributional rank based on the "natural" identity of all KVs to widen alliance possibilities). Persons become aware of, and fight out, these contradictions in terms of symbols which bridge both halves of the contradiction by altering stress (for example, KV blood).

NOTES

1. David M. Schneider, *American Kinship: A Cultural Account* (Englewood Cliffs, N.J.: Prentice-Hall, 1969).
2. See especially J. Silverberg (ed.), *Social Mobility in the Caste System in India*, Supplement III of *Comparative Studies in History and Society* (The Hague: Mouton, 1968); and M. N. Srinivas, "Mobility in the Caste System," in *Structure and Change in Indian Society*, eds. Milton Singer and Bernard S. Cohn (Chicago: Aldine, 1968).
3. Louis Dumont, *Homo Hierarchicus: An Essay on the Caste System* (Chicago: University of Chicago Press, 1970), pp. 229–230.
4. M. Singer, "The Indian Joint Family in Modern Industry," in Singer and Cohn, *Structure and Change*, pp. 438–439.
5. Lloyd L. Rudolph and Susanne H. Rudolph, *The Modernity of Tradition* (Chicago: University of Chicago Press, 1967).
6. Max Weber, *The Religion of India* (Glencoe, Ill.: Free Press, 1958).
7. M. Singer, "Cultural Values in Indian Economic Development," *Annals of the American Academy of Political and Social Science* 5 (May 1956), p. 305.
8. E. R. Leach, "Introduction," in *Aspects of Caste in South India, Ceylon, and North-West Pakistan*, ed. E. R. Leach (Cambridge: Cambridge University Press, 1960).
9. T. Scarlett Epstein, *Economic Development and Social Change in South India* (Manchester: Manchester University Press, 1962).
10. Dumont, *Homo Hierarchicus*, p. 219.
11. Keeping in mind that the more a theory risks, the greater its testability and potential significance. K. Popper, *The Logic of Scientific Discovery* (Glencoe, Ill.: Free Press, 1956).

12. S. Barnett, *The Structural Position of a South Indian Caste* (Doctoral thesis, University of Chicago, 1970); and B. Stein, "Brahman and Peasant in Early South Indian History," *Adyar Library Bulletin* 31–32 (1967–1968).
13. E. Irschick, *Politics and Social Conflict in South India* (Berkeley: University of California Press, 1969).
14. Dumont, *Homo Hierarchicus*, p. 222.
15. For an extended discussion of natural identity and codes for conduct see Schneider, *op. cit.*
16. Dumont, *Homo Hierarchicus*, p. 222.
17. I use "bilateral kindred" in Yalman's sense as a bounded group, *not* an ego-oriented network. See Nur Yalman, "The Structure of the Sinhalese Kindred: A Re-Examination of the Dravidian Terminology," *American Anthropologist* 64, no. 3 (1962).
18. Dumont, *Homo Hierarchicus*, p. 219.
19. H. Gould, "Is the Modernity-Tradition Model All Bad?" *Economic and Political Weekly* 5, no. 29–30 (Special Number, July 1970), especially p. 4. See also a passing mention in M. Marriott, "Multiple Reference in Indian Caste Systems," in Silverberg, *Social Mobility*, p. 107.
20. For an elaboration of the ideas and data of this section, see S. A. Barnett, "Blood Symbolism and Urban Kinship Networks," in *Urban Socio-Cultural Systems*, ed. L. Keiser (forthcoming).
21. D. Kumar, *Land and Caste in South India* (Cambridge: Cambridge University Press, 1965). See also J. Dupris, *Madras et le Nord du Coromandel* (Paris: Librarie d'Amérique et d'Orient,1960).
22. Epstein, *Economic Development*; J. Mencher, "A Tamil Village: Changing Socioeconomic Structure in Madras State," in *Change and Continuity in India's Villages*, ed. K. Ishwaran (New York: Columbia University Press, 1970); S. A. Barnett, "The Process of Withdrawal in a South Indian Caste," in *Entrepreneurship and the Modernization of Occupations in South Asia*, ed. M. Singer (forthcoming).
23. A. Béteille, "The Green Revolution in Tanjore," paper prepared for a July 1969 University of London (School of Oriental and African Studies, Centre of South Asian Studies) "Study Conference on Tradition in Indian Politics and Society." For data suggesting *lower* yields for various periods in certain other regions of South India, see Kumar, *Land and Caste*, p. 192; and R. Ratnam, *Agricultural Development in Madras State Prior to 1900* (Madras: New Century Bookhouse, 1966).
24. G. Woodruff, "Family Migration into Bangalore," *Economic and Political Weekly* 12 (1960). On a related subject, see N. Gist, "Selective Migration in South India," *Sociological Bulletin* 4 (1955).
25. M. Singer, "The Great Tradition in a Metropolitan Center: Madras," in *Traditional India: Structure and Change*, ed. M. Singer, vol. 71, no. 281 of *Journal of American Folklore* (1958), pp. 347–389.
26. J. J. Berna, *Industrial Entrepreneurship in Madras State* (New York: Asia Publishing House, 1960).
27. M. Mines, "Tamil Muslim Merchants in India's Industrial Development," in *Entrepreneurship and the Modernization of Occupations*, ed. M. Singer (forthcoming).
28. The Madras School of Social Work has completed a number of mimeographed studies of urban slums (and factory conditions).

29. M. R. Barnett, "Ideology, Caste, and Politics in South India," paper prepared for the 1970 American Political Science Association convention. She discusses the recent new signification of the symbol *sudra* in a political context, adding to the examples of symbolic persistence with new meanings given South Indian change.

30. There is a considerable literature on this development; for a bibliographic summary and the most comprehensive account see M. R. Barnett, "Masses and Elites: A Study of Ideology and Leadership in an Indian State" (Doctoral dissertation, University of Chicago, 1971).

31. K. Gough, "Palakkara: Social and Religious Change in Central Kērala," in Ishwaran, *Change and Continuity*, p. 155.

32. Epstein, *Economic Development*, p. 310.

33. S. Epstein, "Productive Efficiency and Customary Rewards in Rural South India," in *Themes in Economic Anthropology*, ed. R. Firth (London: Tavistock, 1967). ASA Monographs, no. 6.

34. K. Gough, "The Social Structure of a Tanjore Village," in *Village India*, ed. M. Marriott, vol. 57, no. 3, pt. 2, memoir no. 83 of *American Anthropologist* (June 1955), p. 46.

35. Barnett, "The Process of Withdrawal." See also J. Mencher, "Past and Present in an Ex-Untouchable Community of Chingleput District, Madras," paper presented to the April 1967 Wenner-Gren Conference on "The Untouchable in Contemporary India."

36. Epstein, *Economic Development*, pp. 185–189.

37. *Ibid.*, p. 309.

38. Gough, "Pālakkara," p. 164.

39. E. Harper, "Social Consequences of an 'Unsuccessful' Low Caste Movement," in Silverberg, *Social Mobility*, pp. 63–65.

40. Dumont, *Homo Hierarchicus*, p. 235.

41. Gough, "Social Structure of a Tanjore Village," p. 48; Barnett, "Process of Withdrawal."

42. S. Hanchett, "Myth and Mechanics: Two South Indian Festival Processions," paper prepared for the November 1969 American Anthropological Association meeting.

43. A. Béteille, *Caste, Class, and Power* (Berkeley: University of California Press, 1965); D. Sivertsen, *When Caste Barriers Fall* (New York: Humanities Press, 1963).

44. Béteille, *Caste, Class, and Power*, p. 187.

45. A. M. Klausen, *Kerala Fishermen and the Indo-Norwegian Pilot Project* (Oslo: Scandinavian University Books, 1969), p. 179.

46. I am suggesting that networks of differing kinds (kindred, caste, on the job, friendship) may be seen differently by South Indians. They may see one in transactional, another in attributional, terms. One might have to do with ties of blood, another with ideological agreement ("tamilization"). Marriott's idea of "multiple reference in caste" ably puts the problem, but we are still faced with the basic issue: How do men conceptualize these multiple references and how do they move from one network to another? One suggestion, developed throughout this essay, is that shifts in meanings of the same symbols might provide one vehicle for multiple reference. Given network change, the study of voluntary organizations becomes essential. We have almost no infor-

mation about Chit funds, sports clubs, "recreation" (rummy, carrom) clubs, amateur acting societies, unions.

47. A. Aiyappan, *Social Revolution in a Kerala Village* (New York: Asia Publishing House, 1965), p. 173.
48. Epstein, *Economic Development*, pp. 310, 314–315.
49. Mencher, "A Tamil Village," p. 198.
50. Epstein, *Economic Development*, p. 322.
51. One hypothesis is that joint family persistence is one class of phenomena that continue to the extent that joint families "bridge" structures.
52. M. Singer, "The Radha-Krishna Bhajanas of Madras City," in *Krishna: Myths, Rites, and Attitudes*, ed. M. Singer (Honolulu: East-West Center Press, 1966); and M. Singer, *When a Great Tradition Modernizes* (New York: Praeger, 1972).
53. For data on equivalence during bhajanas, see R. K. Venkateswaran, "Rādhā-Krishna *Bhajanas* of South India: A Phenomenological, Theological, and Philosophical Study," in Singer, *Krishna*, p. 170.
54. E. K. Gough, "Cults of the Dead Among the Nayars," in Singer, *Traditional India*, p. 270.
55. D. Mandelbaum, *Society in India* 2 (Berkeley: University of California Press, 1970), p. 460.
56. A. K. Ramanujan, "The Structure of Variation: A Study in Caste Dialects," in Singer and Cohn, *Structure and Change*.
57. How can I write of both fusion and class conflict? I am thinking of a two-stage process where cross-caste networks (probably among adjacent castes at the outset) develop first, for only then can conflict emerge. The question of caste versus class networks then becomes critical. Do persons perceiving class conflict maintain caste networks across class lines? Or does caste inhibit the development of class consciousness in certain cases? There seems to be a marked lack of enthusiasm for unions among KV factory workers who also own rural land. They know of landless agricultural worker organization in Tanjavur and dread its appearance in Chingleput.
58. Parenthetically, the relation of caste to substance is misconstrued by C. Lévi-Strauss in *The Savage Mind* (Chicago: University of Chicago Press, 1966), chap. 4 ("Totem and Caste"). His ingenious transformation of totemism to caste never reaches caste as a hierarchical order, but only substantializes equivalent units (by shifting the nature-culture relation to a homology between one species and one group). Substantialized, equivalent units have been called ethnic groups in this essay. To move to hierarchy we must remove substance, thus stressing holism and the ranking of castes oriented toward the whole.
59. Dumont, *Homo Hierarchicus*, pp. 230–231.
60. The background for this view derives from similarities in the work of L. Dumont and M. Marriott. Of course there are profound differences between them. See M. Marriott, "Review of *Homo Hierarchicus*," *American Anthropologist* 71 (1969), pp. 1166–1175; and L. Dumont, "Marriott's Review of Dumont's *Homo Hierarchicus*: A Comment," *American Anthropologist* 72 (1970), pp. 468–469.
61. For an important, initial attempt, see A. Bopegamage and P. V. Veeraghavan, *Status Images in Changing India* (Bombay: Manaktalas, 1967), pp. 103–194.
62. Marriott, "Multiple Reference," p. 114.

63. See note 12 above.
64. B. E. F. Beck, *Peasants of Konku: A Study of Right and Left Castes in South India* (Vancouver: University of British Columbia Press, 1972).
65. Studies of change in single castes are rare. See S. A. Barnett, *From Structure to Substance: Change in a South Indian Caste* (forthcoming); and R. Hargrave, *The Nadars of Tamilnad* (Berkeley: University of California Press, 1969). Hargrave analyzes processes discussed here: changes in the size and definition of a caste as it gains economic and political strength.
66. J. R. Marr, "The Position of Brahmans in Tamilnad in the Twentieth Century," paper prepared for a July 1969 University of London (School of Oriental and African Studies, Centre of South Asian Studies) "Study Conference on Tradition in Indian Politics and Society." And for an important discussion of British rule and Brahman political and economic advance, see R. V. Subramaniam, "The Tamil Brahmans: Some Guides to Research on Their Emergence and Eclipse," *Economic and Political Weekly* (forthcoming).
67. C. G. Diehl, *Church and Shrine: Intermingling Patterns of Culture in the Life of Some Christian Groups in South India* (Uppsala, Sweden: Acta Universitatis, Historia Religionum, no. 2, 1965).
68. "South Asia in Turmoil," *Bulletin of Concerned Asian Scholars* 4 (Winter 1972). We do have one detailed longitudinal study of a Mysore village: A. R. Beals, "Interplay Among Factors of Change in a Mysore Village," in Marriott, *Village India*; and A. R. Beals, "Nāmahaḷḷi, 1953–66: Urban Influence and Change in Southern Mysore," in Ishwaran, *Change and Continuity*, pp. 57–73. Beals's emphasis on networks, changing relations to the land, and rural-urban contact all have significance for the analysis here.
69. Gould, "Is the Tradition-Modernity Model All Bad?"
70. R. Fox, "Resiliency and Change in the Indian Caste System: The Umar of U.P.," *Journal of Asian Studies* 26 (1967).

Sociolinguistics Research in South India: Achievements and Prospects

FRANKLIN C. SOUTHWORTH
University of Pennsylvania

The Scope of Sociolinguistics

Since its inception, the modern field of linguistics has been concerned with the discovery of the abstract structure of language—the linguistic system presumed to be shared by all speakers of a language. "Pure linguistics" includes the specific rules operating in particular languages, the general principles governing the operation of rules, and the processes of change undergone by such systems. Combining a number of humanistic concerns, including the logical, psychological, and mathematical, linguists have in recent years come to concentrate more and more on language as an intellectual activity. They have taken as their field of study the potential utterances of a language, without regard to whether there exist any real speakers who might ever produce these utterances in any real situations. A key assumption of this approach, which has been with us since people first began to discuss language, is that any act of speech can be characterized as grammatical (correct, well formed) or ungrammatical, without reference to the social context in which it is used. Linguists have posited the existence of an "ideal speaker-hearer" who can produce, interpret, and judge the correctness of any utterance without being affected by emotional or social factors. Much recent work in linguistics has, in fact, made use of linguistic material produced by linguists without the normal social context which accompanies speech events, in order to reduce the effects of "external" factors such as interruptions, mishearing, false starts, and the like which occur in normal speech. This type of restricted data, though useful for the purpose of isolating certain formal structures, leads the linguist to posit much greater uniformity in usage than is actually observable in normal speech.

The term *sociolinguistics* refers to a variety of approaches to the study of language behavior which attempt to integrate the concerns of linguistics (identification of the linguistic system) with other concerns of social science. In a more restricted sense (as used, for example, by William Labov), sociolinguistics can be considered a variety of linguistics which shares the goals of "pure" linguistics, as stated at the outset of this essay, but makes different assumptions about the nature of the linguistic system and uses different methods of collecting and analyzing data. Sociolinguists assume that certain kinds of variation are inherent in linguistic behavior and that these are not "external" to the language but must be described as part of the linguistic system. For example, a speaker of Tamil belonging to a nonvegetarian community from the northern part of Tamil Nadu will have several words to convey the meaning "meat": he would use *kaṟi* in ordinary colloquial conversation with members of his own community, but might use *māmisam* (Sanskrit *māṁsa-*) in some formal contexts or in talking with Brahmans or members of other vegetarian castes. If he is educated, he may also on occasion use the term *eracci* (the usual colloquial word for "meat" in the southern part of Tamil Nadu) or *pullāl* (a word restricted to written or formal Tamil).[1] Ramanujan cites *irukku* ("it is") and *pōradu* ("it goes") as the usual colloquial forms for educated Iyengar Brahman speakers, in contrast to the forms *irukkudu* and *pōvudu* used by Mudaliars.[2] Other forms also may occur, but they are restricted to particular geographical regions. In formal speech and in writing, all Tamilians use the standard literary forms *irukkiratu* and *pōkiratu*.

Before the development of current approaches to sociolinguistics, linguists had two ways of dealing with such variations. They could be treated as "free variation," that is, as insignificant and randomly distributed differences which are not part of the systematic structure of the language. Alternatively, they could be regarded as belonging to different "dialects," each of which is presumed to be describable as a separate system. Both these approaches fail to deal with the fact that individual speakers react predictably to a variety of situational cues in selecting different phonological, grammatical, and lexical variants. Thus the sociolinguist considers it his task to describe not only which forms occur but also the ways in which different social contexts affect their occurrence.

Sociolinguistics as narrowly defined concerns itself with the implications of variation for the structure of the linguistic system and for processes of linguistic change. The term *sociolinguistics* is also used in a broader sense to include studies of language within the matrix of social or cultural behavior. One way of approaching this broader study is to ask the question:

What does the speaker say about himself (in terms of his social identification and his relationship to others present) when he uses particular variants? In this sense, sociolinguistics can be said to encompass both what has been called the sociology of language—that is, studies of language use in a population with respect to other social variables—and what Dell Hymes has called the ethnography of communication[3]—the study of language as part of a cultural system. To the extent possible, the following discussion will attempt to cover both the narrower and the broader aspects of sociolinguistic work in South India.

South Asian Languages and Sociolinguistics

South Asia has provided a great deal of data for the study of linguistic variation, and in fact the field of sociolinguistics derived much of its initial stimulus from studies of South Asian languages. The volume entitled *Linguistic Diversity in South Asia*[4] contains a number of important early studies of sociolinguistic variation in different South Asian languages, including Tamil[5] and Kannada[6] among Dravidian languages. Though considerable work has been done since that time, the papers in that volume are still worthy of study. Addressed both to linguists and nonlinguists, the volume includes an introduction describing the principal types of variation to be found in South Asia and elsewhere.

Three principal types of variation can be distinguished: geographical, social, and functional (or stylistic). Of these, geographical variation is the best known and has been pursued in the West for over a century under the name of dialect geography or dialectology. In India, Sir George Grierson's monumental *Linguistic Survey of India*[7] marks the beginning of dialect study. Grierson presented specimens and grammatical sketches of dialects of most of the major languages of India but unfortunately did not cover the old Madras Presidency, which means that most of the Dravidian area has been omitted. He does, however, present specimens of Tamil, Malayalam, Kannada, Telegu, Kurukh, Malto, Kui, Brahui, Kolami, and the "semi-Dravidian" languages Ladhadi and Bharia. Dravidian languages are dealt with in the introductory volume[8] and in volume IV.[9]

As noted by Gumperz and Ferguson,[10] Grierson did not attempt to give detailed maps of linguistic features but only indicated what he considered to be the boundaries of major dialect areas. Dialect studies since that time have consisted mostly of descriptions of individual dialects, though some attempts have been made to survey larger areas (see below).

The term *social dialect* refers to varieties of a language which coexist in the same region with other varieties but are differentiated on the basis of social factors. Differences of the type noted above for Iyengar and Mudaliar Tamil abound in India and have given rise to the term *caste dialect.*

Although there are plenty of data on linguistic differences correlating with caste and some evidence that this correlation is independent of geographical variation,[11] caste is only one of the social variables affecting speech variation. Differences correlating with other factors, such as religion, professional status, age, sex, and residence (urban versus rural) are also found. We do not yet know enough about the relationships among these. In particular, we do not know the relative importance of such major factors as caste, social class, education, and urbanization in the contemporary picture.

Functional variation involves differences in the style of speech of the same individual or group, relating to different situations or roles. Whereas in the case of geographical and social dialects it is normally expected that a person speaks one dialect or another, functional variation coexists in the speech of the same individuals. Thus the difference between Iyengar *irukku* and Mudaliar *irukkudu* ("it is") is a case of social variation, but the (formal) functional variant *irukkiratu* exists for both groups. This type of variation is also known as "superposed variation" since the more prestigious or formal variety is in a sense superposed on the lower or informal varieties of the same language.

Such variation appears to exist in all stratified societies. Generally speaking, the higher variety (H) is one which requires more attention to pronunciation and rigid adherence to grammatical rules than the lower (L) variety. Tamil and Bengali are well known for the sharp distinctiveness of their H varieties, known respectively as *sen tamil* ("pure Tamil") and *sadhu bhāṣa* ("decent speech"). Though the differences are perhaps less sharp in other South Asian languages, they still tend to be more marked than in most European languages (though Modern Greek has a similar distinction). Functional variation can be said to involve complementary varieties of a language in the sense that an individual needs control of more than one variety in order to fulfill all his expected social roles. A corollary of this principle is that, in societies characterized by such variation, individuals who control only one variety are limited in the roles they can fulfill.

When functional varieties are sharply distinguished, as in the case of Tamil and Bengali, the situation is described as involving *diglossia*.[12] This term applies not only to situations like those of Tamil, Bengali, and Modern Greek but also to multilingual societies or groups when the different languages are functionally differentiated. Thus in India many immigrant groups have bilingual diglossia. The Iyers of Kerala, for example, generally use a form of Tamil for in-group communication but use Malayalam for contact with the larger society and even within their own group for discussions on some subjects. The majority of educated Indians are in the same position with regard to English and their home language. Studies of bilingualism and language contact form an important part of the subject matter of sociolinguistics.

Sociolinguistic Studies in South India

As noted below, South India shares certain features with the rest of South Asia but also has certain characteristics of its own—linguistically as well as culturally. The following sections discuss the achievements and prospects of sociolinguistic work in Dravidian languages but are not strictly confined to that area. Some of the most interesting data for sociolinguistic study come from language-contact situations such as that on the Mysore-Maharashtra border discussed by Gumperz[13] or that of Saurashtri speakers in Tamil Nadu described by Pandit.[14]

Studies of Regional Dialects

The following information regarding dialect studies in South India has been provided to me by Dr. N. Sivaramamurthy of the Department of Linguistics, University of Kerala, in the form of a brief to appear in the *International Journal of Dravidian Linguistics.*

The Linguistic Survey Project of Deccan College, Poona, has surveyed dialects of Kannada, Telegu, and Marathi (including dialects of Marathi spoken in the Dravidian area). The Kannada Dialect Survey, guided by Dr. D. N. S. Bhat, has produced descriptive grammars of Kannada dialects by Acharya,[15] Mahadevan,[16] and Upadhyaya.[17] The survey of Marathi dialects, under Dr. A. M. Ghatage, has produced descriptions of the Konkani spoken in south Kanara[18] and of the Marathi of Kasargode[19] among others. Other materials on dialects of Kannada and Marathi have been published from time to time in the *Linguistic Survey Bulletin of the Deccan College*, Poona.

The Tamil Dialect Survey conducted by the Department of Linguistics of Annamalai University has produced a number of descriptive monographs. In addition, a number of studies of Tamil dialects have been done by Kamil Zvelebil.[20]

The Andhra Pradesh Sahitya Akademi has published a series of studies of professional vocabularies in dictionary form. The first of these, by Krishnamurti,[21] deals with agricultural vocabulary. The English introduction to the volume describes the scope and methods of the project.

The small-scale dialect survey project of the Department of Linguistics, Kerala University, under the supervision of Dr. V. I. Subramoniam, aims primarily at the preparation of dialect maps and descriptive grammars of individual dialects. Methodologically it can claim to be the most systematic dialect survey yet attempted for any language of India. Materials are being collected from 950 local administrative units (panchayats), each of which will be visited four times by the survey team before the results are finalized. The work of collecting, analyzing, and preparing the materials for presentation has been organized by caste. Materials have been collected so far from the speech of Tiyyars (Iḷavas) and Nayars, and the study of Harijan speech is currently underway. For the Tiyyar materials, some three hundred maps have been prepared showing isoglosses. Ultimately the department hopes to produce a dictionary of Malayalam dialects.

Some scholars have criticized the organization of this project on the grounds that it gives too much importance to caste distinctions. If such an objection is made on political grounds, social scientists need not be troubled by it, since it is clear that caste distinctions are not waning as fast as politicians would like them to. (See the essay by Mencher and Unni in this volume.) On methodological grounds, however, it may be pointed out that if the design of the survey assumes the existence of "caste dialects" and materials are collected by caste, the results may obscure the relationship between caste and other social variables as factors in speech variation.

Social Dialects

An early study by Gumperz[22] demonstrated the significance of caste differences, as well as other social differences such as locality of residence and religious orthodoxy, in differentiating speech behavior. He concluded that

> the determining factor seems to be informal friendship contacts. . . . Since there are a number of intergroup and intercaste friendships among touchables, there is no barrier to the spread of innovations from one sector to the other. However, these friendships do not extend across the touchable-untouchable line or from one untouchable group to another, and thus account for the linguistic isolation of the untouchables.[23]

On the basis of this finding, Gumperz found it necessary to revise a long-accepted notion of Bloomfield's regarding "density of communication," which holds that the speech of individuals in a society tends to be similar in proportion to the amount of communication taking place between them. Since the linguistic differences in this case correlated with friendship groups and not with other social groupings (such as work groups, which normally contain a greater range of castes), clearly not only the amount of contact matters but also the kind of contact.

Though the village on which this study was based is in North India, Gumperz's general conclusion about the importance of friendship groups and caste distinctions in determining linguistic variations is presumably valid for all of South Asia and probably for many other areas as well. On the basis of data available so far, South India appears to differ from the northern areas primarily in having a greater number of social dialects, with greater distinctiveness. Most studies of social dialects in the south have pointed out the sharp distinctions between Brahman (B) and non-Brahman (NB) speech in phonology, morphology, and lexicon.

The phonological distinctiveness of B speech has been noted for Tamil and Tulu,[24] Telegu,[25] Kannada,[26] and Malayalam.[27] A number of phonological differences involve the use of borrowed forms, in which Brahman speakers reproduce the foreign phonology more faithfully than do non-Brahmans: for example, Tamil B *svāmi*, NB *sāmi* "lord" (Sanskrit *Svāmin-*); Kannada *B kafi*, NB *kāpi* "coffee"; Telegu B *vyawahāraw̃*, NB *vyawāraw̃ /yawwāraw̃* (Sanskrit *vyavahāram*) "business"; Tulu B *gandha*, NB *ganda* (Sanskrit *gandha-*) "fragrance." Both B and NB speech also show hypercorrect forms, in which the foreign phonological element is used wrongly: for example, Tamil B *krāfu* "haircut" (NB *krāppu*, from English *crop.*)[28] Apart from such cases, there are also differences in native phonology between B and NB speech, most of which appear to show more conservatism on the B side. For example: Kannada B *hāku*, NB *āku* "put"; Telegu B *veduru*, NB *yeduru* "bamboo" (initial *v* is the older form, Subbarao 9); Tamil B *vāḻappaḻam*, NB *vāzappaḷam/ vāḷappaḷam/ vāḷappaḷam/ vāyappayam* "banana"; Tulu B *sikk-*, NB *tikk-* "be obtained."

Brahman and non-Brahman speech also differ in morphology and in lexicon. Morphological variants include such points as the differences in verb endings reported for Tamil by Ramanujan,[29] differences in verb and noun endings noted by McCormack[30] for Kannada, the different B and NB genitive suffix in Tulu described by Bright and Ramanujan,[31] and certain verb endings noted by Subbarao for Telegu.[32] In most cases, the differences described consist of different forms for the "same" endings; that is, the descriptions appear to imply that the same morphological categories are represented by different forms in the B and NB varieties. McCormack[33] notes: "Differences in the phonemic shape of suffixes which occur in identical morphemic environments with noncontrastive meaning are among the most important differences in the speech of Brahmins and non-Brahmins." Thus he lists Kannada B/e, NB/ae as the first person singular ending of verbs in certain circumstances; B/e: vi/, NB/i:vi as first person plural.

Differences of this type would appear to be what linguists nowadays are calling differences in surface structure. Some of the variations mentioned, on the other hand, indicate differences in underlying semantic structure: for example, in discussing locative suffixes McCormack lists the following two cases: (1) B/ae-ka/, NB/ige, (2) B/ukka/, NB/ige/, suggesting that the B variety of Kannada makes a distinction not made in the NB variety. Similarly, Bright and Ramanujan[34] note that while the NB variety of Tulu has a single genitive suffix *-da*, the B variety makes a distinction between a form *-no* (used with "rational" nouns) and a form *-nte* (used with "irrational" nouns). Ramanujan also mentions some fairly extensive semantic differences in the B and NB pronoun systems of Tamil.[35] Other cases may also turn out, on closer investigation, to involve differences of this kind. This distinction between surface grammar and underlying (semantic) structure is important in studying the different social functions of linguistic variants.

Lexical differences are also said to involve two types of cases: in one type, the different varieties have "different words for the same thing," such as Tulu B *puruṣe* (Sanskrit *puruṣa-*), NB *kaṇḍane* "husband." Other cases which might appear at first glance to be of this type actually involve semantic differences: for example, foreigners learning Tamil are sometimes told by NB speakers that the B word for cooked rice is *sādam* and the NB equivalent is *cōru*. As Ramanujan[36] mentions, B speakers also use *cōru* but in a different meaning ("useless rice, rice fit for beggars"). Other examples of this second type can also be found; a careful study of such cases could presumably reveal a great deal about the social dynamics of intergroup relations.[37]

A study of comparative semantic structure of Tamil and other South Asian language suggests that lexical differences in the speech of different caste groups tend to be less prominent in the areas of the lexicon which are most often discussed in public.[38] In this study, which is currently in the analysis stage, fewer intercaste differences have been found in the vocabulary of agriculture than in those areas which are most likely to be discussed within the family or within the caste group—such as food and eating, kinship, marriage, and other rituals. Thus Tamil *nellu* ("paddy") and *arici* ("husked rice") are shared by B and NB speakers whereas the terms for "cooked rice" are different as noted above.

M. S. Pillai's study of variations in kinship terms in a Tamil village[39] shows a picture of four of five groups which are distinguishable purely on the basis of kinship terms, with Muslims, Brahmans, and Mudaliars being clearly distinguishable from each other and from the rest. (In studies of this kind, Muslims and Christians appear to function like distinct castes, and it is probably useful to extend the term *caste* to include such groups.) Thus caste boundaries appear to function like other cultural boundaries in their effect on lexical structure. For example, the difference between B and NB speakers with regard to the terms for rice and paddy can be compared with the difference found between the rice-eating and wheat-eating areas of the Hindu-Urdu region: in the eastern rice areas, it is normal to distinguish between *bhāt* ("cooked rice") and *cāval* ("rice in general") whereas in the western wheat areas the distinction is much less common and normally *cāval* is used to refer to rice in all forms.[40]

Apte, in a study of varieties of Marathi spoken by people of various backgrounds in Bombay City, concludes that "the Marathas and others who belong to the higher castes do show a different speech from the speech of Brahmins, especially at the level of phonology."[41]. He notes differences in borrowed words (for example: B *varṣa*, NB *varsa* "year"; compare with Sanskrit *varṣa*) and in native vocabulary (for example: B *ek*, NB *yek* "one"). He also notes some differences in morphology between B and NB speech, but there are not sufficient data at present to control for regional differences in these cases since many of the speakers in his sample came from other parts of Maharashtra. One of his general conclusions is that "the differences between the 'standard Brahmin' dialect and other dialects is more noticeable than the difference between the non-Brahmin castes."[42] The similarities between the type of variation reported for Marathi and that which has been reported for the Dravidian area are quite striking (see below for a comparison with North India). It would appear to make sense to include Maharashtra (at least tentatively) at part of South India for the purposes of sociolinguistic study. The historical basis for this inclusion, and the historical implications, are discussed below.

Where the NB varieties have been studied, even superficially, they show low-caste (LC) varieties which are distinct from the other NB varieties; thus a tripartite division seems to be the general picture throughout South India. Unni has commented explicitly on the three-way division in phonology in Malayalam: "There are again variations in pronunciation which broadly fall into three—that of Nambudiris, of non-Brahmins above polluting castes, and of middle and low group of polluting castes." McCormack makes the following comment on the situation in Kannada: "The majority of differences between the speech style of backward classes in Dharwar and the speech styles of the other two social classes appear to be differences in the phonemic shape of verbal suffixes. . . . There are also differences in the use of compound verbal bases. . . . There are some distinctive forms of address and kinship nouns. . . . But. . . the vocabulary of the Harijans' speech appears from this study to be practically identical with that of other non-Brahmins in Dharwar."[43]

Subbarao notes a number of cases, including systematic phonological and morphological variants, where the LC speech in Telegu differs from that of other NB speakers. For Marathi, Apte comments: "Among the non-Brahmin speakers, it is not possible to assign any particular features to any one caste. This situation therefore may be compared and contrasted with that described by William McCormack in his article Social Dialects in Dharwar Kannada."[44] It seems to me, however, that the more striking contrast is between the situation described above, as found in Maharashtra and the south, and that revealed for North India by the village studies of Gumperz[45] and Levine.[46] These show rather significant differences (mainly in phonology) between the touchable and untouchable castes, without any sharp breaks within the whole touchable group (though Gumperz's study shows differences among the three untouchable groups living in separate hamlets).

As for Marathi, there seems to be a need for more data, since Apte's study was confined to urban speakers and therefore did not take into account those situations in which the untouchables are required to live in their traditional physical isolation. What I am suggesting is that the existence of a separate "lower" linguistic variety may well be a pan-Indian feature—at least in those areas where untouchables are physically isolated —but that the presence of a distinct "upper" variety (mainly Brahman but sometimes including other high castes as well) is a characteristic of the south, including Maharashtra.

We do not yet have adequate information on the identity of the groups using the LC varieties. It is often said that untouchables are recognizable by their speech, but we do not know the extent to which other factors such as dress or manners contribute to this identification. In M. S. Pillai's study cited above, the "low" group contains ten castes, including low Harijans and high Pillais, with no sharp linguistic boundaries. Clearly there are differences in the extent of distinctiveness of different groups, and few generalizations can be made without further detailed study.

In cases where their speech has been observed, Muslims also constitute a distinct group. In Pillai's study, the Muslims constitute the most distinct group in the village. The other studies mentioned above have not included Muslims, but informants report substantial differences between Muslim and Hindu speech in various parts of the south. An informant from north Malabar, P. V. Kunhikannan, has informed me that Muslims in his area substitute /l/ for /r/ and have certain morphological and lexical differences as well. He offered the following sample sentence ("Raghavan, what are you doing?") as an illustration of some of these differences:

Nayar: *rāgava, endā ceyunnadu*
Muslim: *lāgava, dettā kāṭṭannu(du)*

(Though these are not the observations of a trained linguist, the informant is an excellent mimic and his observations were offered spontaneously.) For North India, Gumperz reports no phonological characteristics of Muslim speech and combines "Hindu and Muslim touchable castes" as speakers of the standard, while noting that there are some vocabulary differences and that Hindu-Muslim differences are said to be greater elsewhere.[47]

Linguistic variation according to caste (or social class) is only one type. It has generally been assumed, in most cases covertly, to be the principal kind of sociolinguistic variation, but until more systematic studies have been done which take other variables into account, this is only an assumption. Education is, naturally, one of the most important variables in this regard. In general, it can be expected that an educated person's speech will approximate the prestige variety of the language more clearly than the speech of an uneducated person of similar background. Urbanization, that is, the exposure to people of a variety of backgrounds in an urban environment where many of the restrictions on intercaste contacts are losing their traditional force, may be expected to have a similar leveling effect—though the direction of change may not necessarily be toward the most prestigious variety.

McCormack noted that, in eliciting informant judgments about caste on the basis of tape-recorded samples of Kannada, "the four backward class speakers were almost never correctly identified, and the reason for this was that they spoke a mixture of Brahmin, Lingayat and literary forms which effectively masked their own distinctive class dialect. Some urbanized backward class speakers regularly use such a mixture when they speak before a member of other social classes."[48] He also notes that the use of a literary style of speech tends to predispose the listener to classify the speaker as a Brahman.

Apte, in a similar experiment with Marathi speakers in Bombay, reached similar conclusions. He notes that "very few of the informants were able to identify the exact castes of the persons whose speech was played to them, with the exception that 'better or pure' speech was usually associated with either Brahmins or Marathas, in most cases, Brahmins,"[49] Apte concludes that "education and urbanization are very significant in keeping the morphological and syntactic differences to a minimum, and with some reservations, this may also be true of the phonology."[50] A study of sociolinguistic variation in the town of Phaltan by Maxine Bornsten, currently underway, apparently shows that certain linguistic variants correlate better with education than with caste (personal communication).

Functional Variation

In attempting to assess the importance of such factors as caste, class, and education in molding speech patterns, we must keep in mind that an individual's speech often varies according to the social situation. McCormack's phrase "when they speak before a member of other social classes" is an important cue because the use of a high-caste variety of a language by low-caste people in certain public circumstances is no guarantee that the distinctive low-caste variety has been eliminated. The phenomenon of "switching" has been documented by a number of investigators in a number of different speech communities,[51] but it is as prevalent in India as in any other society so far reported on. This brings us to another major factor in linguistic variation, namely, the situation in which speech takes place. Since we know that people's style of speaking differs considerably depending on who is present and that speakers of a low-prestige group will generally modify their speech in the direction of the prestige variety, we cannot consider any investigation of this type complete until we have determined the whole range of an individual's speech in all circumstances.

Traditionally, in many areas low-caste speakers were discouraged from imitating the speech of members of the higher castes, just as they were discouraged from imitating high-caste modes of dress or other behavior. This could mean that a person's speech might vary considerably depending on whether he was speaking to an equal or to a higher-caste person. Unni reports on an extreme form of this, which was until recently prevalent in Kerala and still exists to some extent. This is the custom known by the name of *ācāram paḻayal* or "conduct speech," according to which "a range of vocabulary prevalent among higher castes [is] forbidden to be used by the lower," with the consequences that "the free social emulation of higher groups in the field of speech is not possible" and that "each caste . . . keeps itself conscious of its lowly rank."[52]

The examples given by Unni of terms avoided by lower castes consist mainly of references to the person, his dwelling, his kin, and certain domestic activities such as eating, cooking, and bathing. A low-caste person refers to himself as *aḍiyan* ("slave") in talking to a higher-caste person, and he refers to the latter by one of a set of prescribed terms (such as *tamburān* "protector" or *yajamān* "master"). A low-caste person's house is *kuppāḍu* ("refuse place"). Terms for the high-caste person's house include *illam* (for Nambudiris), *mana* (for Nambudiripads), *maḍam* (for immigrant Brahmans), and *vīdu* (for Nayars). Avoidance terms used by low castes include such words as *veḷuttadu* ("the white thing") for *mōru* ("buttermilk"); *karikkādi* (compare with *kari* "coal") for *nellu* ("paddy"); *kallari* ("stony rice") for *ari* ("raw rice"); and *tenginmel kāya* ("fruit of the coconut tree") for *tenga* ("coconut"). Such differences in status vocabulary are not uncommon in other parts of India but have not been adequately studied.

The ingredients of the speech situation include not only the social composition of the group speaking but also the situation (for example, the degree of formality of the occasion) and the subject matter of the conversation. Variation according to degree of formality has been discussed extensively by Labov,[53] who has proposed a variety of techniques for eliciting speech of different degrees of formality in interview situations.

Differences between formal and informal speech in Hindi-Urdu have been discussed by Gumperz and Naim.[54] In general, South Asian languages appear to vary considerably along the formal-informal dimension.

Informal speech situations are characterized by a minimum of concern about matters of status or of linguistic propriety and a maximum emphasis on interaction, verbal and otherwise. Formal speech situations involve, on the other hand, a maximum emphasis on the appropriateness and propitiousness of the words uttered. Some data are available on the linguistic differences involved between H and L varieties of South Asian languages, in the form of grammatical descriptions of different styles of speech published in *Indian Linguistics* and other linguistics journals. As for lexicographical work, it has been based largely on the literary or formal varieties of regional languages, with little attention paid to functional variants. For example, a recently published Hindi-English dictionary contains the words *lekin, par, magar, kintu,* and *parantu,* all of which can be translated as "but," with no indication of the differences in situational usage. (The first two words are used most commonly in informal conversation, the last two primarily in formal.) This was fairly typical of lexicographical work in most parts of the world until fairly recently, so this remark does not imply any special criticism of South Asian lexicographers.

When we come to the sociological correlates of functional variation, our ignorance is most obvious. We know in a general way that formal situations trigger certain linguistic responses which are different from those triggered by informal or intimate situations, but no attempt has yet been made to measure the difference in response or to specify the sociological factors responsible. The methodology for such work is still being developed, and it is probable that future work in South Asian languages will have important consequences for its development. The practical importance of such studies is discussed below under Applications.

Multilingualism

Since the publication of the 1961 Census of India, which included material on bilingualism, a good deal of attention has been given to multilingualism in India. From a narrow sociolinguistic point of view, interest in multilingualism centers on the interaction between different linguistic systems and the changes they undergo as a result of contact. P. B. Pandit's studies of Saurashtri, a form of Gujarati spoken in and near Madurai, illustrate the absorption of grammatical patterns of Tamil by Saurashtri speakers resulting in the complete transformation of parts of the grammar, such as the numeral system, without any changes in the surface forms of words.[55] Upadhyaya's study of Bidar Kannada[56] presents interesting though fragmentary data on the extreme effects of Urdu influence on the Kannada spoken in the northernmost part of Mysore. Gumperz's study[57] of convergence in local varieties of Kannada and Marathi in the Mysore-Maharashtra border area suggests that stable bilingualism can lead to virtual identity in grammatical structure. Regarding the social function of such convergence, Gumperz comments: "Such codes seem ideally suited for communication in societies which stress cultural distinctions, while at the same time requiring regular and frequent interaction."[58]

In terms of broad sociolinguistic interests, studies are needed of the origins of multilingual communities, the social functions of stable bilingualism, and the factors that perpetuate or discourage it. Background studies of interest on the all-India level include Bose,[59] Apte,[60] and Khubchandani.[61] The detailed study of multilingual groups is still in its infancy, though Khubchandani's pioneering study[62] provides an excellent model for further work. We look forward to the publication of the results of Apte's current study of Marathi speakers in Tanjore and other parts of the Tamil-speaking area.

Historical Study

Historical linguistics, the study of the changes undergone by linguistic systems, derived its initial stimulus in the early nineteenth century from the discovery of the historical connection between Sanskrit and the classical languages of Europe. There followed over a century of intense concentration on the historical study of Sanskrit and its relationships to its forebears, to its contemporary sister languages, and to its middle Indo-Aryan daughter languages and its modern Indo-Aryan granddaughter languages. Only in the 1950s and 1960s was there any general realization among linguists and indologists that this work had been taking place in a vacuum, though Burrow's work on Dravidian influences on Sanskrit had begun to appear in the 1940s.[63] Emeneau's "Linguistic Prehistory of India"[64] and "India as a Linguistic Area"[65] were key works in producing an awareness among linguists and others of the extent of interaction between Dravidian and Indo-Aryan, which must have been going on since the earliest period of contact. These studies, along with others, have stimulated a number of studies of contact among South Asian languages, especially between Dravidian and Indo-Aryan. In addition to those mentioned in the previous section, two collections of papers on contact and convergence are currently in an advanced stage of preparation.[66] Thus it is unlikely that Dravidianists will fall into the same error that students of Sanskrit did for so many decades: that of treating their language in a vacuum.

Historical linguistics is concerned with changes in the formal system of a language and has traditionally dealt mainly with rather long spans of time. Sociolinguistics, by taking into account the inherent variation within the linguistic system, adds a dynamic dimension which makes possible the detailed study of social factors in relation to linguistic change. Some early studies, such as those of Fischer[67] and Labov,[68] show clearly the possibility of identifying such elements as intragroup solidarity, intergroup tensions, and group expectations as important factors in sound change. Several of the studies mentioned above attest to the crucial importance of such factors in the South Asian scene. Gumperz[69] and Ramanujan[70] indicate the powerful role of caste boundaries in discouraging diffusion of innovations from one group to another and also in stimulating distinctive innovations within a group.

Such studies provide sufficient motivation for the differences in social dialects which we observe, but they do not account for the unexpected similarities which have been repeatedly pointed out. When two unrelated languages, such as Kannada and Marathi, can have the same grammatical structure, we have a situation which cannot be accommodated within the assumptions of classical historical theory. It has traditionally been assumed that languages borrowed words from each other but kept their own grammatical and semantic patterns basically intact. In South Asia the reverse seems to have happened, and on a gigantic scale: many grammatical, phonological, and semantic features can be found which cover the whole subcontinent. Compared to this, the amount of lexical borrowing has been fairly restricted, except that all the literary languages (with the exception of the most prestigious written form of Tamil) borrow copiously from Sanskrit.

Gumperz suggests that this situation may arise from the needs of people living in multicaste villages. Just as differences in dress and ritual observances emphasize the distinctiveness of different communities, differences in consciously observable features of speech have a similar function. On the other hand, the less easily observable features (rules of word order, semantic distinctions) appear to tend toward similarity because of the need for economic cooperation, particularly in agriculture. It has been pointed out that agricultural operations in some parts of India, particularly in rice-growing areas, traditionally involve a complex pattern of cooperation among high-caste landowners, intermediate-caste tenants, and low-caste laborers. The common grammatical and semantic basis thus serves to facilitate communication in spite of considerable differences in the overt forms of the languages.

Writing the sociolinguistic history of South Asia, then, means developing a model of the linguistic communication patterns of earlier periods which will explain the remarkable linguistic fusion which has taken place, in slightly different forms, many in different parts of the subcontinent. In this endeavor, we can make use of every kind of evidence available, including studies of social variation in contemporary society and descriptions of such variation by earlier writers; philological studies (such as that of George Hart in this volume); and the evidence of linguistic history, archaeology, and physical anthropology. A preliminary attempt to examine the sociolinguistic background of Marathi, which shows a greater similarity to Dravidian than do most other Indo-Aryan languages, provides detailed evidence of the large-scale fusing of Indo-Aryan lexical material with grammatical and semantic patterns which originated in Dravidian.[71] This linguistic fusion appears to be one manifestation of the social fusion process which created the typical multicaste settlements of India, often integrating groups from different geographical and ethnic backgrounds into economically viable units.[72]

Ethnography of Communication

Several of the studies mentioned above contribute to our general understanding of communicative behavior in South Asia, including the social functions of linguistic variation and diglossia and the effects of urbanization and education.[73] But we still do not know enough about the ways in which people in this part of the world accomplish the variety of communicative tasks their lives require. The following paragraphs touch on a few areas in which work is needed.

The study of constraints on communicative behavior—who can say what, when, and to whom—has not been undertaken systematically for any part of South Asia. Thus we have only general impressions to go on at present. For example, many visitors to the area have observed that younger members of a family tend to keep quiet in the presence of their elders unless instructed to speak. An extension of this type of constraint can also be observed outside the family, for example in business or government offices and in academic contexts, with regard to the reluctance of junior staff members to initiate communication except on routine matters. The same behavior seems to hold by and large in classrooms, from the elementary school to the college level, where communication is almost entirely from teacher to student except when a student is asked a direct question. We do not know how prevalent this behavior is, in what other cultural situations it occurs, or to what extent (and in which contexts) it may be undergoing change. And this is only one type of constraint. In many other situations (such as rituals, intercaste functions, formal meetings, and marriage negotiations, to name a few) other restrictions no doubt exist.

From what has been said here, it is clear that diglossia of one kind or another is the norm rather than the exception in South Asian society. Multilingual individuals and groups are common in all areas, both urban and rural. Even functional diglossia is not the exclusive prerogative of the educated. Since in most cases a person's home language binds him to a particular regional and social identification, the tendency toward diglossia can be considered almost universal in South Asia. The ways in which this tendency is realized, however, are very complex and insufficiently known at present.

Some notion of the complexities involved can be obtained from the following brief description of the situation in south Malabar in the present and the recent past. Dr. K. Raman Unni, a social anthropologist who is from that region and who did field work there in the mid-1950s and again in 1971, provided this information in a recent conversation. Though impressionistic, it gives a picture of a number of factors which deserve fuller investigation. Apart from regional and social dialects of Malayalam, one must distinguish at least the following varieties: anglicized Malayalam (AM), sanskritized Malayalam (SM), and English (E). (My own observations suggest that, in certain urban contexts, one might also add EM, a style of switching in which full sentences in both English and Malayalam occur.)

Anglicized Malayalam refers to a range of styles in which English words are used, in varying quantities, within a basic Malayalam framework. Though English words are required in some cases because there is no convenient equivalent (for example, such words as *current, fuse wire*, and *transformer* are unavoidable in talking with an electrician), this factor does not begin to account for the extent of usage. In urban contexts, knowledge of a few English terms is useful in order to establish one's status as a sophisticated and knowledgeable person. But apart from this, a great deal of the use of AM (and also of E) appears to have the function of avoiding the need to make certain traditional distinctions. This is often in the context of new communication situations which did not exist in the traditional picture and which result mostly from the spread of school education. For example, Unni noted that during the 1950s when he did field work in this region, he could conveniently avoid the need to observe *ācāram paḷayal* when talking with Nambudiri Brahmans by using AM or E where necessary. This was accepted because of his status as an educated man.

In another type of situation, it is common to use English words to replace Malayalam terms belonging to particular domains such as kinship, food, and worship, which often are linked closely to particular caste or religious groups. Thus the words *father, uncle, brother-in-law,* and *wife* are commonly heard in Malayalam, especially in mixed groups such as might be found in a college hostel. English terms are also frequently used in medical contexts and in discussions of family planning and similar matters. In these contexts, the use of such terms as *sexual relations, private parts, delivery,* and *breast feeding* avoids the possibility of embarrassment which might be caused by using the Malayalam terms. It may be pointed out here that, though official statistics list only about one percent of India's population as knowing English, the use of anglicized forms of regional languages for purposes such as these is widespread.

The status-raising function of AM was filled by sanskritized Malayalam for many speakers of earlier generations. For example, specialists such as astrologers and master carpenters received technical training based on traditional Sanskrit texts. Though of low caste, their ability to use Sanskrit words in their everyday conversation lent them somewhat greater mobility. Among well-to-do Nayars, girls were expected to receive enough Sanskrit education to enable them to read such works as the *Ramayana* and the *Mahabharata*. Thus they were also able to spice their conversation with Sanskrit, just as modern women spice theirs with such English words as *fashion, decency, love, marriage*, and the like.[74]

Written English is used on signboards, on formal communications such as wedding invitations (sometimes accompanied by Malayalam), for salutations and closing in personal letters, and similar uses. (It is not uncommon for a personal letter in Malayalam to begin with "Dear Brother" and close with "Your affectionate.") English (or EM) is an accepted spoken medium in government and business offices, in academic contexts, and on the telephone. In the rural context, the use of English is particularly appropriate when one wishes to give recognition that a person's status has changed from uneducated to educated. Thus a well-to-do man may make a point of speaking in English to the educated son of his uneducated tenant. I observed a similar situation in a Madras village when the panchayat president, an educated man, spoke to my assistant (a Harijan with an M.A. in social work) exclusively in English. In such situations, the use of English not only serves to avoid the traditional mode of interaction among people of different social backgrounds, but also serves a positive function of symbolizing equality of status.

A similar picture, though differing in details, may be found in most other parts of South Asia. Apart from inquiring into the interregional differences, there are a number of specific questions which would need to be pursued in studying this subject further. What changes are currently taking place in these patterns? Is the use of sanskritized Malayalam on the radio and in the press having any effect on the relative prestige of A.M. and S.M.? Is the alleged support of the use of AM by Marxists having any visible impact? In general, what are the contexts in which changes appear to be taking place and in what other contexts do changes seem likely?

From the point of view of individuals in the society, we do not know enough about the ways in which diglossia is acquired. Spoken fluency in any medium other than the home language is generally not obtained as a result of formal education or parental training but probably more through peer-group interaction. Though formal education is probably crucial for the acquisition of a written command of English, it may be of minimal importance for a spoken command. Along with the question of acquisition, there is a need for a typology of individual linguistic repertories. It is not uncommon to find individuals, either educated or uneducated, who control three or four languages. Though we know in general the circumstances under which such multilingualism appears (mainly as a result of occupational experience or residence in different areas), we have no adequate information on its incidence.

Studies of code-switching (see above under Multilingualism) have provided information of use in the study of linguistic change but have not focused on the factors that determine which code will be used in a particular situation. Several factors have already been mentioned: avoidance (of traditional class and caste distinctions and delicate subjects), content of the conversation, symbolization of change in status, and type of situation (office, telephone conversation). Other factors can no doubt be identified. What is needed is a detailed study of individual behavior in a variety of situations to discover the factors affecting the choice of medium for speakers of different backgrounds. An important part of this study would be to observe changes that occur as the composition of a group changes or as new groups (local governmental bodies, labor unions, college social groups) come into being.

An important area of study within the ethnography of communication (some would consider it a separate field) is ethnographic semantics. Generally such studies focus on a particular semantic domain, such as medical or botanical terminology, and examine the principles of classification implicit in the terms used and how this classification relates to other cultural behavior. A few studies of this type have been done in South India, though none is yet available in published form. Susan Bean's Columbia University doctoral dissertation, based on a study of forms of personal reference and address in Kannada, provides valuable information on the differences between actual and reported usage in this domain. Stanley Regelson's dissertation on food terms in Kannada, also for Columbia University, examines food vocabulary in an ethnographic context.

In 1970 work was begun on comparative study of semantic structure in Tamil, Malayalam, Marathi, Hindi-Urdu, and Indian English. This study (sponsored by the National Science Foundation of the U.S.) focuses on the domain of food, agriculture, work, personal reference, and respect status. Its purpose is to examine the underlying semantic structure of these semantic domains in order to discover similarities and differences among the languages studied. The materials collected for this project consist largely of transcribed conversations, which not only provide copious examples of works and expressions pertaining to the chosen semantic domains but also contain rich data on the verbal interaction in social groups of varying composition. A general view of the results of this research has been completed.[75]

Within ethnographic semantics, an area of growing importance is the semantics of social change. This includes the study of ways of talking about change, ways of making explicit the differences between new and old particles, and also ways of talking which mask a lack of change. The term *Harijan* ("scheduled caste"), for example, is symbolic of change, but in areas where the circumstances of untouchables have not changed substantially, the use of such terms serves mainly to cover up the unpleasant truth. The study of such terms, if done in conjunction with observations of ongoing changes, may make a singificant contribution to our understanding of change processes and attitudes toward change.

Applications

A number of the points discussed here have a fairly direct bearing on such practical concerns as language education, adult literacy programs, and the choice of the medium for mass communication. Differences in language background appear to account for a certain amount of educational difficulties, particularly those of low-caste or lower-class children. It is necessary to identify and quantify the factors involved if meaningful remedies are to be proposed. Differences in home dialect are presumably only part of the picture. Attitudes toward the use of language, particularly toward the need to use "proper" language in certain contexts, may possibly account for some problems. In addition, attitudes and expectations on the part of teachers may enter in.

I was told by teachers in a school in Madras City that children of the "servant class" (that is, Harijans), when they first come to the school, often do not know even the simplest words: "They do not even know *ukkāru* ('sit down')—we have to tell them *kundu* ('squat')." Such differences are found throughout South Asia, and even when teachers are prepared to accept such children without prejudice and give them special attention, they are not trained for such work. There has been no systematic study of the differences between the dialects of these children and the form of the language taught in the schools, and teachers are given no training in dealing with such differences. Basic study of these differences can therefore be of great practical value.

An additional factor relates to the question of acquisition of linguistic competence mentioned above. An understanding of the relative importance of formal training and other exposure may be of importance in planning elementary language education. If the role of informal exposure is as important in transmitting competence as some observers have suggested, then it might be worthwhile experimenting with methods to introduce more informal peer-group interaction into the educational process.

The gulf between the "standard" form of the regional language, as taught in schools, and the everyday spoken varieties has often been blamed for students' difficulties in learning language. These "standard" forms, usually highly sanskritized (or highly classicalized, as in the case of Tamil), are bolstered by various traditional arguments, and it is generally assumed that any variety of the language which is closer to ordinary spoken language would not be viable for the whole linguistic region because of regional and social differences. This is not necessarily true, because of the tendency (mentioned above) to adopt features of urban speech such as anglicization. Thus it is possible that a standard colloquial form may be evolving spontaneously in many linguistic regions, among the middle-class urban population, which could function for the region as a whole. It is worth investigating to what extent such standards are emerging and what their linguistic characteristics are.

Addendum

Cited here are references to works I was not able to consult before submitting this essay. They are from the Proceedings of the First All-India Conference of Dravidian Linguists, which was held in Trivandrum in May 1971, and from the first two issues of the *International Journal of Dravidian Linguistics*, which began publication in January 1972.

B. Gopinathan Nair's study of social dialects in Kerala, based on the work of the dialect survey of Kerala,[76] is a useful though preliminary discussion of phonological, morphological, and lexical differences. These are given in the form of a comparison of the "literary dialect," the "Brahmin dialect," the "Ezhava dialect," the "Nair dialect," the "Harijan dialect," the "Christian dialect," and the "Muslim dialect." The paper concludes that the last-named dialect is the "most divergent." Though the material presented is most interesting, several objections must be raised to the approach used. Since there is no evidence that any attempt was made to control for other social variables besides caste, the suspicion must remain that this study started with the assumption that caste dialects exist and therefore took the speech of individuals from each caste to be representative of each "caste dialect." In some cases, for example among

Harijans and Christians, who are far from being homogeneous groups, the assumption that there is a single dialect for the whole group certainly should not be taken for granted. In addition, the evidence given suggests that the specimens of high-caste (Brahman and Nayar) speech were restricted to the formal style of educated speech, thus exaggerating the differences between these "dialects" and others.

Susheela P. Upadhyaya's study of the Malayalam spoken by Muslims who have migrated from Malabar to south Kanara provides much-needed data.[77] In her exposition, the main focus is on the influence of Tulu on the speech of the Muslims in this area. M. Shanmugam Pillai's paper[78] on address terms in Tamil presents valuable and interesting new data on the use of address terms, their relationships with other forms of interpersonal behavior, and on the use of substitute forms for tabooed terms (name of a woman's husband). Other relevant work includes R. Solomon's study[79] of Tamil-Malayalam bilingualism, a study of language contact by T. Elizarenkova,[80] and a number of studies of regional dialects of Dravidian: see especially the papers by C. Isaacs, U. P. Upadhyaya, P. S. Nair, M. V. Sreedhar, L. Koshy, K. R. Savithry, J. Neethivanan, and R. V. K. Thampuran.[81]

NOTES

1. Franklin C. Southworth, "On the Semantic Unity of a Speech Community: Some (Socio) Linguistic Implications of a Study of Tamil Food Categories," *International Journal of Dravidian Linguistics* (forthcoming).
2. A. K. Ramanujan, "The Structure of Variation: A Study in Caste Dialects," in *Structure and Change in Indian Society*, ed. Milton Singer and Bernard Cohn (New York: Viking Fund Publications in Anthropology, 1968), p. 47.
3. John J. Gumperz and Dell H. Hymes, *The Ethnography of Communication*, vol. 66, no. 6 of *American Anthropologist* (1964).
4. John J. Gumperz and Charles A. Ferguson (eds.), *Linguistic Diversity in South Asia* (Bloomington: Indiana University Research Center in Anthropology, Folklore, and Linguistics, 1960).
5. M. Shanmugam Pillai, "Tamil—Literary and Colloquial," in Gumperz and Ferguson, *op. cit.*
6. William Bright, "Linguistic Change in Some Indian Caste Dialects," in Gumperz and Ferguson, *op. cit.*; William McCormack, "Social Dialects in Dharwar Kannada," *ibid.*
7. In ten volumes, originally published in 1927; (reprinted in Delhi by Motilal Banarsidass, 1967).
8. Gierson, *op. cit.*, I, pp. 81–93.
9. *Ibid.*, IV, pp. 277–645.
10. *Op. cit.*, p. 8.
11. Ramanujan, *op. cit.*, p. 462.
12. Charles A. Ferguson, "Diglossia," in *Language in Culture and Society*, ed. Dell Hymes (New York: Harper and Row, 1964).

13. John J. Gumperz, "On the Linguistic Markers of Bilingual Communication," in *Problems of Bilingualism*, ed. John MacNamara, vol. 23 of *Journal of Social Issues* (1967), pp. 48–58.
14. Prabodh B. Pandit, *India as a Sociolinguistic Area* (Poona: University of Poona, 1971).
15. A. S. Acharya, *Halakki Kannada* (Poona: Deccan College, 1967).
16. R. Mahadevan, *Gulbarga Kannada* (Poona: Deccan College, 1968).
17. U. P. Upadhyaya, *Nanjangud Kannada* (Poona: Deccan College, 1968).
18. A. M. Ghatage, *Konkani in South Kanara* (Bombay: State Board for Literature and Culture, Government of Maharashtra, 1963).
19. A. M. Ghatage, "Marathi in Kasaragod," *Indian Linguistics* 31 (1970), pp. 138–144.
20. Kamil Zvelebil, *Dialects of Tamil*, vols. 27 and 28 of *Archiv Orientalni* (Prague) (1959–1960); "Some Features of Dindigul Tamil," *T. P. Meenakshisundaram Commemorative Volume* (Annamalainagar, Madras: Annamalai University, 1961); "Tamil," *Current Trends in Linguistics*, ed. Thomas A. Sebeok *et al.*, vol. 5 (The Hague: Mouton, 1969).
21. Bhardriraju Krishnamurti (ed.), *Māṇḍalika Vrittipadakōśam* I (Hyderabad: Andhra Pradesh Sahitya Akademi, 1962).
22. John J. Gumperz, "Dialect Differences and Social Stratification in a North Indian Village," *American Anthropologist* 60 (1958), pp. 668–682.
23. *Ibid.*, p. 681.
24. William Bright and A. K. Ramanujan, "Sociolinguistic Variation and Language Change," in *Proceedings of the Ninth International Congress of Linguists*, ed. Horace G. Lunt (The Hague: Mouton, 1964), pp. 1107–1114.
25. K. V. Subbarao, "Varieties of Telegu" (manuscript: Urbana, University of Illinois).
26. Bright, *op. cit.*
27. K. Raman Unni, "Caste in Southern Malabar" (Doctoral thesis, University of Baroda, 1959).
28. Bright and Ramanujan, *op. cit.*, p. 1110.
29. Ramanujan, *op. cit.*
30. McCormack, *op. cit.*
31. Bright and Ramanujan, *op. cit.*
32. Subbarao, *op. cit.*
33. McCormack, *op. cit.*, p. 83.
34. Bright and Ramanujan, *op. cit.*, p. 1112.
35. Ramanujan, *op. cit.*, pp. 466–467.
36. *Ibid.*, p. 472.
37. Southworth, "On the Semantic Unity of a Speech Community."
38. Franklin C. Southworth, "Final Report on GS-2838: South Asian Semantic Structures (Research Project Sponsored by the National Science Foundation)," mimeographed (Philadelphia: South Asia Center of the University of Pennsylvania, 1973).
39. M. Shanmugan Pillai, "Caste Isoglosses in Kinship Terms," *Anthropological Linguistics* 7 (1965), pp. 59–66.
40. Southworth, "Final Report . . . South Asian Semantic Structures."
41. Mahadeo L. Apte, "Linguistic Acculturation and Its Relation to Urbanization and Socioeconomic Factors," *Indian Linguistics* 23 (1962), pp. 5–25.
42. *Ibid.*, p. 23.

43. McCormack, *op. cit.*, p. 88.
44. Apte, *op. cit.*, p. 8.
45. Gumperz, "Dialect Differences and Social Stratification."
46. Lewis Levine, "Speech Variation and Social Structure in a Group of North Indian Villages," (Doctoral thesis, Columbia University, 1959).
47. Gumperz, "Dialect Differences and Social Stratification."
48. McCormack, *op. cit.*, p. 81.
49. Apte, *op. cit.*, pp. 22–23.
50. *Ibid.*, pp. 23–24.
51. For example: Gumperz, "On the Linguistic Markers of Bilingual Communication"; and "Hindi-Punjabi Code Switching in Delhi," in *Proceedings of the Ninth International Congress of Linguists*, pp. 1115–1124.
52. Unni, *op. cit.*
53. William Labov, *The Social Stratification of English in New York City* (Washington: Center for Applied Linguistics, 1966).
54. John J. Gumperz and C. M. Naim, "Formal and Informal Standards in the Hindi Regional Language Area, "in Gumperz and Ferguson, *op. cit.*
55. Pandit, *op. cit.*
56. U. P. Upadhyaya, "Effects of Bilingualism on Bidar Kannada," *Indian Linguistics* 32 (1971), pp. 132–138.
57. Gumperz, "On the Linguistic Markers of Bilingual Communication."
58. *Ibid.*, p. 56.
59. Ashish Bose, "Some Aspects of the Linguistic Demography of India," *Language and Society in India* (Simla: Indian Institute of Advanced Study, 1969).
60. Mahadeo L. Apte, "Some Sociolinguistic Aspects of Interlingual Communication in India," *Anthropological Linguistics* 12 (1970), pp. 63–82.
61. Lachman M. Khubchandani, "Language Planning in a Multilingual Communication Network: A Study of the Indian Situation," *Actes du* Xe *Congres International des Linguistes* I (Bucharest, 1967), pp. 591–597; "Mother Tongue in Multilingual Societies: An Interpretation of Indian Census Returns," *Economic and Socio-Cultural Dimensions of Regionalization*, ed. B. K. Roy Burman (New Delhi: Registrar General of India, 1971).
62. Lachman M. Khubchandani, "The Acculturation of Indian Sindhi to Hindi: A Study of Languages in Contact" (Doctoral thesis, University of Pennsylvania, 1963).
63. See the bibliography in Murray B. Emeneau, "Dravidian and Indo-Aryan: The Indian Linguistic Area," in *Symposium on Dravidian Civilization*, ed. Andrée Sjoberg (Austin: Center for Asian Studies of the University of Texas, 1971).
64. *Proceedings of the American Philosophical Society* 98 (1954).
65. *Language* 32 (1956).
66. John J. Gumperz, J. F. Staal, *et al.*, *The Peacock-Tailed Horses of Indra: Studies in Grammatical and Semantic Convergence in South Asian Languages* (Berkeley: University of California Press, 1972); Franklin C. Southworth and M. L. Apte, "Contact and Convergence among South Asian Languages" (forthcoming).
67. John Fischer, "Social Influence on the Choice of a Linguistic Variant," *Word* 14 (1958), pp. 47–56.
68. William Labov, "The Social Motivation of a Sound Change," *Word* 19 (1963).

69. Gumperz, "Dialect Differences and Social Stratification."
70. Ramanujan, *op. cit.*
71. Franklin C. Southworth, "Detecting Prior Creolization: An Analysis of the Historical Origins of Marathi," in *Pidginization and Creolization of Languages*, ed. Dell Hymes (Cambridge: Cambridge University Press, 1971).
72. Southworth and Apte, *op. cit.*, "Introduction."
73. See particularly: Apte, *op. cit.*; Bright and Ramanujan, *op. cit.*; Jyotirindra Das Gupta and John Gumperz, "Language, Communication and Control in North India," in *Language Problems of Developing Nations*, ed. Joshua A. Fishman, Charles A. Ferguson, and J. Das Gupta (New York: Wiley, 1968); Gumperz and Naim, *op. cit.*; McCormack, *op. cit.*; Ramanujan, *op. cit.*; Andrée Sjoberg, "Co-existent Phonemic Systems in Telegu; A Socio-Cultural Perspective," *Word* 18 (1962), pp. 269–279; Southworth as cited above; and John J. Gumperz, "Sociolinguistics in South Asia," in Sebeok, *op. cit.*, pp. 597–606.
74. C. V. Kala, "Hybrid Conversational Malayalam—The Role of English in the Kerala Social Situation" (manuscript in preparation).
75. Southworth, "Final Report . . . South Asian Semantic Structures."
76. B. Gopinathan Nair, "Caste Dialects of Malayalam," in *Proceedings of the First All India Conference of Dravidian Linguists*, ed. V. I. Subramoniam and E. Valentine (Trivandrum: Dravidian Linguistic Association, Department of Linguistics, University of Kerala, 1971), pp. 409–414.
77. Susheela P. Upadhyaya, "Mapila Malayalam," in Subramoniam and Valentine, *op. cit.*, pp. 468–479.
78. M. Shanmugan Pillai, "Address Terms and Social Hierarchy of the Tamils," in Subramoniam and Valentine, *op. cit.*, pp. 424–432.
79. R. Solomon, "The Tense Markers of Bilingual Speech," in Subramoniam and Valentine, *op. cit.*, pp. 396–401.
80. T. Elizarenkova, "Influence of Dravidian Phonological System on Sinhalese," *International Journal of Dravidian Linguistics* I, no. 2 (1972), pp. 126–138.
81. All of which appear in Subramoniam and Valentine, *op. cit.*

Index

Archaeology in South India (Clarence Maloney)

agriculture, 5, 6, 9. *See also* rice
Andhra, early civilisation of, 26–27
Black and Red Ware, 6, 7, 8, 13–14, 24, 30
  range of, 10
bricks, 31, 32
brick structures, 15, 22, 29, 30–31
burials
  Iron Age, 7–8, 10, 11
  megalithic, 13
  Neolithic, 6
Chalcolithic. *See* Neolithic/Chalcolithic
coins
  Chinese, 31
  markers of trade route, 16–17
  punchmarked, 19–20, 21, 28, 29, 32
  Roman and Sātāvahana, 24–25, 26
  ship design, 27
Dravidian languages, 9–10, 11
  archaeological inferences from, 9
  spread of, 10, 33
early stone age archaeology, 1–3
food-producing cultures, impact of, 4–5
hand axes, 1–2
Indus civilization, 4–5
Iron Age
  culture, 6–7
  language of people, 10–11
  See also burials, megalithic
iron implements, 6, 7
Karṇāṭaka, early civilization of, 24–26
Kērala, early civilization of, 27–28
Late Stone Age, 3–4
Lustrous Red Ware, 5
megaliths, of Iron Age, 7–8. *See also* burials, megalithic
microliths, 3, 4, 22
Middle Stone Age, 2, 3
Neolithic/Chalcolithic, 4–5
  culture, 4–5, 6
  first phase, 4–5
  second phase, 5
  third phase, 6
Ptolemy, 13, 18, 27, 33
rice, 8, 10
  as agricultural basis, 12–13
Roman influence, 16–17, 18, 19, 21–22, 29, 30
Rouletted ware, 13, 24, 26, 27
Russet-coated ware, 6, 27
Śaṅgam period, 11–24
  acculturation, 21–24
  buildings, 15–16
  religion, 18–19, 28
  rice and agriculture, 12–13
  society, structure and diversity, 17–18
  state or government, 19–20
  trade, 16–17
  urbanization, 13–15
  writing and literature, 20–21
Sri Lanka, 3, 9, 20, 22–24
Tamiḻ Nāḍu, 1, 3, 9, 11, 21–22
  buildings of, 15–16
  excavated coastal sites of, 28–30
  Iron Age findings of, 6
  potential sites, 31–33
wooden structures, 14–15, 16

Ancient Tamil Literature (George L. Hart III)

ancient Dravidians
  invaders, 56
  names in music, 48
  religion, 43–44
ancient Tamil literature
  as reflective of daily life, 41–42
  closeness of Maharashtrian literature, 45–46
Aryan elements, 42, 43–44, 58–59
astrology, 50
Brahmans, 41–42, 43, 58–59
  as cultural assimilators, 59–60
  as dominant and powerful, 50–51, 52, 53
burial practices, 56–57
caste, 44
  abundances of, 57–58
  as indigenous, 44
Cilappatikāram, 41
dancing women, 47
early Tamil literature, 51–52
  description of agricultural organization, 51

The State and the Agrarian Order in Medieval South India (Burton Stein)

Geography and the Study of South India (Brian J. Murton)

Anthropological and Sociological Research in Kerala (Joan P. Mencher and K. Raman Unni)

Approaches to Changes in Caste Ideology in South India (Stephen A. Barnett)

Sociolinguistics Research in South India (Franklin C. Southworth)

Participants

SSIS CONFERENCE, UNIVERSITY OF WISCONSIN
7–9 April 1970

E. Annamalai, University of Chicago
Stephen A. Barnett, Princeton University
V. K. Bawa, Indian Administrative Service, Hyderabad, India
John B. Carman, Harvard University
Joseph W. Elder, University of Wisconsin
Albert B. Franklin, Kansas State University
Robert E. Frykenberg, University of Wisconsin
George L. Hart III, University of Wisconsin
Eugene F. Irschick, University of California, Berkeley
Clifford R. Jones, University of Pennsylvania
James M. Lindholm, University of Chicago
McKim Marriott, University of Chicago
William McCormack, University of Calgary
Clarence Maloney, Montclair State College
Joan P. Mencher, Lehman College and Columbia University
Robert J. Miller, University of Wisconsin
Brian J. Murton, University of Hawaii
T. S. Rama Rao, University of Madras
A. K. Ramanujan, University of Chicago
Lloyd I. Rudolph, University of Chicago
Suzanne H. Rudolph, University of Chicago
Burton Stein, University of Hawaii
Guy R. Welbon, University of Pennsylvania
Theodore P. Wright, Jr., State University of New York, Albany

Orders for Asian Studies at Hawaii publications should be directed to The University Press of Hawaii, 2840 Kolowalu Street, Honolulu, Hawaii 96822. Present standing orders will continue to be filled without special notification.

Asian Studies at Hawaii

(No. 1) *Bibliography of English Language Sources on Human Ecology, Eastern Malaysia and Brunei.* Compiled by Conrad P. Cotter with the assistance of Shiro Saito. September 1965. Two parts. Out of print.

(No. 2) *Economic Factors in Southeast Asian Social Change.* May 1968. Robert Van Niel, editor. Out of print.

No. 3 *East Asian Occasional Papers (1).* Harry J. Lamley, editor. May 1969.

(No. 4) *East Asian Occasional Papers (2).* Harry J. Lamley, editor. July 1970.

No. 5 *A Survey of Historical Source Materials in Java and Manila.* Robert Van Niel. February 1971.

(No. 6) *Educational Theory in the People's Republic of China: The Report of Ch'ien Chung-Jui.* Translation by John N. Hawkins. May 1971. Out of print.

No. 7 *Hai Jui Dismissed from Office.* Wu Han. Translation by C. C. Huang. June 1972.

No. 8 *Aspects of Vietnamese History.* Edited by Walter F. Vella. March 1973.

No. 9 *Southeast Asian Literature in Translation: A Preliminary Bibliography.* Philip N. Jenner. March 1973.

No. 10 *Textiles of the Indonesian Archipelago.* Garrett and Bronwen Solyom. October 1973.

No. 11 *British Policy and the Nationalist Movement in Burma, 1917–1937.* Albert D. Moscotti. February 1974.

No. 12 *Aspects of Bengali History and Society.* Edited by Rachel Van M. Baumer. In press.

No. 13 *Nanyang Perspective: Chinese Students in Multiracial Singapore.* Andrew W. Lind. June 1974.

No. 14 *Political Change in the Philippines: Studies of Local Politics Preceding Martial Law.* Edited by Benedict J. Kerkvliet. November 1974.